Seeds of the Church

FCCT | Free Church, Catholic Tradition

Barry Harvey and Bryan C. Hollon, editors

PUBLISHED VOLUMES:

Jeff W. Cary
Free Churches and the Body of Christ: Authority, Unity, and Truthfulness

Scott W. Bullard
Re-membering the Body: The Lord's Supper and Ecclesial Unity in the Free Church Traditions

Derek C. Hatch
Thinking with the Church: Toward a Renewal of Baptist Theology

Seeds of the Church

Towards an Ecumenical Baptist Ecclesiology

EDITED BY
Teun van der Leer, Henk Bakker,
Steven R. Harmon, and Elizabeth Newman

FOREWORD BY *Neville Callam*

CASCADE *Books* · Eugene, Oregon

SEEDS OF THE CHURCH
Towards an Ecumenical Baptist Ecclesiology

Free Church, Catholic Tradition 4

Copyright © 2022 Wipf and Stock Publishers. All rights reserved. Except for brief quotations in critical publications or reviews, no part of this book may be reproduced in any manner without prior written permission from the publisher. Write: Permissions, Wipf and Stock Publishers, 199 W. 8th Ave., Suite 3, Eugene, OR 97401.

Cascade Books
An Imprint of Wipf and Stock Publishers
199 W. 8th Ave., Suite 3
Eugene, OR 97401

www.wipfandstock.com

PAPERBACK ISBN: 978-1-6667-1837-9
HARDCOVER ISBN: 978-1-6667-1838-6
EBOOK ISBN: 978-1-6667-1839-3

Cataloguing-in-Publication data:

Names: van der Leer, Teun, editor. | Bakker, Henk, 1960–, editor. | Harmon, Steven R. (Steven Ray), editor. | Newman, Elizabeth, 1960–, ditor. | Callam, Neville, foreword.

Title: Seeds of the church : towards an ecumenical baptist ecclesiology / edited by Teun van der Leer, Hank Bakker, Steven R. Harmon, and Elizabeth Newman ; foreword by Neville Callam.

Description: Eugene, OR : Cascade Books, 2022 | Series: Free Church, Catholic Tradition 4 | Includes bibliographical references.

Identifiers: ISBN 978-1-6667-1837-9 (paperback) | ISBN 978-1-6667-1838-6 (hardcover) | ISBN 978-1-6667-1839-3 (ebook)

Subjects: LCSH: Baptists—History. | Baptists—Doctrines | Church—Unity. | Ecumenical movement. | Church—Catholicity.

Classification: BX6331.3 .S38 2022 (print) | BX6331.3 .S38 (ebook)

All Scripture quotations, unless otherwise noted, are from the New Revised Standard Version Bible, © 1989 by Division of Christian Education of the National Council of the Churches of Christ in the United States of America. Used by permission. All rights reserved.

For Anthony R. Cross, *in memoriam*

Table of Contents

Abbreviations ix

List of Contributors xi

Foreword xiii
Neville Callam

Preface xv
*Teun van der Leer, Henk Bakker, Steven R. Harmon,
    and Elizabeth Newman*

1   A Response to *The Church: Towards a Common Vision* 1
    *Baptist World Alliance Commission on Baptist Doctrine
    and Christian Unity*

2   The Baptistic Ecclesial Voice 24
    Teun van der Leer

3   Covenanting Churches 32
    Paul S. Fiddes

4   Discerning Churches 44
    Henk Bakker

5   Gathering Churches 55
    Jan Martijn Abrahamse

6   Befriending Churches 67
    Lina Toth

7   Proclaiming Churches 78
    Ruth Gouldbourne

Table of Contents

8   Equipping Churches 88
    Uwe Swarat

9   Baptizing Churches 97
    Anthony R. Cross

10 Discipling Churches 109
    Marion L. S. Carson

11 Caring Churches 119
    Frank Rees

12 Theologizing Churches 131
    Amy L. Chilton

13 Scattering Churches 143
    Daniël Drost

14 Remembering Churches 155
    Elizabeth Newman

Abbreviations

BEM	*Baptism, Eucharist and Ministry*
BUGB	Baptist Union of Great Britain
BWA	Baptist World Alliance
TCTCV	*The Church: Towards a Common Vision*
TTL	*Together towards Life*
WCC	World Council of Churches

List of Contributors

Jan Martijn Abrahamse is tutor in systematic theology and ethics at Ede Christian University of Applied Sciences and Research Fellow at the Dutch Baptist Seminary in Amsterdam, Netherlands.

Henk Bakker is professor at the Vrije Universiteit Amsterdam, Netherlands, and James Wm. McClendon Chair for Baptistic and Evangelical Theologies.

Marion L. S. Carson is a freelance theologian and writer who lives in Glasgow, Scotland.

Amy L. Chilton is senior pastor of Phillips Memorial Baptist Church in Cranston, Rhode Island, USA and adjunct professor of theology at Fuller Theological Seminary in Pasadena, California, USA.

Anthony R. Cross† was adjunct PhD supervisor, IBTS Centre Amsterdam, Netherlands.

Daniël Drost is tutor at the Dutch Baptist Seminary in Amsterdam, Netherlands.

Paul S. Fiddes is professor of systematic theology at Oxford University in Oxford, UK.

Ruth Gouldbourne is pastor at Grove Lane Baptist Church in Cheadle Hulme, UK, and senior research fellow at IBTS Centre Amsterdam, Netherlands.

Steven R. Harmon is professor of historical theology at Gardner-Webb University School of Divinity in Boiling Springs, North Carolina, USA.

List of Contributors

Teun van der Leer is tutor at the Dutch Baptist Seminary in Amsterdam, Netherlands.

Elizabeth Newman teaches in The Baptist House of Studies, Union Presbyterian Seminary, Richmond, VA, USA, is adjunct professor of theology at Duke University Divinity School in Durham, North Carolina, USA, and chairs the Baptist World Alliance Commission on Baptist Doctrine and Christian Unity.

Frank Rees is associate professor at the University of Divinity in Melbourne, Australia.

Uwe Swarat is professor of systematic theology and history of dogma at Theologische Hochschule Elstal in Elstal, Germany.

Lina Toth is assistant principal and lecturer in practical theology at Scottish Baptist College, University of the West of Scotland, Paisley, Scotland.

Foreword

Neville Callam

THE MULTILATERAL PROCESS LEADING to the publication in 2013 of *The Church: Towards a Common Vision* (*TCTCV*) benefited from three major sources, namely, the extensive process of reception of *Baptism, Eucharist and Ministry*; the fruit of the Fifth World Conference on Faith and Order convened in Santiago de Compostela, Spain, in 1993, and especially its affirmation of *koinonia* as the key image under which to conceive the subject of ecclesiology in relation to the unity of the church; and the convergence yielded by bilateral dialogue between Christian World Communions.

This book, *Seeds of the Church: Towards an Ecumenical Baptist Ecclesiology*, provides one example of the reception of *TCTCV* within the Baptist community. It begins with a general response crafted after wide consultation among members of the Commission on Baptist Doctrine and Christian Unity of the Baptist World Alliance. After this, it offers constructive perspectives on specific dimensions of the ecclesiological vision shared in *TCTCV* in the light of special emphases treasured by Baptists. *Seeds of the Church* illustrates how Baptists may learn from, and contribute to, an emerging convergent ecumenical ecclesiological vision through a process of giving and receiving among different church traditions.

Seeds of the Church represents a new departure from previously published multiauthored works exploring Baptist ecclesiological perspectives. It is the first case of such a Baptist publication dealing with aspects of ecclesiology using an ecumenical convergence text as its starting point and whose multiple authors from several countries adopt the stance of receptive ecumenism. The writers are familiar with the continuing stream of reflection within the Baptist family around the issues they analyze. Yet, recognizing the gifts that perceived contesting ecclesiologies may offer each other, they engage dialogically with perspectives from *TCTCV*, sometimes embracing, sometimes offering suggestions toward the strengthening of the proposal Faith and Order presents.

Seeds of the Church opens a window on what is possible when Baptists engage with people of other Christian traditions in the exploration of the common heritage of people belonging to the one household of faith. In explicating *TCTCV*, it unveils new horizons for typical Baptist convictions on the church and its unity. In the process, the authors evince contours of an emerging Baptist multivoiced ecclesiological vision, within a primary Western post-Christendom and postmodern context. Based on the authors' conviction that *TCTCV* is the work of fellow pilgrims on a single pilgrimage of faith, this book also offers a reading of an ecumenical text in a Baptist key and paves the way for ecclesiological renewal in the authors' own communion.

Seeds of the Church shows the possibility of reading and reflecting on an ecumenical text by creatively analyzing the gifts of one's communion in the light of gifts offered by other church communions, not so as to engage in a process that yields comparison and contrast, not merely to highlight similarity and difference, but to benefit from, and contribute to, efforts to envision the unity we seek in the one, holy, catholic, and apostolic church.

Preface

IN HIS PRESENTATION "*THE Church: Towards a Common Vision*: Baptistic Responses" on July 6, 2018, at the final session of the annual meeting of the Commission on Baptist Doctrine and Christian Unity of the Baptist World Alliance in Zürich, Switzerland, Teun van der Leer showed how few the Baptist responses to the 2013 WCC convergence text *The Church: Towards a Common Vision* actually were. Some of them were substantial, but there was no coherent communal reaction. Therefore, the commission decided to write a response together before the end of 2020 and to add a sketch of Baptist ecclesiology as a contribution to the ecumenical discourse about the church. In this volume we present the outcome of the shared effort, and the editorial team is grateful for the support of so many esteemed colleagues, men and women from three continents, and even more for the result, because the fruit of the tree planted in Zürich 2018 tastes good.

With this volume the worldwide Baptist community makes a contribution to the ongoing discussion on changing patterns of ecumenical engagement, not only on a global scale but also at grassroots level. We observe that Baptist churches throughout the global scene take up the invitation to participate in local (and "glocal") initiatives to share in the richness of ecumenical, and for that matter, catholic, involvement. To be sure, Baptists do not join forces easily. There is an inherent hesitance, even reluctance, in the ecclesial heredity to welcome neighboring Christians. As a consequence, Baptist churches tend to become easily isolated, even though they may be surrounded by many brothers and sisters who show hospitality without raising that many thresholds.

The editors of this volume are more aware than ever that local churches have to find creative ways to share their presence with believers and nonbelievers, regardless of what their opinions or convictions may be. Denominational boundaries may increasingly be less sharply defined

Preface

in a world shaped not only by secularism but also by the ongoing effects of the COVID-19 pandemic. These times of loss, sadness, and uncertainty may carry with them the momentum for the church to reach out to the world with one voice. The worldwide church is breached, and it needs both "visible unity" and "legitimate diversity" to voice its message to the world. What Baptists bring with them in terms of this bifocal vision (visible unity and legitimate diversity), fourteen Baptist authors attempt to collect and represent in this volume.

The reader will find that the common denominator in the listed contents of this book consists of practices expressed by a verbal noun (gerund), starting with "responding" to the WCC convergence text *The Church: Towards a Common Vision*. In addition to the response (written by Steven R. Harmon, incorporating input from the BWA Commission on Baptist Doctrine and Christian Unity), the contributors present twelve complementary practices, also formulated in the gerund, which more or less reflect the lived Baptist faith from its very beginnings up to now: covenanting, discerning, gathering, befriending, proclaiming, equipping, baptizing, discipling, caring, theologizing, scattering, and remembering. The dynamics of Baptist ecclesiology, as well as its ecumenical potential, are encapsulated in the immediacy of these characteristics, which are active practices. The local church, then, is considered a vibrant laboratory for lived Baptist theology, as it also informs the outlines for any sort of ecumenical Baptist ecclesiology.

The list of characteristics may (and possibly does) apply to all types of churches. We consider the interrelationship of these twelve practices, however, to be typically Baptist. They may be summarized with another verbal noun, namely "investing." Jesus refers to the kingdom of God as an enterprise in which the church should invest by using its opportunities and "setting it to work" (Matt 25:16). Therefore, the kingdom is to be compared to a seed. The list of Baptist practices explored in this volume merely comprises a limited selection of "seeds," as the title of the book indicates, representing a fraction of its richness. We are aware of that, and yet, we as Baptists expectantly sow and invest, what we have, looking forward to the harvest time, unaware of the things to come. With good reason the book of Ecclesiastes says, "Sow your seed in the morning, and at evening let your hands not be idle, for you do not know which will succeed" (Eccl 11:9).

When we were in the final stages of preparing this book for publication, we received the sad news of the untimely death of our contributor

Preface

Anthony R. Cross, whose scholarship in the field of Baptist studies sowed many seeds that are watered by his fellow contributors herein. May the fruit of our enterprises, along with those of the communion of saints in which we continue to be united with Anthony, be a blessing for the church catholic.

Teun van der Leer, Henk Bakker, Steven R. Harmon, and Elizabeth Newman
The Season after Pentecost ("The Time of the Church"), 2022

1

A Response to *The Church: Towards a Common Vision*

BY THE BAPTIST WORLD ALLIANCE COMMISSION ON BAPTIST DOCTRINE AND CHRISTIAN UNITY[1]

IN RESPONSE TO THE invitation of the WCC Commission on Faith and Order to the churches to submit official responses to *The Church: Towards a Common Vision* (*TCTCV*), the Baptist World Alliance Commission on Baptist Doctrine and Christian Unity is pleased to make the following contribution to the process of reception of this important convergence text, in the hope that our churches and all churches might live into its vision of an ecclesial communion that receives from the communion of the Triune God "both the gift by which the Church lives and, at the same time, the gift that God calls the Church to offer to a wounded and divided humanity in hope of reconciliation and healing."[2]

---

1. Drafted by Steven R. Harmon; revised in light of input from the membership of the BWA Commission on Baptist Doctrine and Christian Unity meeting in Nassau, The Bahamas, 8–12 July 2019.

2. WCC, *TCTCV*, §1.

A Response to The Church: Towards a Common Vision

1. The Baptist World Alliance and the Status of This Response

1.1. Founded in 1905, the Baptist World Alliance (BWA) is a fellowship of 240 Baptist conventions and unions located in 125 countries and territories, including 168,491 local congregations and 47,500,324 members.[3] According to its constitution, "The Baptist World Alliance, extending over every part of the world, exists as an expression of the essential oneness of Baptist people in the Lord Jesus Christ, to impart inspiration to the fellowship, and to provide channels for sharing concerns and skills in witness and ministry. This Alliance recognizes the traditional autonomy and interdependence of Baptist churches and member bodies." One of the objectives of the BWA articulated in its constitution is "to promote understanding and cooperation among Baptist bodies and with other Christian groups, in keeping with our unity in Christ."[4]

1.2. One of the commissions of the BWA is the Commission on Baptist Doctrine and Christian Unity, which is charged with the following work:

> The Commission on Baptist Doctrine and Christian Unity identifies, reflects on, and clarifies issues of doctrine that are important to Baptists. It analyzes the causes of disunity among Baptists and promotes ways to overcome this disunity. It shares in theological conversations between the BWA and other Christian communities, in furtherance of Jesus' prayer for the unity of the church. It also participates in programs to improve inter-church understanding and cooperation. The Commission makes its findings available to the wide Baptist family.[5]

---

3. These statistics for the total number of local congregations and individual church members affiliated with the BWA were current as of Dec. 31, 2017; the number of 240 member unions reflects the reception of one additional member union by the BWA during its 2019 General Council meeting (Baptist World Alliance, "Statistics"). Since Baptist churches do not include in their membership statistics children whose families participate in the life of the congregation but who have not yet been baptized, the actual number of persons affiliated with churches included in the global fellowship of the BWA is significantly larger than 47,500,324 members.

4. Preamble and §2, "Objectives," in BWA, "Constitution of the BWA." While the largest national union of Baptists in the world, the Southern Baptist Convention—which was instrumental in the founding of the BWA in 1905—ceased to be a member union of the BWA in 2004, Southern Baptists nevertheless continue to participate individually in the commissions and gatherings of the BWA.

5. BWA, "Commissions."

A Response to The Church: Towards a Common Vision

As an instrument by which the BWA relates to other Christian traditions, the Commission on Baptist Doctrine and Christian Unity supplies the members of Baptist delegations to the joint commissions of international bilateral ecumenical dialogues, receives updates on these dialogues, and offers responses to multilateral proposals for ecumenical convergence such as *Baptism, Eucharist and Ministry* (*BEM*) and *TCTCV*.

1.3. While the BWA itself is not a member body of the World Council of Churches (WCC), eight Baptist unions were founding members of the WCC in 1948: the Baptist Union of Great Britain, the Northern Baptist Convention (now American Baptist Churches, USA), the National Baptist Convention (USA), the Seventh Day Baptist General Conference (USA), the Baptist Union of New Zealand, the Union of Baptist Congregations in the Netherlands, the Burma Baptist Missionary Convention, and the China Baptist Council.[6] Today twenty-seven Baptist unions are WCC-members.[7] Representatives of these Baptist WCC member unions, as well as representatives of the BWA itself, have served on commissions of the WCC, including the WCC Commission on Faith and Order and its working groups, which have been responsible for drafting and offering input into the Faith and Order study documents and convergence texts.

1.4. While the WCC Commission on Faith and Order has commended to the churches for study numerous study documents among the more than two hundred Faith and Order papers issued by that commission since 1948 and has invited the churches to offer responses to them, only two have been designated as "convergence texts": *BEM* (1982) and *TCTCV* (2013). The introduction to *TCTCV* explains the status of a convergence text in this manner:

> Our aim is to offer a convergence text, that is, a text which, while not expressing full consensus on all the issues considered, is much more than simply an instrument to stimulate further study. Rather, the following pages express how far Christian communities have come in their common understanding of the Church, showing the progress that has been made and indicating work that still needs to be done.[8]

The preface to *TCTCV* invites both "ecclesial responses" from "the churches that are members of the Commission [on Faith and Order] and

---

6. Payne, "Baptists and Ecumenical Movement," 263.
7. WCC, "Baptist Churches."
8. WCC, *TCTCV*, 1.

the fellowship of churches in the World Council of Churches" and "responses from ecclesial bodies, such as national and regional councils of churches and the Christian World Communions, whose official dialogues among themselves have contributed so much to the convergence reflected in *The Church* [*TCTCV*]."[9] When a similar call accompanied the publication of *BEM*, nine Baptist unions issued official ecclesial responses.[10] In the category of responses from ecclesial bodies such as Christian World Communions, the BWA Commission on Baptist Doctrine and Interchurch Cooperation (now the Commission on Baptist Doctrine and Christian Unity) received an initial response to *BEM* drafted by George Beasley-Murray, Morris West, and Robert Thompson, which was subsequently expanded by William R. Estep.[11] This response detailed Baptist affirmation of aspects of *BEM* along with Baptist concerns about other elements of that convergence text: for example, appreciation for *BEM*'s recognition, informed by ecumenical biblical and historical scholarship, of the biblical, historical, and theological priority of believer's baptism, but also concern about what seemed to be an *ex opere operato* (i.e., automatically conferred) connection between baptism and salvation; an appreciation for the biblically rich development of the meaning of the Eucharist, but again reservations about a stronger connection between the Eucharist and the experience of salvation than Baptists would typically make; and appreciation for the attention to the ministry of the whole people of God in the section on ministry, but disappointment that *BEM* seemed to make reconciliation with the historic episcopate (i.e., apostolic succession) a condition for visible unity.[12]

---

9. WCC, *TCTCV*, viii–ix.

10. These Baptist ecclesial responses are published in Thurian, *Churches Respond to "Baptism."* They include the Baptist Union of Great Britain and Ireland (1:70–77), All-Union Council of Evangelical Christians-Baptists in the USSR (3:227–29), Baptist Union of Scotland (3:230–45), Baptist Union of Denmark (3:246–53), Covenanted Baptist Churches in Wales (3:254–56), American Baptist Churches, USA (3:257–63), Burma Baptist Convention (4:184–90), Union of the Evangelical Free Churches in the GDR (Baptists) (4:191–99), and Baptist Union of Sweden (4:200–213).

11. Kerstan and Burke, *Out of Darkness*, 146–55; Estep, "Response to *Baptism*." The earlier version prepared by George Beasley-Murray, Morris West, and Robert Thompson is noted by Manley, "Survey."

12. While Estep's expanded response was presented to the BWA Commission on Baptist Doctrine and Interchurch Cooperation and published in the collected papers of the Study and Research Division for 1986–90, it was not published in the six volumes of responses to *BEM* (Thurian, *Churches Respond to "Baptism"*).

1.5. While the present document is presented as a response to *TCTCV* by the BWA Commission on Baptist Doctrine and Christian Unity, it is not the first effort of this commission to participate in the process of reception of *TCTCV*. At the meeting of the Commission on Baptist Doctrine and Christian Unity in Ocho Rios, Jamaica, July 1–6, 2013, three responses to different sections of *TCTCV* (in one case, to a section of its 2005 predecessor *The Nature and Mission of the Church: A Stage on the Way to a Common Statement*) were presented to and discussed by the commission. These responses were subsequently published in the collected papers of the BWA Division of Mission, Evangelism, and Theological Reflection for the quinquennium 2010–15.[13] In addition, other individual Baptist theologians have published independent responses to *TCTCV*.[14] The present response draws in part on these previous instances of Baptist participation in the reception of *TCTCV* as well as on the input of the current membership of the BWA Commission on Baptist Doctrine and Christian Unity.

1.6. This response is in the category of "responses from ecclesial bodies, such as national and regional councils of churches and the Christian World Communions"[15] solicited by the WCC, but its status as a response from the BWA needs some qualification. It is the product of the work of the BWA Commission on Baptist Doctrine and Christian Unity as an expression of its charge to share "in theological conversations between the BWA and other Christian communities, in furtherance of Jesus' prayer for the unity of the church" and to make "its findings available to the wide Baptist family."[16] As such, it has a status similar to that of the reports written by the joint commissions to the international bilateral ecumenical dialogues with BWA participation. The note on "The Status of This Report" appended to the preface of the report from phase 2 of the dialogue between the BWA

---

13. Freeman, "Church of Triune God"; Newman, "Church"; Fiddes, "*Koinonia*." While the subtitle of the volume in which these responses appear refers to a "Commission" on Mission, Evangelism, and Theological Reflection, its proper designation during this period was the "Division of Mission, Evangelism, and Theological Reflection," a division that included multiple study commissions of the BWA, among them the Commission on Baptist Doctrine and Christian Unity.

14. Hatch, "*Koinonia* as Ecumenical Opening"; Searle, "Moving towards an Ecumenism"; Abramov et al., "Importance, Relevance, and Challenge"; Baban, "Four Views and Response"; Van der Leer, "*Church*"; Harmon, "How Might We Envision."

15. WCC, *TCTCV*, viii–ix.

16. BWA, "Commissions."

and the Catholic Church (2006–10) also applies to the status of this response in relation to the BWA and its member unions:

> The Report published here is the work of the International Conversations between the Catholic Church and the Baptist World Alliance. It is a study document produced by participants in the Conversations. The authorities who appointed the participants have allowed the Report to be published so that it may be widely discussed. It is not an authoritative declaration of either the Catholic Church or of the Baptist World Alliance, who will both also evaluate the document.[17]

2. *The Church: Towards a Common Vision* in Baptist Ecclesiological Perspective

2.1. The introduction to *TCTCV* invites the churches to respond to this convergence text in light of five questions, the first of which is "To what extent does this text reflect the ecclesiological understanding of your church?"[18] While the Baptist ecclesiological principle of congregational freedom to follow the leadership of the Spirit in discerning the mind of Christ about what it will mean for the congregation to be the body of Christ in its particular context makes it difficult to generalize about Baptists' ecclesiological self-understanding, there are multiple dimensions of the Baptist ecclesial vision that may be recognized in the vision of church articulated by *TCTCV*.

2.2. Apart from the ecclesial vision expressed in the text of *TCTCV*, Baptists may recognize themselves also in the process that led to it. The previous paragraph mentioned the Baptist ecclesiological principle of congregational freedom to follow the leadership of the Spirit in discerning the mind of Christ about what it will mean for the congregation to be the body of Christ in its particular context. One way in which Baptists have sought to exercise this freedom is in the practice of ecclesial discernment. Ideally this practice entails deep listening, not only to all voices within the congregation—including (perhaps especially including) minority or marginalized voices—but also to various voices from other contexts beyond the local church.[19] A parallel to this Baptist practice of ecclesial discernment

---

17. BWA and Catholic Church, "Word of God."
18. WCC, *TCTCV*, 3.
19. Baptist theologian Paul Fiddes has explained the embodied "Baptist experience"

through listening deeply to the input of multiple voices is the process by which the WCC Commission on Faith and Order solicited and received responses from a wide range of ecclesial voices to the successive drafts of the convergence text that became *TCTCV*: *The Nature and Purpose of the Church* (1998), *The Nature and Mission of the Church* (2005), and three successive additional drafts that made continued improvements in light of ongoing input on the way to the reception by the WCC Central Committee in September 2012 of the new convergence text, now titled *TCTCV* and published in 2013.

2.3. Baptists may especially see themselves in the way *TCTCV* attended to the voices of those who have been marginalized in their contexts. Baptists began as a persecuted religious minority, and this formative experience has led them historically to be advocates for religious liberty, not only for themselves but for other marginalized minorities, and to work for the just treatment of all persons. We confess that there have been notable Baptist failures to embody these convictions regarding freedom and justice. But at their best, Baptists have sought to live in light of the insistence of Baptist minister and theologian Martin Luther King Jr. that "injustice anywhere is

---

that informs Baptist efforts to bring their faith and practice under the rule of Christ in this way: "The liberty of local churches to make decisions about their own life and ministry is not based in a human view of autonomy or independence, or in selfish individualism, but in a sense of being under the direct rule of Christ who relativizes other rules. This liberating rule of Christ is what makes for the distinctive 'feel' of Baptist congregational life, which allows for spiritual oversight (*episkopē*) both by the *whole* congregation gathered together in church meeting, and by the minister(s) called to lead the congregation. . . . Since the same rule of Christ can be experienced in assemblies of churches together, there is also the basis here for Baptist associational life, and indeed for participating in ecumenical clusters" (Fiddes, *Tracks and Traces*, 6). Elsewhere Fiddes elaborates what it means for the whole congregation to seek together the mind of Christ in what British Baptists call "church meeting": "Upon the whole people in covenant there lies the responsibility of finding a common mind, of coming to an agreement about the way of Christ for them in life, worship and mission. But they cannot do so unless they use the resources that God has given them, and among those resources are the pastor, the deacons and (if they have them) the elders. The church meeting is not 'people power' in the sense of simply counting votes and canvassing a majority. . . . The aim is to search for consent about the mind of Christ, and so people should be sensitive to the voices behind the votes, listening to them according to the weight of their experience and insight. As B[arrington] White puts it, 'One vote is not as good as another in church meeting,' even though it has the same strictly numerical value" (Fiddes, *Tracks and Traces*, 86). Cf. also Broadway et al., "Re-Envisioning Baptist Identity." For an exploration of the theological practice by local churches of discernment through intercontextual listening to a wide range of voices beyond the local church, see Chilton and Harmon, *Sources of Light*.

a threat to justice everywhere."[20] The ongoing commitment of the global Baptist community to seeking liberty and justice for the oppressed and marginalized is reflected in the existence of BWA commissions devoted to Religious Freedom; Racial, Gender, and Economic Justice; and Human Rights, Peacebuilding, and Reconciliation. In addition, the BWA awards an annual Human Rights Award that reflects this commitment.[21] When members of the Plenary Commission on Faith and Order meeting in Crete in October 2009, with Baptist representatives among them, offered their perspectives on the draft statement *The Nature and Mission of the Church* and suggestions for revising it, one speaker critiqued the way that draft text treated biblical images of the church in purely doctrinal terms, without sufficient attention to their sociological dimensions and implications for the liberation of the dispossessed and the disempowered.[22] Baptists who pray and work for liberty and justice for the dispossessed and disempowered will rejoice that this critical voice was heard by the drafting committee. It is reflected in the insistence of *TCTCV* that "the Church needs to help those without power in society to be heard," "must become a voice for those who are voiceless," and is impelled "to work for a just social order, in which the goods of this earth may be shared equitably, the suffering of the poor eased and absolute destitution one day be eliminated,"[23] as well as in its assertion

---

20. King, "Letter from Birmingham Jail."

21. During years in which the quinquennial Baptist World Congress is held, the award is designated as the BWA Congress Quinquennial Human Rights Award; in non-Baptist World Congress years, the prize is awarded as the Denton and Janice Lotz Human Rights Award, named after a former general secretary of the BWA and his wife.

22. Syrian Orthodox Metropolitan Geevarghese Mar Coorilos of India called the dispossessed and disempowered "the actual church amongst communities of people in their struggle for the fullness of life," going on to say, "In India, for the ['untouchable' members of the Dalit caste] who form the majority of the Indian church, the body of Christ is a Dalit body, a 'broken body' (the word Dalit literally means 'broken' and 'torn asunder'). Jesus Christ became a Dalit because he was torn-asunder and mutilated on the cross. The Church as 'body of Christ,' in the Indian context, therefore, has profound theological and sociological implications for a Dalit ecclesiology. . . . [*The Nature and Mission of the Church*], however, fails to strike chords and resonate with such contextual theological challenges. . . . In other words, the text fails to encounter the real *ecclesia* among communities of people in pain and suffering" (Coorilos, "Nature and Mission"). Also at the meeting of the Plenary Commission on Faith and Order in Crete, members of the Plenary Commission recommended that those responsible for drafting "shorten the text and . . . make it more contextual, more reflective of the lives of the churches throughout the world, and more accessible to a wider readership" (WCC, *TCTCV*, 45).

23. WCC, *TCTCV*, §64.

that "after the example of Jesus, the Church is called and empowered in a special way to share the lot of those who suffer and to care for the needy and the marginalized."[24]

2.4. Baptists welcome one feature of *TCTCV* that seems most obviously an advance beyond *BEM*: its reengagement of the roots of the modern ecumenical movement in the modern missions movement. The 1910 Edinburgh World Missionary Conference that led to the founding of the ongoing International Missionary Conference in 1921 was in some sense anticipated a century earlier by pioneering Baptist missionary to India William Carey (1761–1834), who in 1806 suggested that "a general association of all denominations of Christians from the four quarters of the earth" meet each decade at the Cape of Good Hope.[25] In *TCTCV*, the quest for Christian unity is framed as a participation in God's mission in the world in its opening chapter, "God's Mission and the Unity of the Church." The opening paragraph ends with these two sentences:

> The Church, as the body of Christ, acts by the power of the Holy Spirit *to continue his life-giving mission in prophetic and compassionate ministry and so participates in God's work of healing a broken world*. Communion, whose source is the very life of the Holy Trinity, is both the gift by which the Church lives and, at the same time, the gift that God calls the Church to offer to a wounded and divided humanity in hope of reconciliation and healing.[26]

This first chapter sees the *missio dei* as carried out in the sending of the Son, defined by the earthly ministry of Jesus, extended in the church as the body of Christ that continues his mission, and empowered by the Holy Spirit sent upon the church and into the world. In the next chapter on "The Church of the Triune God," the church "is by its very nature missionary, called and sent to witness in its own life to that communion which God intends for all humanity and for all creation in the kingdom."[27] Whereas the title of the earlier text on *The Nature and Mission of the Church* suggested that one could somehow differentiate the church's nature and the church's mission, *TCTCV* now conceives of mission as essential to the nature of the church—a strengthening of a long-developing trajectory in ecclesiology and ecumenical theology that appropriates the missiological concept of

---

24. WCC, *TCTCV*, §66.
25. Hinson, "William Carey and Ecumenical Pragmatism," 76–77.
26. WCC, *TCTCV*, §1 (emphasis added).
27. WCC, *TCTCV*, §13.

the *missio dei* in which the church participates and becomes more fully the church whenever it does so. Johann Gerhard Oncken (1800–1884), the German "Father of Continental Baptists" who adopted as his motto "Every Baptist a missionary," would have been pleased by this aspect of *TCTCV*.[28]

2.5. A second notable advance beyond *BEM* is the way *TCTCV* roots the unity of the church in the unity of the Triune God: "Communion, whose source is the very life of the Holy Trinity, is both the gift by which the Church lives and, at the same time, the gift that God calls the Church to offer to a wounded and divided humanity in hope of reconciliation and healing."[29] The text advances this Trinitarian rationale and framework for conceiving of the church and its unity not only in its second chapter, titled "The Church of the Triune God," but throughout the document. It does so especially in terms of the biblical concept of *koinonia*, which the subsequent Christian theological tradition has developed both as a Trinitarian concept and as an ecclesiological concept, and it is influenced in particular by recent constructive retrievals of these developments.[30] *TCTCV* reaps the harvest of this Trinitarian ecclesiological ferment as a deepening of a theme long present in ecumenical theology,[31] but it is also a theme that had already featured prominently in international bilateral ecumenical dialogues with Baptist participation—in particular, phase 2 of the dialogue between the BWA and the Catholic Church (2006–10). A "common language" of an ecclesiology rooted in Trinitarian *koinonia* enabled Baptists and Catholics together to make affirmations such as the following in the report of this dialogue, "The Word of God in the Life of the Church":[32]

> Jesus Christ is thus God's self-revelation who draws us into the communion of God's own triune life and into communion (*koinonia*) with each other.[33]
>
> The church is thus to be understood as a *koinonia* . . . which is grounded in the *koinonia* of the triune God. Believers are joined in *koinonia* through participation in the communion of Father,

---

28. Luckey, *Johann Gerhard Oncken*.
29. WCC, *TCTCV*, §1.
30. E.g., Fuchs, *Koinonia and the Quest*.
31. Second Vatican Council, *Unitatis Redintegratio*, §2.
32. BWA and Catholic Church, "Word of God," §8: "In recent years this [the *koinonia* of the Triune God as the foundation for the communion of the church] has become our common language, whether Catholic or Protestant, or specifically Baptist."
33. BWA and Catholic Church, "Word of God," §7.

> Son and Holy Spirit . . . [and] are in *koinonia* through their participation in the community of believers gathered by Christ in his church.³⁴
>
> The principle of *koinonia* applies both to the church gathered in a local congregation and to congregations gathered together. . . . We agree that the local fellowship does not derive from the universal church, nor is the universal a mere sum of various local forms, but that there is mutual existence and coinherence between the local and universal church of Christ.³⁵

The Baptists recognized in such an ecclesiology of *koinonia* a convergence with the concept of "covenant" emphasized in Baptist ecclesiology, in which the church is constituted by participatory divine-human and human-human relationships that extend beyond the local church to include trans-local ecclesial relationships.³⁶ While *TCTCV* does not make this connection between *koinonia* and covenant, it is in particular the communion ecclesiology of *TCTCV* that makes it possible for Baptists to see *TCTCV* as a basis for growth in unity, a matter addressed in the next major section of this response.

2.6. Baptists are also able to appreciate a third strand in this ecumenical vision that *TCTCV* brings into sharper focus: its development more strongly than *BEM* of the church's ecumenical imperative in eschatological terms, which *TCTCV* sees as inseparable from the mission of the Triune God, who is the source of ecclesial unity. The three strands come together in the opening paragraph of *TCTCV*, which concludes with the insistence that "communion, whose source is the very life of the Holy Trinity, is both the gift by which the Church lives and, at the same time, the gift that God calls the Church to offer to a wounded and divided humanity *in hope of reconciliation and healing.*"³⁷ *TCTCV* portrays the church that has this eschatological hope as "an eschatological reality, already anticipating the kingdom, but not yet its full realization." Therefore, it is also "a pilgrim community" on a "journey towards the full realization of God's gift of communion."³⁸

---

34. BWA and Catholic Church, "Word of God," §11.
35. BWA and Catholic Church, "Word of God," §12.
36. See BWA and Catholic Church, "Word of God," §§16–19.
37. BWA and Catholic Church, "Word of God," §1 (emphasis added).
38. BWA and Catholic Church, "Word of God," §§33, 35, 37. This thoroughly eschatological pilgrim church motif had already been expressed in the Vatican II "Decree on Ecumenism," which said that the church "makes its pilgrim way in hope toward the goal of the fatherland above," with that goal defined in the next sentence as "the sacred

This vision of a pilgrim church articulated by *TCTCV* may be the feature of this convergence text that most fully reflects the ecclesiological self-understanding of Baptists. The Baptist ecclesial ideal is the church that is fully under the rule of Christ, which Baptists locate somewhere ahead of them in a not-yet-arrived-at future rather than in any past or present instantiation of the church.[39] Baptists are relentlessly dissatisfied with the present state of the church in their pilgrim journey toward the community that will be fully under the reign of Christ, and *TCTCV* gives expression to the same sort of holy dissatisfaction with the ecclesial status quo. The acknowledgment that the whole church both shares in past and present ecclesial failures to realize God's gift of communion and in a pilgrim journey toward a visible manifestation of communion that has yet to be fully realized makes it possible for Baptists to see the vision of *TCTCV* as a basis for mutual growth toward a more fully visible unity.

---

mystery of the unity of the Church" (Second Vatican Council, *Unitatis Redintegratio*, §2). This pilgrim church conception of ecclesial identity, however, belongs broadly to the modern ecumenical movement and all churches that participate in it. The concept was clearly expressed in reports and documents issued in connection with assemblies of the WCC that preceded and followed the Second Vatican Council—Evanston in 1954 and New Delhi in 1961, as well as Uppsala in 1968. The New Delhi assembly issued a "Report on Witness" that urged "a reappraisal of the patterns of church organization and institutions inherited by the younger churches" so that "outdated forms . . . may be replaced by strong and relevant ways of evangelism." It offered this as an example of "how the Church may become the Pilgrim Church, which goes forth boldly as Abraham did into the unknown future, not afraid to leave behind the securities of its conventional structure, glad to dwell in the tent of perpetual adaptation, looking to the city whose builder and maker is God." The New Delhi assembly also proposed a vision of the ecumenical future toward which the pilgrim church journeys in its definition of the unity sought by the modern ecumenical movement: "We believe that the unity which is both God's will and [God's] gift to [God's] Church is being made visible as all in each place who are baptized into Jesus Christ and confess him as Lord and Savior are brought by the Holy Spirit into one fully-committed fellowship, holding the one apostolic faith, preaching the one Gospel, breaking the one bread, joining in common prayer, and having a corporate life reaching out in witness and service to all and who at the same time are united with the whole Christian fellowship in all places and all ages, in such wise that ministry and members are accepted by all, and that all can act and speak together as occasion requires for the tasks to which God calls [God's] people" ("Report of the Section on Unity," in WCC, *New Delhi Report*, 116).

39. Cf. Harmon, *Baptist Identity*, ch. 9, "The Theology of a Pilgrim Church," 213–42.

3. *The Church: Towards a Common Vision* as Basis for Growth in Unity

3.1 *TCTCV* also invites response to the question "To what extent does this text offer a basis for growth in unity among the churches?" In Baptist perspective, the communion ecclesiology developed within the framework of Trinitarian *koinonia* noted in the previous section makes it possible to envision a movement toward visible unity that has a place not only for Baptists and their own ecclesiological convictions but also for all the other churches with which Baptists do not currently have full communion, without any of the traditions being required to surrender the distinctive ecclesial gifts that have been uniquely preserved in each of the divided traditions. Without the exchange of these gifts, none of the divided churches can become fully catholic (in the sense not only of quantitative catholicity, which describes the totality of the one church to which all who belong to Christ belong, but also of qualitative catholicity, which describes the fullness of certain qualities of faith and faithfulness that mark the one church fully under the rule of Christ).[40]

3.2. *TCTCV* insists that "each local church contains within it the fullness of what it is to be the Church."[41] This emphasis of *TCTCV* on the presence in the local church of the catholic fullness of what it means to be church (in both senses of catholicity noted in the preceding paragraph of this response), without prioritizing the universal church over the local church, invites a growth toward unity that happens at the grassroots. This develops further the locality of growth toward visible unity envisioned by the 1962 New Delhi assembly of the WCC in its definition of "The Unity We Seek": "We believe that the unity which is both God's will and [God's] gift to [God's] Church is being made visible as *all in each place* who are baptized into Jesus Christ and confess him as Lord and Savior are brought by the Holy Spirit into one fully-committed fellowship."[42] This emphasis on the local church makes space for the contributions of difference and diversity to the growth toward unity, and it helps ensure that growth toward unity is not merely a matter of negotiating mergers between trans-local unions of

---

40. On the distinction between "quantitative" and "qualitative" catholicity, see Congar, *Chrétiens désunis*, 115–17; Congar, *Divided Christendom*, 93–94.

41. WCC, *TCTCV*, §31.

42. "Report of the Section on Unity," in WCC, *New Delhi Report*, 116 (emphasis added).

churches, which themselves play an important role in the traditioning of healthy diversity within the body of Christ.

3.3. The affirmation of *TCTCV* that "each local church contains within it the fullness of what it is to be the Church" quoted in the preceding paragraph of this response continues, "It [the local church] is wholly Church, but not the whole Church. Thus, the local church should not be seen in isolation from but in dynamic relation with other local churches."[43] This application of the *koinonia* ecclesiology of *TCTCV* helps the churches to imagine the possibility of a form of future visible unity that is neither ecclesial merger nor a movement "home to Rome" (or Constantinople), but rather a communion of communions in which each communion is able to conserve and offer to the whole church its diversity of distinctive ecclesial gifts while having full communion with the other communions. Such "full communion" would entail the conditions envisioned by the New Delhi statement referenced above: a full communion of the churches with each other in which all baptized Christians fully belong to one another in a covenanted community that is both local and worldwide, marked by common confession of the broad contours of the historic faith of the church, common celebration of the Eucharist in which table fellowship is fully extended to all members of all churches, joint engagement in mission and

---

43. WCC, *TCTCV*, §31. The BWA has previously embraced this conception of the interdependency of the local church and expressions of church beyond the local church. In conjunction with the German Union of Free Evangelical (Baptist) Churches, the BWA sponsored a Symposium on Baptist Identity and Ecclesiology in Elstal, Germany, Mar. 21–24, 2007, that addressed the question "Are Baptist Churches Autonomous?" Among the five affirmations agreed upon by the sixty-plus conference participants were these two: "That for Baptists, the local church is wholly church but not the whole church," and "That our local churches and Conventions/Unions are participants in the one church that God has called into being as we anticipate the full revelation of the children of God." This language derives from Allmen, "L'Église locale," 512, who as a Reformed ecumenist insisted that the local church is "wholly the church, but not the whole church," language closely echoed in the Elstal affirmation. (The statement from the Elstal symposium and the press release reporting on its proceedings are no longer available online at the BWA website, but the affirmation referenced here is quoted and engaged by Newman, "Are Local Baptist Churches." This statement by the BWA, along with the papers from this symposium, are published in Freeman, *Congregational Independence—Associational Interdependence*; see "Statement from the Baptist World Alliance Symposium on Baptist Identity and Ecclesiology (Are Baptist Churches Autonomous?)"; the editorial introduction by Freeman, "Wholly Church but not the Whole Church"; and the articles "Words Are Inadequate to Express Our Convictions: The Problem of the Autonomy of the Local Church" by William H. Brackney and "Are Baptist Churches Autonomous?" by Nigel G. Wright.)

service, mutual recognition of the baptisms and ordinations performed by one another's churches, and a unified prophetic voice. The communion ecclesiology of *TCTCV* offers a theological framework within which such full communion may more easily be envisioned, and in a manner that may seem much more inviting to the churches that have a history of reticence about Faith and Order ecumenical proposals.

3.4. The *koinonia* ecclesiology of *TCTCV* also makes ecclesial space for the practice of "receptive ecumenism" as a paradigm for ecumenical convergence. It invites the churches "not only to work untiringly to overcome divisions and heresies but also to preserve and treasure their legitimate differences in liturgy, custom and law and to foster legitimate diversities of spirituality, theological method and formulation in such a way that they contribute to the unity and catholicity of the Church as a whole."[44] While the language of receptive ecumenism is recent in ecumenical theology,[45] as a practice it has long been practiced in the recognition that there are gifts of liturgy, spirituality, theology, and other ecclesial practices present in other traditions that may be received into one's own tradition to help it become more fully catholic, more fully under the rule of Christ, without relinquishing the good gifts that have been distinctively stewarded in one's own tradition. The reception of *TCTCV* by the churches can help the practice of receptive ecumenism become more intentional. When practiced over time by the churches, it may lead to the future realization that our churches have so remarkably converged toward one another through the exchange of these gifts that full communion is now possible in ways not previously envisioned, as the gift of the Spirit at work in the churches rather than as a blueprint for convergence engineered by ecumenists.

---

44. WCC, *TCTCV*, §30.

45. Receptive ecumenism is a more recent approach to ecumenical dialogue according to which the communions in conversation with one another seek to identify the distinctive gifts that each tradition has to offer the other and which each could receive from the other with integrity, but in which "the primary emphasis is on learning rather than teaching . . . each tradition takes responsibility for its own potential learning from others and is, in turn, willing to facilitate the learning of others as requested but without dictating terms and without making others' learning a precondition to attending to one's own" (quotation is from a briefing document distributed to participants in an international conference on receptive ecumenism held at Durham University [UK] in 2006 and included in Walter Cardinal Kasper's foreword to Murray, *Receptive Ecumenism*, vii).

4. Challenges to Baptists

4.1. The next question which *TCTCV* poses to the churches is "What adaptations or renewal in the life of your church does this statement challenge your church to work for?" Receptive ecumenism is not merely the addition of gifts received from other churches to the store of gifts already possessed by one's own church. Sometimes the recognition of the desirability of these gifts carries with it the realization of deficiencies in one's own church that must be rectified by altering aspects of faith and practice in light of a current shortcoming that another tradition's gift reveals. At other times, a gift recognized in another tradition leads to the re-reception of a gift that has previously marked the life of one's own communion but that has been neglected or forgotten and therefore must be renewed.

4.2 After noting the interdependence that marked the first-century Christian communities described in the New Testament, *TCTCV* rightly insists:

> This communion of local churches is thus not an optional extra. The universal Church is the communion of all local churches united in faith and worship around the world. It is not merely the sum, federation or juxtaposition of local churches, but all of them together are the same Church present and acting in this world. Catholicity . . . refers not simply to geographic extension but also to the manifold variety of local churches and their participation in the fullness of faith and life that unites them in the one *koinonia*.[46]

While Baptists are able to recognize their emphasis on the primacy of the local church in the refusal of *TCTCV* to prioritize the universal church over the local church, serious consideration of the *koinonia* ecclesiology of *TCTCV* will remind Baptists that while "the local church is wholly church, it is not the whole church" and that there is therefore something intrinsically deficient about the local church when it is not living into the fullest possible extension of its interdependence with the whole church.

4.3. Baptists have often seen themselves as ecumenical in the sense that they value their spiritual connection that they already have with other followers of Jesus Christ in other churches from which Baptists are visibly divided. They recognize that with these other Christians they share "one body and one Spirit . . . one hope . . . one Lord, one faith, one baptism, one God" (Eph 4:4–6) in what has been termed a "spiritual ecumenism."

---

46. WCC, *TCTCV*, §31.

While this is an important recognition as a starting point for ecumenical engagement, Baptists have too often been content with affirming spiritual ecumenism and neglecting or even disavowing the visible unity of the followers of Jesus, which is the clear implication of Jesus's prayer "that they may all be one . . . so that the world may believe that you have sent me" (John 17:21). The insistence of *TCTCV* that visible unity is the goal of ecumenical convergence challenges Baptists beyond being content with the spiritual ecumenism they already affirm.

5. Opportunities for *Koinonia* in Life and Mission

5.1. The introduction to *TCTCV* asks, "How far is your church able to form closer relationships in life and mission with those churches which can acknowledge in a positive way the account of the Church described in this statement?" While Baptist ecclesial diversity precludes generalizing about Baptists' perspectives on particular ecclesiological proposals, in general, Baptists will be able both to affirm the vision of the church articulated by *TCTCV* and to recognize churches that can join them in affirming this vision as churches with which "closer relationships in life and mission" can be formed.

5.2. The Lund Principle proposed at the Third World Conference on Faith and Order in Lund, Sweden, in 1952, according to which churches should "act together in all matters except those in which deep difference of conviction compel them to act separately," serves as a useful means of self-examination regarding the extent to which Baptist churches have developed missional partnerships with other churches in living into the vision of *TCTCV* for a more visible unity.[47]

5.3. In the context of international bilateral dialogue, delegated representatives of the BWA have already affirmed the Lund Principle as a guideline for entering into missional partnerships with other churches. The first of eleven recommendations at the conclusion of the report from the dialogue between the BWA and the World Methodist Council is this:

> Around the world Baptists and Methodists share joint work through theological education, social ministry, youth programs, evangelistic meetings, joint communion services, and they often participate in each other's churches when there is no congregation of their own denomination in the area. Because such widespread

---

47. WCC, *Third World Conference*, 15–16.

shared life already exists, we recommend that at every geographical level from the global to the local congregation, Baptists and Methodists always seek to follow the Lund principle that "to manifest the oneness of the people of God [they should] act together in all matters except those in which deep differences of conviction compel them to act separately."[48]

Therefore, inasmuch as there are other churches beyond Baptist churches and Methodist churches that embrace the ecclesial vision of *TCTCV* in which Baptists can recognize themselves and which Baptists can affirm, this application of the Lund Principle to Baptist-Methodist relationships can be applied to Baptist relationships with these other Christian churches as well.

6. Baptist Questions and Suggestions for the Commission on Faith and Order

6.1. Finally, *TCTCV* invites response to the question "What aspects of the life of the Church could call for further discussion and what advice could your church offer for the ongoing work by Faith and Order in the area of ecclesiology?" While there is much that Baptists could propose for work by the Commission on Faith and Order, in this response we focus on some ways in which from our perspective the *koinonia* ecclesiology of *TCTCV* could be fruitfully applied to matters not sufficiently developed in this convergence text.

6.2. Although *One Baptism: Towards Mutual Recognition* (2011) represented a fuller development of *BEM*'s recognition of the historical and theological priority of believer's baptism that Baptists were able to appreciate,[49] this did not receive as thorough an exploration as might have been desired in *TCTCV*. This convergence text also did not apply the insights of its emphasis on *koinonia* to the ongoing divisions between churches that baptize only believers and those that also baptize the infant children of believing parents. Proposals that focus on the "mutual recognition of baptism," which is the language employed also by *TCTCV*,[50] remain problematic from a Baptist perspective. However, the international bilateral dialogues that the BWA has held with the Anglican Communion,

---

48. BWA and World Methodist Council, *Faith Working through Love*.
49. Harmon, "'One Baptism.'"
50. WCC, *TCTCV*, §41.

the Catholic Church, and the World Methodist Council have explored the possibilities for a mutual recognition of journeys of initiation in which the emphasis is shifted from chronological orderings of faith, baptism, and formation in faith to a focus on the whole journey of Christian initiation in the company of the church.[51] As one response to *TCTCV* by an individual Baptist theologian has suggested, a theology of *koinonia* makes it possible to appreciate the manner in which different orderings of events in whole journeys of initiation nonetheless draw those who are baptized into participation in the communion of the Triune God in the communion of the church.[52] We believe that a fully ecumenical exploration of these possibilities for a mutual recognition of journeys of initiation in light of the *koinonia* ecclesiology expressed in *TCTCV* would be a fruitful endeavor for future work by the WCC Commission on Faith and Order.

6.3. In light of the convergence between an ecclesiology rooted in Trinitarian *koinonia* and a Baptist covenantal ecclesiology explored in bilateral dialogues with BWA participation noted earlier in this response (2.5), we suggest that further study of the parallels between covenantal ecclesiologies and communion ecclesiology would invite a wider embrace of the vision of *TCTCV* not only by Baptists but also by other churches in the broader Free Church tradition.

6.4. The WCC Commission on Faith and Order recently has been giving attention to the matter of ecclesial moral discernment, which is becoming a concern for Faith and Order ecumenism because disagreements over ethical issues are increasingly a cause of ecclesial division.[53] It has been noted that the section of *TCTCV* on "The Moral Challenge of the Gospel"[54] lacks any connection with the overarching theme of *koinonia*. The application of the framework of Trinitarian *koinonia* to moral discernment in the churches might supply this ecclesial practice with a theological framework that "can point all people towards the possibility of a life in which relations are the most important thing, where all persons and even the natural environment are interconnected, and where human beings can actively and

---

51. BWA and Anglican Consultative Council, *Conversations around the World 2000-2005*, §§40-52 (pp. 44-51); BWA and Catholic Church, "Word of God," §§101-6; BWA and World Methodist Council, *Faith Working through Love*, §§70-80.

52. Fiddes, "Koinonia," 43-44.

53. WCC, *Moral Discernment*.

54. WCC, *TCTCV*, §§61-63.

intentionally participate more deeply in movements of love and justice in which they are already immersed by living in the world."[55]

7. Recommendations for Baptist Reception of *The Church: Towards a Common Vision*

Toward the end of facilitating reception of *TCTCV* among Baptists, the BWA Commission on Baptist Doctrine and Christian Unity makes the following recommendations:

7.1.1. The text of *TCTCV* and this response to it need to be disseminated widely in the global Baptist community if there is to be a Baptist reception of what is proposed by this convergence text. Links to the electronic version of *TCTCV* on the website of the WCC Commission on Faith and Order and to this response from the BWA Commission on Baptist Doctrine and Christian Unity should be posted on the websites of the BWA and its regional fellowships.

7.1.2. The Baptist reception of the ecumenical ecclesiology articulated by *TCTCV* will be aided by posting the statement from the 2007 Elstal Symposium on Baptist Identity and Ecclesiology once again on the BWA website (see 3.3 above).

7.2. In the absence of ecumenical officers and other structures tasked with promoting ecumenical engagement, in the Baptist tradition it is institutions of theological education that have the greatest opportunity for facilitating Baptist reception of *TCTCV*. We recommend that the BWA encourage Baptist theological educators to make use of *TCTCV* and this response to it as texts in courses that include attention to ecclesiology and that institutions of theological education provide continuing education opportunities for ministers that introduce them to *TCTCV*.

7.3. At the local level, we encourage Baptist ministers to study *TCTCV* themselves and to form local study groups with ministers of neighboring churches from other traditions to read and discuss *TCTCV* and to contemplate the possibilities for living into its vision locally in the relationships between their churches.

7.4. We appeal to local Baptist churches, to Baptist associations and unions, and to the BWA itself to give serious, prayerful consideration to the Lund Principle, according to which churches should "act together in all matters except those in which deep difference of conviction compel them

---

55. Fiddes, "*Koinonia*," 46.

to act separately," as a call to seek a fuller, more visible participation in the Trinitarian *koinonia* imagined by *TCTCV* wherever manifestations of this *koinonia* are recognized.

Bibliography

Abramov, Alexander, et al. "The Importance, Relevance, and Challenge of 'The Church: Towards a Common Vision.'" *Journal of European Baptist Studies* 15 (2015) 28–33.

Allmen, Jean-Jacques von. "L'Église locale parmi les autres Églises locales." *Irénikon* 43 (1970) 512–37.

Baban, Octavian D. "Four Views and a Response on WCC Church Vision." *Journal of European Baptist Studies* 15 (2015) 34–45.

Broadway, Mikael, et al. "Re-Envisioning Baptist Identity: A Manifesto for Baptist Communities in North America." *Baptists Today* (1997) 8–10.

———. "Re-Envisioning Baptist Identity: A Manifesto for Baptist Communities in North America." Duke Divinity, May 1997. http://divinity.duke.edu/sites/divinity.duke.edu/files/documents/faculty-freeman/reenvisioning-baptist-identity.pdf.

———. "Re-Envisioning Baptist Identity: A Manifesto for Baptist Communities in North America." *Perspectives in Religious Studies* 24 (1997) 303–10.

BWA. "Commissions." Baptist World Alliance, n.d. https://baptistworld.org/commissions/.

———. "Constitution of the BWA." Baptist World Alliance, July 2020. https://secureservercdn.net/50.62.89.49/07e.4a3.myftpupload.com/wp-content/uploads/2020/08/BWA-Constitution-and-Bylaws-2020.pdf.

———. "Statistics." Baptist World Alliance, n.d. https://web.archive.org/web/20200318081247/https://www.bwanet.org/about-us2/stats.

BWA and Anglican Consultative Council. *Conversations around the World 2000–2005: The Report of the International Conversations between the Anglican Communion and the Baptist World Alliance.* London: Anglican Communion Office, 2005.

BWA and Catholic Church. "The Word of God in the Life of the Church: A Report of International Conversations between the Catholic Church and the Baptist World Alliance 2006–2010." *American Baptist Quarterly* 31 (2012) 28–122.

———. "The Word of God in the Life of the Church: A Report of International Conversations between the Catholic Church and the Baptist World Alliance 2006–2010." Christian Unity, n.d. http://www.christianunity.va/content/unitacristiani/en/dialoghi/sezione-occidentale/alleanza-battista-mondiale/dialogo-internazionale-tra-la-chiesa-cattolica-e-l-alleanza-batt/documenti-di-dialogo/2010-la-parola-di-dio-nella-vita-della-chiesa/testo-del-documento-in-inglese.html.

———. "The Word of God in the Life of the Church: A Report of International Conversations between the Catholic Church and the Baptist World Alliance 2006–2010." *Pontifical Council for Promoting Christian Unity Information Service* 142 (2013) 20–65.

BWA and World Methodist Council. *Faith Working through Love: Report of the International Dialogue between the Baptist World Alliance and the World Methodist Council.* Baptist World Alliance, 2018. https://www.bwanet.org/images/MEJ/Final-Report-of-the-International-Dialogue-between-BWA-and-WMC.pdf.

Chilton, Amy L. and Steven R. Harmon, eds. *Sources of Light: Resources for Baptist Churches Practicing Theology*. Perspectives on Baptist Identities 3. Macon, GA: Mercer University Press, 2020.

Congar, Yves. *Chrétiens désunis: principes d'un "oecuménisme" catholique*. Unum Sanctam 1. Paris: Cerf, 1937.

———. *Divided Christendom: A Catholic Study of the Problem of Reunion*. Translated by M. A. Bousfield. London: Centenary, 1939.

Coorilos, Geevarghese Mar. "The Nature and Mission of the Church: An Indian Perspective." In *Called to Be the One Church: Faith and Order at Crete*, edited by John Gibaut, 188–92. Faith and Order 212. Geneva: WCC, 2012.

Estep, William R. "A Response to *Baptism, Eucharist and Ministry*: Faith and Order Paper No. 111." In *Faith, Life and Witness: The Papers of the Study and Research Division of the Baptist World Alliance 1986–1990*, edited by William H. Brackney and R. J. Burke, 2–16. Birmingham: Samford University Press, 1990.

Fiddes, Paul S. "'Koinonia: The Church in and for the World': Comment on the Final Part of *The Church: Towards a Common Vision* (Faith and Order Paper 214)." In *Papers of the Commission on Mission, Evangelism and Theological Reflection of the Baptist World Alliance 2010–2015*, edited by Eron Henry, 37–47. Baptist Faith & Witness 5. Falls Church, VA: Baptist World Alliance, 2015.

———. *Tracks and Traces: Baptist Identity in Church and Theology*. Studies in Baptist History and Thought 13. Milton Keynes, UK: Paternoster, 2003.

Freeman, Curtis W. "'The Church of the Triune God': A Baptist Response to *The Nature and Mission of the Church: A Stage on the Way to a Common Statement* (Faith and Order Paper 198)." In *Papers of the Commission on Mission, Evangelism and Theological Reflection of the Baptist World Alliance 2010–2015*, edited by Eron Henry, 7–24. Baptist Faith & Witness 5. Falls Church, VA: Baptist World Alliance, 2015.

———, ed. *Congregational Independence—Associational Interdependence*. Thematic issue of *American Baptist Quarterly* 38 (Spring 2019).

Fuchs, Lorelei. *Koinonia and the Quest for an Ecumenical Ecclesiology: From Foundations through Dialogue to Symbolic Competence for Communionality*. Grand Rapids: Eerdmans, 2008.

Harmon, Steven R. *Baptist Identity and the Ecumenical Future: Story, Tradition, and the Recovery of Community*. Waco, TX: Baylor University Press, 2016.

———. "How Might We Envision the Unity We Have? Engaging *The Church: Towards a Common Vision*, Part 1." Keynote address, Louisiana Interchurch Conference, Wesley Center, Woodworth, LA, Mar. 2–3, 2015.

———. "'One Baptism': A Study Text for Baptists." *Baptist World: A Magazine of the Baptist World Alliance* 58 (2011) 9–10.

———. "What Can We Do about the Unity We Envision? Engaging *The Church: Towards a Common Vision*, Part 2." Keynote address, Louisiana Interchurch Conference, Wesley Center, Woodworth, LA, Mar. 2–3, 2015.

Hatch, Derek C. "*Koinonia* as Ecumenical Opening for Baptists." *Ecumenical Review* 71 (2019) 175–88.

Hinson, E. Glenn. "William Carey and Ecumenical Pragmatism." *Journal of Ecumenical Studies* 17 (1980) 73–83.

Kerstan, R. J., and R. J. Burke, eds. *Out of Darkness into the Light of Christ: Official Report of the Fifteenth Baptist World Congress, Los Angeles, California, USA, July 2–7, 1985*. McLean, VA: Baptist World Alliance, 1985.

King, Martin Luther, Jr. "Letter from Birmingham Jail." Martin Luther King, Jr. Research and Education Institute, Apr. 16, 1963. http://okra.stanford.edu/transcription/document_images/undecided/630416-019.pdf.

Luckey, Hans. *Johann Gerhard Oncken und die Anfänge des deutschen Baptismus*. 3rd ed. Kassel, Germ.: Oncken, 1958.

Manley, Ken. "A Survey of Baptist World Alliance Conversations with Other Churches and Some Implications for Baptist Identity." Paper presented to the joint meeting of the BWA Baptist Heritage and Identity Commission and Doctrine and Interchurch Cooperation Commission, Seville, Spain, July 11, 2002. https://archive.org/details/bwa-2002-manley-conversations.

Murray, Paul D., ed. *Receptive Ecumenism and the Call to Catholic Learning: Exploring a Way for Contemporary Ecumenism*. Oxford, UK: Oxford University Press, 2008.

Newman, Elizabeth. "Are Local Baptist Churches Wholly Autonomous?" *Baptist News Global*, June 12, 2007. https://baptistnews.com/article/opinion-are-local-baptist-churches-wholly-autonomous/#.Yxkt4S-B1QI.

———. "'The Church: Growing in Communion': Response to Chapter III of *The Church: Towards a Common Vision* (Faith and Order Paper 214)." In *Papers of the Commission on Mission, Evangelism and Theological Reflection of the Baptist World Alliance 2010–2015*, edited by Eron Henry, 25–36. Baptist Faith & Witness 5. Falls Church, VA: Baptist World Alliance, 2015.

Payne, Ernest A. "Baptists and the Ecumenical Movement." *Baptist Quarterly* 8 (1960) 258–67.

Searle, Joshua T. "Moving towards an Ecumenism of *Koinonia*: A Critical Response to 'The Church: Towards a Common Vision' from a Baptistic Perspective." *Journal of European Baptist Studies* 15 (2015) 17–27.

Second Vatican Council. *Unitatis Redintegratio* [Decree on ecumenism]. Vatican, Nov. 21, 1964. http://www.vatican.va/archive/hist_councils/ii_vatican_council/documents/vat-ii_decree_19641121_unitatis-redintegratio_en.html.

Thurian, Max, ed. *Churches Respond to "Baptism, Eucharist and Ministry."* 6 vols. Geneva: World Council of Churches, 1986–88.

Van der Leer, Teun. "*The Church: Towards a Common Vision*: A Believers Church Response." *Journal of European Baptist Studies* 15 (2015) 21–31.

WCC. "Baptist Churches." Oikoumene, n.d. https://www.oikoumene.org/en/church-families/baptist-churches.

———. *The Church: Towards a Common Vision*. Faith and Order 214. Geneva: WCC, 2013. https://www.oikoumene.org/sites/default/files/Document/The_Church_Towards_a_common_vision.pdf.

———. *Moral Discernment in the Churches: A Study Document*. Faith and Order 215. Geneva: WCC, 2013.

———. *The Nature and Mission of the Church: A Stage on the Way to a Common Statement*. Faith and Order 198. Geneva: WCC, 2005.

———. *The Nature and Purpose of the Church: A Stage on the Way to a Common Statement*. Faith and Order Paper 181. Geneva: WCC, 1998.

———. *The New Delhi Report: The Third Assembly of the World Council of Churches, 1961*. New York: Association, 1962.

———. *The Third World Conference on Faith and Order, Lund 1952*. Edited by Oliver S. Tomkins. London: SCM, 1953.

2

The Baptistic Ecclesial Voice

Teun van der Leer

Introduction

In November 1952 Lesslie Newbigin, the then-bishop of Madurai-Ramnad in the (ecumenical) Church of South India, delivered the Kerr Lectures at Trinity College in Glasgow, Scotland, on the nature of the church. One year later they were published as what was to become a classic in ecumenical ecclesiology, *The Household of God*. In this book he discerns and discusses three types of church, characterizing them as manners of our ingrafting or incorporation into Christ. He names them, in this order, *protestant* (incorporated by hearing and believing the gospel), *catholic* (incorporated by sacramental participation in the life of the historically continuous church), and *pentecostal* (incorporated by receiving and abiding in the Holy Spirit).[1] Here—without explicitly mentioning him—Newbigin follows Angus Dun, who talks about three different ways of embodying the vision of the church, naming them catholic (the church as a "great society"),

---

1. Newbigin, *Household of God*, 9. Although Newbigin uses a capital letter for Protestant, Catholic, and Pentecostal, I use the lower case to make it clear that we are not talking about denominations but about types. Newbigin also uses the word *types* on pp. 30 and 111.

classical protestant (the church as the community that receives the word of God in faith), and "the fellowship of the Spirit" (the church as a community of the Spirit-led life in Christ).² In a similar way Franklin Littell, in defining the Free Church, talks about a "'third force' in Western Christianity, a force just as original as Roman Catholicism or 'magisterial Protestantism.'"³ James McClendon, following Newbigin, chooses "baptist" as the name for what he calls "a third type of Christian community, a third understanding of 'church,'" which is "local, Spirit-filled, mission-oriented, its discipleship always shaped by a practice of discernment."⁴ He believes the type to be distinctive, having "its own role and destiny in the Kingdom of Christ."⁵

In this chapter I want briefly to delineate the baptistic ecclesial voice as part of this third type or third force, seeing this type as the distinctive third voice in the ecumenical discourse on the nature of the church. First, I will give a short historical overview of the development of the terms and descriptions used for this type of Christian community. Second, I will show that the type is distinctive but not exclusive, and part of the "one, holy, catholic, and apostolic church." Finally, I will explain that the Baptist vision of the church is best defined by its core practices, which as a lived theology show us what the church is called to be. As such this chapter functions as an introduction to the purpose of this book: to contribute to the ecumenical ecclesiological search for a common vision of the church by presenting the singularity of a Baptist ecclesiology through its core practices.

The Third Type

The use of types goes back to the works of Weber and Troeltsch at the beginning of the twentieth century, both using *sect* to describe the "baptist"

---

2. Dun, *Prospecting for Uniting Church*, 46–58. Cf. Parushev, *Christianity in Europe*, 15.

3. Littell, "Historical Free Church Defined," 78. Shelly, without referring to Littell, also uses the term *third force* (Shelly, "Deliberation on 'Believers Church,'" 1078).

4. McClendon, *Doctrine*, 343. He introduces this idea for the first time in his essay "What Is a 'Baptist' Theology?" and explores it further in "The Baptist Vision." This latter essay, which is adapted from the graduation address at the International Baptist Theological Seminary (IBTS), Rüschlikon, Switzerland, April 25, 1985, was found in the archives of the IBTS in Prague (now located since 2014 in Amsterdam) and published in its original form in 2014. A significant revised and expanded version of this text was published as "The Mennonite and Baptist Vision."

5. McClendon, "Baptist Vision," 26.

type of church, over against *church* for the established church.[6] The difference in a nutshell is that "one is born into a church, but *joins* a sect."[7] In their descriptions of the sect both emphasize regenerate membership and voluntarism: in the words of Troeltsch, "the sect is a voluntary society, composed of strict and definite Christian believers bound to each other by the fact that all have experienced 'the new birth.'"[8] The "third type churches" themselves use names that point to the alternatives they represent: Free Church (and not State Church),[9] Believers' Church (and not National Church),[10] Gathered or Gathering Church (and not Given Church)[11] and Congregationalist (and not Episcopal or Presbyterian).[12] Of course all of them are ideal types, meant to *clarify*, not to *classify*.[13] They are used as constructions to understand and analyze different ways of being church. Common characteristics for the third type can be found in the gathering of consciously committed believers, the separation of church and state, living under the rule of Christ in a "congregational way" and a deep desire to be a "New Testament Church." So here the church is first and foremost a

---

6. Max Weber talks about "Puritan sects" and "Baptist sects" in his *Protestant Ethic*. A couple of years later Ernst Troeltsch introduces here his famous tripartite "church, sect and mysticism" in *The Social Teaching of the Christian Churches*.

7. Paul Fiddes formulates the essential difference in this way in "Church and Sect," 34.

8. Troeltsch, *Social Teaching*, 993. Fiddes thinks that Weber's almost exclusive focus on the element of "voluntarism" overlooks the Baptist theology of covenant. Fiddes's conclusion is that while the behavior of the early Baptists "sometimes showed the marks of a sect, their covenant theology supplied a momentum towards 'free-church' which was unstoppable" (Fiddes, "Church and Sect," 60).

9. Littell, *Free Church*.

10. Durnbaugh defines them as "the covenanted and disciplined community of those walking in the way of Jesus Christ" (Durnbaugh, *Believers' Church*, 33). The term *Believers' Church* (BC) as such dates back to Max Weber who in 1904 in the first edition of his *Protestantische Ethik* introduced this (English) term (rather than a German equivalent), defining it "solely as a community of personal believers of the reborn, and only these" ("eine Gemeinschaft der persönlich Gläubigen und Wiedergeborenen rund nur dieser") (Weber, *Protestant Ethic*, 93).

11. Williams uses *gathered* over against *given* (Williams, "Believers' Church"). Keith Jones prefers *gathering* over *gathered*, being more dynamic and "under construction," rather than "fixed" (Jones, *Believing Church*, 64; Jones, "Rethinking Baptist Ecclesiology," 8; Jones, *European Baptist Federation*, 2).

12. Jenkins, *Congregationalism*; Nuttall, *Visible Saints*; Sell, *Saints*.

13. Durnbaugh, *Believers' Church*, 24.

communio fidelium, constituted "from below," the (local) gathering community of (personal) believers.¹⁴

Baptist and Catholic

The three types of church Newbigin identifies are far from being mutually exclusive, since "all of them can obviously make effective appeal to Scripture ... and are rooted in the very nature of the Gospel itself." He even goes so far as to say that "the denial of any of them leads to the disfigurement of the Church and the distortion of its message."¹⁵ For him this has to do with the eschatological depth of our incorporation in Christ, so the church can never be defined in terms of what it is now, for "the Church is the pilgrim people of God.... Therefore, the nature of the Church is never to be finally defined in static terms, but only in terms of that to which it is going."¹⁶ This eschatological dimension prompts us to relativize our ecclesial identity and makes each type only provisional, awaiting "eschatological completion."¹⁷ Avery Cardinal Dulles, in his well-known *Models of the Church*, notes that *ekklesia* as used in the New Testament is an eschatological term and that only in the eschaton will the church "truly come into its own."¹⁸ Dulles also highlights the point that the different types or models (he uses both terms but prefers models) need to supplement each other: "A balanced theology of the Church must find a way of incorporating the major affirmations of

---

14. "There is still no better witness to the Kingdom's reality than a band of men whose heart God has touched, of whom others take knowledge that they have been with Jesus" (Nuttall, *Visible Saints*, 162). "The church is essentially *communio fidelium*, whatever else it may be beyond this. Without faith in Christ as Savior, there is no church." Those that gather in Christ's name "allow their own lives to be determined by Jesus Christ" and the public confession of faith in him "is *the central constitutive mark of the church*," for "that which the church is, namely, believing and confessing human beings, is precisely that which (as a rule) also *constitutes* it" (Volf, *After Our Likeness*, 147, 150, 151). Cf. Bakker, "'We Are All Equal.'"

15. Newbigin, *Household of God*, 31, 111.

16. Newbigin, *Household of God*, 25. Volf talks about a "sojourning church, moving between the historical minimum and the eschatological maximum" (Volf, *After Our Likeness*, 199).

17. McClendon, *Doctrine*, 337. See also Parushev, *Christianity in Europe*, 15–20.

18. Dulles, *Models of the Church*, 96.

each basic ecclesiological type. Each of the models calls attention to certain aspects of the Church that are less clearly brought out by the other models."[19]

So, talking about and looking for the Baptist vision of the church is not meant to be an exclusive act at all, but rather catholic in intent. With their fellow Christians, Baptists confess the "one, holy, catholic, and apostolic church" and see themselves as *part* of the broader body of Christ. Although there have been and still are sectarian tendencies in the Baptist narrative, there is also a clear catholic approach, which can be traced back in Baptist history. For example, in 1678 the General Baptists adopted in article 38 of their Orthodox Creed "the three creeds, viz. Nicene creed, Athanasius's creed, and the Apostles' creed," saying that they "ought thoroughly to be received, and believed."[20] And when in 1905 the *Baptist World Alliance* was founded in London, its first president Alexander Maclaren invited all present to affirm their faith by repeating the Apostles' Creed, "to put aside any doubt that Baptists stood in the tradition of the historic orthodox Christian faith and of the 'Holy Catholic Church.'"[21] Around the turn of this century a growing list of publications on Baptists and catholicity can be found on both sides of the Atlantic Ocean.[22]

So yes, there is a particular baptistic ecclesial voice and it needs to be heard, but it is a partial voice, singing its song in harmony with the choir of "the church of all times and all places." This nonsectarian catholic approach belongs to what I like to call the ecclesial minimum, the minimal requirements needed to speak of "church": a group of people ("two or three") gathering in Jesus's name, confessing him as Lord through preaching, baptism, the Lord's Supper and discipleship, in union with the catholic church of all times and all places.[23] A local church or a regional or nationwide church "on

---

19. Dulles, *Models of the Church*, 2. Nigel Wright interprets the church "as roughly reflecting two tendencies, the catholic and the baptist . . . as being like the twin foci of an ellipse and as representing divergent tendencies in that phenomenon we call global Christianity." For Wright these are not excluding opposites. On the contrary, "the health and the future of the church are in direct proportion to the ability of these broad models of church to interact and interpenetrate" (Wright, *Free Church, Free State*, xxiv).

20. Lumpkin, *Baptist Confessions of Faith*, 326.

21. Pierard, *Baptists Together in Christ*, 24.

22. See, e.g., Freeman, "Confession for Catholic Baptists"; Fiddes, "Church's Ecumenical Calling"; Harmon, *Towards Baptist Catholicity*; Haymes et al., "One Church, Holy, Catholic"; Bakker, "Towards a Catholic Understanding"; Freeman, *Contesting Catholicity*; Harmon, *Baptist Identity*.

23. Van der Leer, "Kerk op haar smalst," 84–86. Cf. Wright, *Free Church, Free State*,

its own" is an oxymoron, just as an isolated Christian, a believer without a community, is an oxymoron: an impossible combination, like a hot snowball. Particularity and universality are mutually dependent. Any particular ecclesial voice is called to tune its sound on the universal (catholic) church, while at the same time contributing to the (worldwide) multivoiced body of Christ. So while in this book we present the baptistic ecclesial voice with conviction and suitable pride, because we do believe that its voice needs to be heard and has something to bring to the ecumenical ecclesial discourse, we are equally convinced that it will only be fertile and meet the demands of the kingdom when it does so with the humble intention to give *and* to receive, to teach *and* to learn; in sum, only as part of a whole.

Core Practices as Lived Theology

How to describe the Baptist vision of the church? Baptists have no episcopal authority, neither do they share authoritative confessional documents as a starting point for their ecclesiology. Baptists seek their starting point in the lived theology of the local church. Accordingly, their way of doing theology is by reflecting on the convictions and practices that we find in these local communities as they share life in Christ and seek to discern his mind. "Faith is lived out before it is thought through."[24] Curtis Freeman calls this "radical catholicity," meaning a way of life that belongs to all churches, being called to discipleship and a certain lifestyle.[25]

So, in this book we will sketch the Baptist vision of the church by describing our core practices and reflecting on them. Accordingly, a baptistic ecclesial narrative will come to the fore, not only in describing these core practices, but also through critically reflecting on them and analyzing how these core practices might both contribute to the ecumenical ecclesiological discourse and be strengthened by meeting other traditions. In this way we can grow not only in self-understanding but also in self-evaluation as part of the worldwide church.

19, and Volf, *After Our Likeness*, 151, 157–58.

24. Freeman, "Introduction," xvii.

25. Freeman, "Introduction," xiii. See also McClendon and Yoder, "Christian Identity," and McClendon, "What Is Southern Baptist." In this latter article McClendon talks about "a unity deeper than words, yes, deeper than theology itself—a unity centered in a shared life" (McClendon, "What Is Southern Baptist," 76).

Bibliography

Bakker, Henk. "Towards a Catholic Understanding of Baptist Congregationalism: Conciliar Power and Authority." *Journal of Reformed Theology* 5 (2011) 159–83.

———. "'We Are All Equal' (*Omnes sumus aequales*): A Critical Assessment of Early Protestant Ministerial Thinking." *Perspectives in Religious Studies* 44 (2017) 353–76.

Dulles, Avery Cardinal. *Models of the Church*. New York: Random House, 1974.

Dun, Angus. *Prospecting for a Uniting Church*. New York: Harper, 1948.

Durnbaugh, Donald. *The Believers' Church: The History and Character of Radical Protestantism*. Eugene, OR: Wipf & Stock, 1968.

Fiddes, Paul S. "Church and Sect: Cross-Currents in Early Baptist Life." In *Exploring Baptist Origins*, edited by Anthony R. Cross and Nicholas J. Wood, 33–60. Centre for Baptist History and Heritage Studies 1. Oxford, UK: Regent's Park College Press, 2010.

———. "The Church's Ecumenical Calling: A Baptist Perspective." In *Tracks and Traces: Baptist Identity in Church and Theology*, 193–22. Milton Keynes, UK: Paternoster, 2003.

Freeman, Curtis. "A Confession for Catholic Baptists." In *Ties That Bind: Life Together in the Baptist Vision*, edited by Gary A. Furr and Curtis W. Freeman, 83–98. Macon, GA: Smyth & Helwys, 1994.

———. *Contesting Catholicity: Theology for Other Baptists*. Waco, TX: Baylor University Press, 2014.

———. "Introduction: A Theology for Radical Believers and Other Baptists." In *Systematic Theology: Ethics*, by James Wm. McClendon Jr., 1:vii–xxxviii. Waco, TX: Baylor University Press, 2012.

Harmon, Steven R. *Baptist Identity and the Ecumenical Future: Story, Tradition, and the Recovery of Community*. Waco, TX: Baylor University Press, 2016.

———. *Towards Baptist Catholicity: Essays on Tradition and the Baptist Vision*. Studies in Baptist History and Thought 27. Milton Keynes, UK: Paternoster, 2006.

Haymes, Brian, et al. "The One Church, Holy, Catholic and Apostolic." In *On Being the Church: Revisioning Baptist Identity*, 180–94. Milton Keynes, UK: Paternoster, 2008.

Jenkins, Daniel. *Congregationalism: A Restatement*. London: Faber & Faber, 1954.

Jones, Keith. *A Believing Church*. Didcot, UK: Baptist Union of Great Britain, 1998.

———. *The European Baptist Federation: A Case Study in European Baptist Interdependency 1950–2006*. Milton Keynes, UK: Paternoster, 2009.

———. "Rethinking Baptist Ecclesiology." *Journal of European Baptist Studies* 1 (2000) 4–18.

Littell, Franklin H. *The Free Church*. Boston: Starr King, 1957.

———. "The Historical Free Church Defined." *Brethren Life and Thought* 9 (1964) 78–90.

Lumpkin, William L. *Baptist Confessions of Faith*. 1959. Reprint, Valley Forge, PA: Judson, 1969.

McClendon, James Wm., Jr. "The Baptist Vision." *Baptistic Theologies* 6 (2014) 23–35.

———. *Doctrine*. Vol. 2 of *Systematic Theology*. Nashville: Abingdon, 1994.

———. "The Mennonite and Baptist Vision." In *Mennonites and Baptists: A Continuing Conversation*, edited by Paul Toews, 211–24. Winnipeg: Kindred, 1993.

———. "What Is a 'Baptist' Theology?" *American Baptist Quarterly* 1 (1982) 16–39.

———. "What Is a Southern Baptist Ecumenism?" *Southwestern Journal of Theology* 10 (1968) 73–78.

———, and John Howard Yoder. "Christian Identity in Ecumenical Perspective," *Journal of Ecumenical Studies* 27 (1990) 561–80.

Newbigin, Lesslie. *The Household of God: Lectures on the Nature of the Church*. London: SCM, 1953.

Nuttall, Geoffrey F. *Visible Saints: The Congregational Way, 1640–1660*. 2nd ed. Weston Rhyn, UK: Quinta, 2001.

Parushev, Parush R. *Christianity in Europe: The Way We Are Now*. Crowther Centre Monographs 9. Oxford: Church Mission Society, 2009.

Pierard, Richard V., ed. *Baptists Together in Christ, 1905–2005*. Falls Church: BWA, 2005.

Sell, Alan P. F. *Saints: Visible, Orderly, and Catholic: The Congregational Idea of the Church*. Allison Park, PA: Pickwick, 1986.

Shelly, Maynard. "Deliberation on the 'Believers Church.'" *Christian Century* 84 (1967) 1077–80.

Troeltsch, Ernst. *The Social Teaching of the Christian Churches*. New York: Macmillan, 1931.

Van der Leer, Teun. "De kerk op haar smalst: Op zoek naar een ecclesiologisch minimum voor de kerk van de eenentwintigste eeuw." MA thesis, Vrije Universiteit, 2006. https://unie-abc.nl/images/seminarium/publicaties/team/TL_060701_De%20kerk%20op%20haar%20smalst_MAthesis.pdf.

Volf, Miroslav. *After Our Likeness: The Church as the Image of the Trinity*. Grand Rapids: Eerdmans, 1998.

Weber, Max. *The Protestant Ethic and the Spirit of Capitalism*. New York: Routledge Classics, 2001.

Williams, G. H. "The Believers' Church and the Given Church." In *The People of God: Essays on the Believers' Church*, edited by Paul Basden and David S. Dockery, 325–32. Nashville: Broadman, 1991.

Wright, Nigel W. *Free Church, Free State: The Positive Baptist Vision*. Milton Keynes, UK: Paternoster, 2005.

3

Covenanting Churches

Paul S. Fiddes

BAPTISTS WERE AMONG THE groups of Christian believers in the wake of the Protestant Reformation who adopted a view of the church that can be called "covenantal." This distinctive ecclesiology has often been neglected by historians of the period, but it should be regarded as the important fourth strand of the Reformation, alongside Lutheran, Reformed, and Anglican forms of the church. In the sixteenth century it was already being expressed by Anabaptists on the continent of Europe and by English Separatists from the Church of England,[1] and it continued in England not only among Baptists but among Independents, who were later called Congregationalists.[2] The idea that churches were to be created by people "covenanting together," or coming into agreement with each other and with God through his covenant-mediator Christ, had large implications for what it meant to live as a Christian believer, and it still characterizes the way that Baptist churches work today. Indeed, it is not too much to claim that covenanting, in the *particular* Baptist form that was worked out in early days, is responsible for what is recognizable as the distinctive flavor of a Baptist church wherever one might meet it in the world today, despite the differences that flourish between, and within, national groups. This is the case whether or not the actual term *covenant* is used—and let us admit that

---

1. See Yarnell, "Covenant Theology," and Fiddes, "Covenant and Inheritance."
2. See Nuttall, *Visible Saints*, 70–100.

it is now often forgotten—or even whether it is properly understood. The shape and the influence of covenant remain in Baptist genes.

Covenant: A Two-Directional Agreement

Covenant, of course, was a widely shared Reformation theme: for Luther—and more especially for Calvin—God had made an eternal covenant of grace with human beings for their salvation. This had priority over any covenant based on religious law, and it had finally become visible in the new covenant established through Christ. But the Reformation groups I have mentioned did something quite original: they took the biblical idea of covenant and worked it out in terms of the actual form and structure of the church "on the ground." Convinced that the existing Catholic Church had violated its covenant with God, and that the newly reformed churches had either followed suit or were in danger of doing so, they particularized the covenant as a relationship between God and distinct local congregations. Each church was to be gathered by a covenant, and so was to "walk together." This covenant was twofold, or we may picture it as having a horizontal and a vertical direction at once: it was made by members with each other and with God.[3]

First and central to the idea of covenant is what we might call a vertical dimension—the rule of Christ, who calls a church into covenant. Though it is essential that faith be voluntary, in response to the initiating grace of God, the church is not regarded as a merely voluntary society, since it gathers in obedience to Christ as the covenant-maker; it does not just decide to gather together but is gathered in the sense of *being* gathered by Christ. Taking up the Reformation stress on Christ as "prophet, priest, and king," and faced by the claims of a state-sanctioned ecclesiastical authority, first Separatists and then Baptists claimed that it was the risen Christ, present in the midst of the congregation in the authority of his threefold office, who gave his people the seal of the covenant, and so the right to celebrate the sacraments (as priests), to call some to the ministry of the word (as prophets), and to exercise a mutual discipline among each other (so sharing the kingly role of Christ).[4]

---

3. See Fiddes, *Tracks and Traces*, 24–31.

4. "Declaration of Faith of English People," art. 9, in Lumpkin, *Baptist Confessions of Faith*, 119; "Confession of Faith, of those Churches" (1644), art. 10, 13, in Lumpkin, *Baptist Confessions of Faith*, 66; "Confession of Faith Put Forth by the Elders" (1677), in

Intersecting with the vertical dimension of covenant with God in Christ is the horizontal dimension of the members' commitment to each other. In Baptist history, it was a pact undertaken and signed when a particular local church was founded and subsequently made by new members on entering it. They promised both to "give themselves up to God" *and* to "give themselves up to each other"; to "walk in the ways of the Lord" *and* "to walk together"; to obey the "rules of Christ" *and* to "watch over each other." The horizontal dimension is well expressed by the covenant made at Gainsborough in 1606 or 1607 by that congregation of English Separatists who were shortly to travel into religious exile in Amsterdam and in 1609 to adopt the practice of believers' baptism and form the first ("General") Baptist church. As William Bradford recalled the event years later in America, the members:

> joined them selves (by a covenant of the Lord) into a Church estate, in the fellowship of the gospel, to walk in all his ways, made known, or to be made known unto them, according to their best endeavours, whatsoever it should cost them, the Lord assisting them.[5]

The early Baptist John Smyth inherited this two-directional theology of covenant from English Separatists, and something similar can be seen, in a separate development, among continental Anabaptists. However, at this point he took a bold and innovative step. He saw that the intersection of the horizontal and the vertical dimensions of covenant must mean that God's eternal covenant of grace is actually *identified* with the covenant-making of a local congregation. While still a Separatist minister in England, Smyth had defined the ecclesial covenant in terms he had received from former Separatists, neatly summarizing the two dimensions of covenant: "A visible communion of Saints is of two, three or more Saints joined together by covenant with God & themselves."[6] By the time of his residence in Amsterdam, however, he had gone further: "We say the Church or two or three faithful people Separated from the world and joined together in a true covenant, have both Christ, the covenant, & promises."[7] Clearly, *the* covenant referred to here, in contrast to *a* covenant, is the eternal covenant of gracious

---

Lumpkin, *Baptist Confessions of Faith*, 260.

5. Bradford, *History of Plymouth Plantation*, 1:20–22. I have modernized the spelling in all seventeenth-century texts.

6. "Principles and Inferences," in Smyth, *Works of John Smyth*, 1:252.

7. "Paralleles, Censures, Observations," in Smyth, *Works of John Smyth*, 2:403.

salvation, containing all God's promises. When people are joined in *a* covenant, they have *the* covenant itself. That John Smyth is envisaging a physical act of covenant-making is clear from his assertion elsewhere that "the outward part of the true forme of the true visible church is a vowe, promise, oath, or covenant betwixt God and the Saints."[8]

Thus, when a local church makes covenant, its members are entering, or entering more deeply, into the new covenant in which they are redeemed by Christ. As the Baptist historian Barrie White put it, "it seems that for [Smyth], in the covenant promise of the local congregation the eternal covenant of grace became contemporary and man's acceptance of it was actualized in history."[9] This running together of eternal and local covenant is confirmed somewhat later in the practice of English Particular Baptists. When Benjamin Keach produced a covenant for his church at Horsley Down (1697), which became the model for many other covenants in Particular Baptist churches, he wrote an opening pledge that significantly appeals to the "everlasting covenant," promising "to give up ourselves to the Lord, in a Church state . . . that he may be our God, and we may be his People, through the Everlasting Covenant of his Free grace, in which alone we hope to be accepted by him, through his blessed Son Jesus Christ."[10]

This depth of theological understanding about covenanting was to have—and still should have among Baptists today—implications for an understanding of baptism, the Lord's Supper, ministry, and the relation of the local church to the wider church. About all this I have some comments to make later, but for the moment we should observe that a covenantal view of church is marked by tensions that are characteristic of Baptist life and can be either its bane or its glory.

Tensions of a Covenantal Church

A covenant ecclesiology gives rise to two tensions of authority in the life of the church. Correspondingly, the presence of these tensions is the evidence of covenant thinking, whether or not the term is actually used, and they are readily observable in Baptist churches all over the world today—usually (but not always) in a fruitful manner. We can see the tensions already embodied in a Baptist confession of 1644, the so-called London Confession,

---

8. "Principles and Inferences," in Smyth, *Works of John Smyth*, 1:254.
9. White, *English Separatist Tradition*, 128.
10. Keach, *Glory of a True Church*, 71.

to which seven Particular Baptist churches in the city subscribed. The first is a tension between the pastoral oversight exercised by the whole church community and the oversight committed to its "officers" or spiritual leaders. As article 44 expresses it:

> And as Christ for the keeping of this Church in holy and orderly Communion, placeth some special men over the Church, who by their office are to govern, oversee, visit, watch; so likewise for the better keeping thereof in all places, by all the members, he hath given authority, and laid duty upon all, to watch over one another.[11]

This article describes a dynamic view of authority in the community, in which oversight flows to and fro between the personal and the communal; the responsibility of "watching over" the church belongs both to *all* the members gathered in a church meeting to find the mind or purpose of Christ, and to the spiritual leader(s). The London Confession expresses this duality without any apparent sense of strain: while all members agree to "watch over" (oversee) each other spiritually, they also recognize that Christ has called some to an office in which they have a special responsibility for oversight. But this tension is not resolved by any rule or formula defining the limits of oversight in each case. The two kinds of oversight are left fluid and open, requiring a relationship of trust. While "discipline" among Baptists of modern times has modulated into general pastoral care, the general tension in authority remains between ordained ministers and congregation and gives a Baptist congregation its recognizable tone. All disciples have spiritual gifts and are called to ministry, and yet some are called by Christ to exercise a particular office of ministry that the congregation recognizes.

The second ecclesial tension we can find in the London Confession is between the local congregation and the associating of churches together. The seven churches, scattered throughout London, confess in article 47 that

> although the particular Congregations be distinct and several Bodies, every one a compact and knit City in itself; yet are they all to walk by one and the same Rule, and by all means convenient to have the counsel and help of one another in all needful affairs of the Church, as members of one body in the common faith under Christ their only head.[12]

---

11. "Confession of Faith" (1644), in Lumpkin, *Baptist Confessions of Faith*, 168.
12. "Confession of Faith" (1644), in Lumpkin, *Baptist Confessions of Faith*, 168–69.

Each congregation makes decisions for its own faith and life, and yet together they are members of "one body," observing "one and the same Rule." The rule is that of Christ, not an ecclesial rule or canon law defining areas of authority, and is discerned on the basis of Scripture when congregations assemble together. Like authority within the single local congregation, this tension can be lived within only by mutual trust.

Because Christ rules in the local congregation, the congregation has a liberty that cannot be infringed by any external ecclesial power. But this is not an untrammelled freedom, such as is often called "autonomy." Since Christ also rules in assemblies of churches when they gather, the local church meeting *must* give serious attention to the way that this wider association has discerned the mind of Christ, to be ready to trust fellow churches, and to have good reason if it is to challenge their proposals.[13] Of course, a single church meeting is still free to recognize that there are good reasons *not* to confirm wider decisions, but there will be an *expectation* that churches together have been seeking the purpose of the Christ who rules among them. In the words of a document about associating accepted by the Baptist Union of Great Britain in 1998: "No local church is complete of itself and does well to seek for that of Christ which is expressed in the wider body.... To fulfil the mission of Christ, churches have to do it together that they may make up for each other's lacks and set forth the whole Christ."[14] This covenantal vision means that, in principle, a local Baptist church could relate to churches of other Christian confessions in the same way as to other Baptist churches, as long as they were willing to live in covenant with it.

Both tensions identified are in fact held within a framework of covenant relations. The tensions arise naturally if the final authority in congregation and association is given to Christ as ruler and covenant-maker in the church, without any scheme where his rule is to be applied in a hierarchical way within society. The two characteristic tensions of authority could (and still can) result in a lapsing towards one side of the polarity or the other—for example, towards the dangers of a claimed autonomy of the local church, of the authoritarianism of leaders, or of the tyranny of the majority of the congregation. If, however, the tensions are held in bonds of trust, they can be truly creative. The diversity of Baptist life throughout the world shows that these tensions have been worked out in ways that are suitable for the context and for the age in which Baptists have lived.

---

13. On early Baptists here, see White, *English Separatist Tradition*, 28.
14. Baptist Union of Great Britain, *Relating and Resourcing*, 4.

Baptism and the Covenant

Like Anabaptists, but unlike Separatists, Baptists have identified covenant-making with the baptism of believing disciples. The restriction of baptism to these disciples defines the distinctive form of covenantal ecclesiology to which Baptists hold, in which baptism normally marks the entry into the covenant community and through which the covenant of God with a particular church is reaffirmed and enlarged. Among many General Baptists, after John Smyth, baptism in fact replaced the signing of a covenant document rather than being complementary to it; Thomas Grantham, for example, called it "the Baptismal Covenant."[15] While Reformed, Lutheran, and Anglican Christian churches have retained infant baptism from the Catholic tradition, largely on the grounds that infants are to be included in the covenant by virtue of the faith of their parents (arguing from the rite of circumcision in the "old covenant"), Baptists have insisted that a covenanted church requires all its members to be disciples of an age to be able to make covenant promises on their own account.

This should not be taken to mean that a person's profession of faith exhausts the meaning of baptism. Baptists have envisaged the act of baptism—usually but not essentially by immersion—in order to set forth the imagery of dying and rising with Christ as a place where divine grace and human faith meet.[16] In the romantic image of Baptist New Testament scholar George Beasley-Murray, baptismal water is a place in the material world that can become a lovers' "trysting-place" with the crucified and risen Christ who is the maker of the new covenant.[17] In fact, in the seventeenth century, the terms *sacrament* and *ordinance* were often used interchangeably by Baptists,[18] the latter term emphasizing that the actions referred to were instituted by Christ himself.

The depth of covenant theology envisaged by Smyth and other early Baptists, where eternal and local covenant came together into one focus, leads to the Baptist conviction that baptism is not only about the person baptized being made a member of the church of Christ, as is found in the baptismal theology of all other Christian churches. In Baptist understanding,

---

15. Grantham, *Christianismus Primitivus*, 23–27.

16. Baptist Union *of Great Britain, Believing and Being Baptized*, 17–20.

17. Beasley-Murray, *Baptism in New Testament*, 305.

18. See "Orthodox Creed" (1679), art. 27, in Lumpkin, *Baptist Confessions of Faith*, 317; Lambe, *Confutation of Infants Baptisme*, 35–39; Keach, *Tropologia*, 425.

the church itself is being *constituted* through this act. Not only is the baptizand being gathered into the church, but the church is being gathered.[19] Whenever someone is baptized, the church is being regathered, and its covenant is being renewed, as it is expanded through the new members. Thus baptism is not an individual, but a corporate, event. Moreover, since in the act of covenanting we are concerned with God's eternal covenant of grace with all who have faith, baptism must be into the whole body of Christ, the church universal, which Baptists have understood to be not only an "invisible" communion of all the redeemed, alive and dead, but as taking "visible" form in the world through the bodies of all living believers.[20] In Baptist understanding of the church, the church universal (and in this sense, "catholic") exists only in its particular forms in local churches; but the universal is not reducible to the local, and as the one body of Christ, it is not merely the sum total of local churches. While rooted in the tension between local and wider forms of church that belongs to the covenant idea, this ecclesiology is also very close to some contemporary Roman Catholic thought that envisages a *perichoresis* or co-inherence between the universal and the local church.[21] Correspondingly, Baptists have understood the minister of a local church (whether called *presbyteros*, "elder," or *episkopos*, "overseer") to be a "minister of the church in general," whose ordination includes a recognition of her or his ministry wider than that of the local church alone.[22]

Some Baptist theologians have considered the sacraments of baptism and the Lord's Supper to be "seals" of the covenant, confirming the gift of the covenant to believers.[23] Others, like John Smyth himself,[24] preferred to identify the Holy Spirit with the covenantal seal and affirmed that this sealing of the Spirit was received *through* the sacraments. John Fawcett, a Particular Baptist minister in fraternal relation with many General Baptists, was to summarize the situation of covenant-making among Baptists at the end of the eighteenth century thus: "It is the custom in many of our

---

19. Grantham, *Christianismus Primitivus*, 41–42.

20. "Orthodox Creed" (1679), art. 29, in Lumpkin, *Baptist Confessions of Faith*, 319; Turner, *Compendium of Social Religion*, 2–4.

21. E.g., Kasper, "On the Church," 927–30.

22. Turner, *Compendium of Social Religion*, 60; Baptist Union of Great Britain, *Meaning and Practice*, 25.

23. So Collins, *Orthodox Catechism*, 25.

24. "The Character of the Beast," in Smyth, *Works of John Smyth*, 2:582–87.

churches to express this [covenant] in writing . . . though this circumstance cannot be thought essentially necessary to the constitution of a church."[25] Whether by simple identification with baptism or in the form of a separate pledge, it was distinctive of early Baptists to find the eternal covenant of grace becoming actual in time and space in the gathering of the local church through covenant, and this meant that the signs of the covenant were a means of grace, or a place where God's gracious presence with people was known and deepened.

The Breadth of Covenant

In the nineteenth century, with the growth of the evangelical movement and increasing cooperation between churches in mission, Baptists wrongly tended to see covenantal language as inward-looking and exclusive. However, in the last fifty years there has been a rediscovery of the breadth of covenant and its outward-looking nature. The Baptist Union of Great Britain produced a covenant renewal service for its churches at the turn of the millenium, in which members covenanted not only in the local setting but with forms of the wider church in associations and union, and this continues to be widely used.[26] The Baptist World Alliance used covenant language in issuing a "Centenary Message" in 2005, pledging that "these things we declare, affirm and *covenant* to the Lord Jesus Christ and to each other, believing the truth found in Him and revealed in the Scriptures,"[27] and followed this up at Ocho Rios, Jamaica, in 2013 with a "Covenant of Intra-Baptist Relations," thus signifying some kind of "ecclesial" or "churchly" relations between its members, while still of course not regarding the BWA itself as a church. Baptists within the Uniting Church of Sweden have agreed with infant-baptizing churches about having opportunities to express "the individual's willingness to live within the covenant of the baptism,"[28] thus healing an agelong breach between Christian groups about the covenantal nature of baptism. Baptists have also paid more attention to the declarations of Scripture that God has made covenant with "every living creature" (Gen

---

25. Fawcett, *Constitution and Order*, 12.

26. Baptist Union of Great Britain, *Covenant* 21.

27. The European Baptist Federation adopted the message as their "Statement of Identity"; see European Baptist Federation, "Statement of Identity."

28. Uniting Church in Sweden, "Theological Foundation," art. 26.

9; Hos 2:18) and have remade their theology of covenant in new concerns for peace and justice in creation.[29]

In ecumenical theology, *covenant* has tended to be used vaguely by non-Baptists for a cooperation between churches that is welcome but falls short of ecclesial commitments. It is a matter of regret that it is not used to describe the nature of the church in *TCTCV*.[30] This "convergence" document does, rightly, center on the language of *koinonia* or *communio*, which has become the term of choice in ecclesiology of recent years, especially on the ecumenical scene. It has, over the last thirty years or so, supplanted the previously preferred phrases "body of Christ" and "people of God."[31] Ecclesially, *koinonia* can describe the relation of an individual believer to a local congregation, the relating of churches together on various levels of human society, the relation between churches and their leaders (pastors and bishops) and leaders with each other, the communal life created by sharing in the Eucharist, the relation of the local to the universal church, and the participation of all these relations (including the partnership of woman and man in creation) in the loving fellowship of Father, Son, and Holy Spirit. In short, it makes clear that the church is a manifestation in time and space of the eternal relational life of God. There is no attempt in this WCC document to place the concept of covenant alongside *koinonia*; but putting these together has been a definite achievement of the recent conversations between the Roman Catholic Church and the Baptist World Alliance. The report aligns the ecumenical convergence on *communio* with the idea of covenant, affirming in an agreed statement that

> The *koinonia* of the church may also be understood as a "covenant community" although this language is less familiar to Catholics than to Baptists. "Covenant" expresses at once both the initiative and prior activity of God in making relationship with his people through Christ, and the willing commitment of people to each

---

29. See, for example, Haymes, "Covenant and Church's Mission"; Fiddes, *Tracks and Traces*, 45–47. On the universal view of the priestly school of theology, see Baptist Old Testament scholar Brett, "Permutations of Sovereignty," and Brett, *Political Trauma and Healing*, 91–109.

30. The word does appear in paras. 10 (local ecumenical covenant), 17–18, and 45 (Old and New Covenants).

31. For this shift in thought, see Hahnenberg, "Mystical Body of Christ," and Kasper, *Harvesting the Fruits*, 72–77.

other and to God. . . . The fellowship or *koinonia* of the church itself is [thus] both a gift and calling.[32]

The Baptist idea of covenant is just as capacious and inclusive as the now-favorite language of *koinonia*, including the Trinitarian dimension of a covenant of love and purpose within the personal relations of God's own being.[33] *Covenant* brings a sense of commitment and discipleship that may sometimes be missing in the affirmation of *koinonia*, rich in meaning though it is, and so perhaps brings a sense of urgency for the church to share in the mission of God to the world.

Bibliography

Baptist Union of Great Britain. *Believing and Being Baptized: A Discussion Document by the Doctrine and Worship Committee*. London: Baptist Union, 1996.

———. *Covenant 21: Covenant for a Gospel People*. London: Baptist Union, 2000.

———. *The Meaning and Practice of Ordination among Baptists*. London: Kingsgate, 1957.

———. *Relating and Resourcing: The Report of the Task Group on Associating*. Didcot, UK: Baptist Union of Great Britain, 1998.

Beasley-Murray, George. *Baptism in the New Testament*. London: Macmillan, 1963.

Bradford, William. *History of Plymouth Plantation, 1620-1647*. 2 vols. Reprint, Boston: Massachussetts Historical Society, 1912.

Brett, Mark. "Permutations of Sovereignty in the Priestly Tradition." *Vetus Testamentum* 63 (2013) 383–92.

———. *Political Trauma and Healing: Biblical Ethics for a Post-Colonial World*. Grand Rapids: Eerdmans, 2016.

BWA, and Catholic Church. "The Word of God in the Life of the Church: A Report of International Conversations between the Catholic Church and the Baptist World Alliance 2006–2010." *American Baptist Quarterly* 31 (2012) 28–122.

Collins, Hercules. *An Orthodox Catechism*. London: N.p., 1680.

European Baptist Federation. "Statement of Identity." European Baptist Federation, 2005. https://www.ebf.org/about.

Fawcett, John. *The Constitution and Order of a Gospel Church Considered*. Halifax: N.p., 1797.

Fiddes, Paul S. "Covenant and the Inheritance of Separatism." In *The Fourth Strand of the Reformation: The Covenant Ecclesiology of Anabaptists, English Separatists, and Early General Baptists*, edited by Paul S. Fiddes, 63–92. Oxford, UK: Regent's Park College Press, 2018.

———. *Tracks and Traces: Baptist Identity in Church and Theology*. Carlisle, UK: Paternoster, 2003.

Grantham, Thomas. *Christianismus Primitivus, or The Ancient Christian Religion*. London: Smith, 1688.

---

32. BWA and Catholic Church, "Word of God," §16.

33. Further, see Fiddes, *Tracks and Traces*, 26–27, 35–37.

Hahnenberg, Edward P. "The Mystical Body of Christ and Communion Ecclesiology: Historical Parallels." *Irish Theological Quarterly* 70 (2005) 3–30.

Haymes, Brian. "Covenant and the Church's Mission." In *Bound to Love: The Covenant Basis of Baptist Life and Mission*, edited by Paul S. Fiddes et al., 63–75. London: Baptist Union, 1985.

Kasper, Walter. *Harvesting the Fruits: Basic Aspects of Christian Faith in Ecumenical Dialogue*. London: Continuum, 2009.

———. "On the Church." *Tablet* 255 (2001) 927–39.

Keach, Benjamin. *The Glory of a True Church, and Its Discipline Display'd*. London: N.p., 1697.

———. *Tropologia: A Key, to Open Scripture Metaphors, in Four Books*. London: Collingridge, 1856.

Lambe, Thomas. *A Confutation of Infants Baptisme*. London: N.p., 1643.

Lumpkin, William L. *Baptist Confessions of Faith*. 1959. Reprint, Valley Forge, PA: Judson, 1969.

Nuttall, Geoffrey. *Visible Saints: The Congregational Way, 1640–1660*. Oxford, UK: Blackwell, 1957.

Smyth, John. *The Works of John Smyth*. 2 vols. Edited by W. T. Whitley. Cambridge: Cambridge University Press, 1915.

Turner, Daniel. *A Compendium of Social Religion*. 2nd ed. London: Ward, 1778.

Uniting Church in Sweden. "A Theological Foundation for Uniting Church in Sweden." Equmeniakyrkan, Dec. 2015. https://equmeniakyrkan.se/wp-content/uploads/2015/12/theological_foundationUCS.pdf.

White, B. R. *The English Separatist Tradition: From the Marian Martyrs to the Pilgrim Fathers*. Oxford Theological Monographs. Oxford, UK: Oxford University Press, 1971.

Yarnell, Malcolm B., III. "The Covenant Theology of the Early Anabaptists." In *The Fourth Strand of the Reformation: The Covenant Ecclesiology of Anabaptists, English Separatists, and Early General Baptists*, edited by Paul S. Fiddes, 15–62. Oxford, UK: Regent's Park College Press, 2018.

4

Discerning Churches

Henk Bakker

Introduction

THE READER OF *TCTCV* is struck by its Christ-oriented content, the frankness of its plurality, and the sincerity of its invitation to participate in the fair quest for unity. There is no theological objective more urgent in the quest for ecclesial transformation than the application of Jesus's words that "they may be one, just as we are one" (John 17:20–23). Unity and wholeness between Christians coming from different ecclesial traditions reflect God's burning desire in Christ. Therefore, as a people of Christ, we should never forsake the intention of enlightening the interconnectedness of the body of Christ. The WCC document explicitly calls for visible unity, not just for mutual acceptance or respect. The goal is set rather high.

> Visible unity requires that churches be able to recognize in one another the authentic presence of what the Creed of Nicaea-Constantinople (381) calls the "one, holy, catholic, apostolic Church."[1]

---

1. WCC, *TCTCV*, §9.

Accordingly, visible unity implies mutual recognition of every church's true intention to embody the "one, holy, catholic, apostolic Church."[2] However, there's a diversity that is legitimate, as it is derived from these four early Christian descriptors.[3] Moreover, legitimate diversity may be a constructive means for the church to learn and prosper, and exactly here the worldwide Baptist denomination may be of help to the church catholic. After all, the church envisaged by WCC is a conciliar church. For example, the WCC text refers to the nascent church of Jews and gentiles in Acts 15 (the Jerusalem Council),[4] to the first ecumenical council (AD 325),[5] and to the second ecumenical council (AD 381)[6]: three synodic events reflecting unity and diversity in early Christian times. In order to be the church, churches reach out to churches. This is not merely an option; this is what churches do.

> Each local church contains within it the fullness of what it is to be the Church. It is wholly Church, but not the whole Church. Thus, the local church should not be seen in isolation from but in dynamic relation with other local churches. . . . This communion of local churches is thus not an optional extra.[7]

Here, I think, the congregational disposition of Baptist churches basically adds up to the church's conciliar awareness. By all means, Baptists have it in their ecclesial DNA and collective memory not to surrender to communal isolation but to structure themselves as discerning communities, prone to hear the voice of God come from every direction, be it from simple church members or from other congregations. This is exactly how Ignatius of Antioch, in whose writings the wording "catholic church" pops up for the first time in Christian literature (ca. AD 110), conceived of the hallmark of catholicity. For him the church "catholic" denotes the whole visible church as, by nature, it resists itself to division.[8] Over against his opponents, those who over-spiritualize the person of Christ as well as the church, he

---

2. Cf. Denzinger and Schönmetzer, *Enchiridion symbolorum*, §150.

3. WCC, *TCTCV*, §12. Cf. Barth, *Kirchliche Dogmatik* IV/1, 753: "legitime . . . Vielheit" (see also 783–95).

4. WCC, *TCTCV*, §§8 and 30.

5. WCC, *TCTCV*, §§30 and 39.

6. WCC, *TCTCV*, §22.

7. WCC, *TCTCV*, §31.

8. Schoedel, *Ignatius of Antioch*, 244; WCC, *TCTCV*, §22 (the reference to *IgnSm.* 6 should be 8,2).

emphasizes the visibility and concreteness of the body of Christ, and for that matter the natural aversion it feels in the face of discord and enmity.

As a consequence, churches quite habitually feel the need to equip themselves to resist division and develop conciliar practices in order to do so. The WCC text is also clear in this regard. Visible communion needs "structures of conciliar relations and decision-making" to be of any value.[9] At all levels of ecclesial life the presence of conciliar awareness and the gift of spiritual discernment do awaken the church to uphold its natural vigilance and resilience.[10]

Differing Approaches on Catholicity and Discernment

Yet, different approaches of the subject matter prevail. But these differences may altogether reflect the legitimate diversity the church catholic looks after. I briefly summarize five avenues taken on the idea of catholicity and discernment, and consequently focus on the Baptist way by digging deep into the history of Reformed conciliar thinking.

Many growing churches, in particular evangelical and charismatic churches (baptists with a small *b*), would seem to have a (1) pragmatic interest in catholicity. They feel connected with other churches, because they have a shared interest in mission, in church growth, or in a certain agenda evolving from such practicalities. Catholicity is something to be done and to be experienced.[11]

However, if expectations are more doctrinally modeled, (2) the doctrinal approach is taken. Before forces can be joined, confessional concurrences should be covered, in particular regarding Christ, the Bible, and salvation. Very often the pragmatic view and the doctrinal view somehow coincide.

Leaving the binary focus of these two aside, (3) the ontological view of the church catholic comes to mind. In late medieval and early Reformation times the dogmatic notion of the universal church had become an extensively elaborated locus. The universal church was to be equated with the church of true believers, consisting of all Old Testament and New Testament believers, and all those who from the beginning of the Christian era

---

9. WCC, *TCTCV*, §37.
10. Cf. WCC, *TCTCV*, §53.
11. Cf. Doornenbal, *Crossroads*, 38, 52, 154–57.

had, by faith, entrusted their lives unto God.[12] The invisible church is the church "as God sees it," not as humankind (especially clergy) sees it.[13] Only in the mind of God is the universal church "one."[14] Furthermore, because the predicate of unity resides only in the true church, the church "as God sees it," the church catholic here on earth, should be aware of intruders, false teachings and false churches. For that reason, the gift of discernment is primarily granted to its ministers, not to its congregation as such.

The idea of the universal church in God's mind originated merely in opposition to (4) the Roman Catholic notion of being the worldwide church. In Catholic thinking the earthly church equals the true church, the church elect, the *communio sanctorum*. As early as Cyprian of Carthage (d. AD 258) much of the basic structure of Catholic ecclesiology had already been developed.[15] Here the existence of the church depends solely on the presence of the episcopate. The church can be one only because the episcopate is.

> The episcopate is one, each part of which is held by each one for the whole. The Church is also one, which is spread abroad far and wide into a multitude by an increase of fruitfulness.[16]

In order to be a true member of the church, it is necessary to enter into communion with an ordained presbyter whose bishop maintains communion with all bishops.[17] As a consequence, church members are not entitled to convene for the sake of the faith and discern the mind of Christ in matters of church polity and conciliarity. Only clergy are entitled to do so.

In (5) the essentialist approach, the very fiber of the church, its *esse*, is not static whatsoever but in the process of becoming (*fieri*). For that matter, there is no definite state to lean back on, neither in God's mind nor by (supposedly) infallible clergy. Essentialists fall back to the church's authenticity as it stretches itself out from its beginning until now. Catholicity, after all,

---

12. Cf. Hodge, *Systematic Theology*, 3:545–46.

13. Berkhof, *Systematic Theology*, 564.

14. "We need to realize that the church of Jesus Christ *is* one church" (Erickson, *Christian Theology*, 1146); and "The Church in its ideal sense . . . is an object of faith rather than of knowledge" (Berkhof, *Systematic Theology*, 565).

15. Cf. Bakker et al., "Introduction."

16. "Episcopatus unus est. . . . Ecclesia unus est" (Cyprian, *De catholicae ecclesiae unitate* 5). Cf. *De catholicae ecclesiae unitate* 4 ("sacramentum unitatis") and 7 ("unitatis sacramentum"). The Latin text is taken from Van den Brink, *S. Caecilii Cypriani*.

17. Brent, *Cyprian and Roman Carthage*, 286–89.

means authenticity. For example, John Macquarrie emphasizes authentic faith as a distinctive marker of root-catholicity, as it seeks conciliar wisdom to identify itself as such.[18] So, churches live the faith of the church of all ages, carry on its legacy, and pass it on as a conciliar treasure.[19] As James McClendon writes, catholic means "authentic Christian existence *fully extended* in space and time."[20] So, in terms of catholicity and conciliarity, Baptists are to be classified as essentialists and henceforth differ in many respects from the other four positions.[21]

Authenticity and Conciliarity: Luther

According to the Baptist view of catholicity (authenticity) and conciliarity, much of the church's authenticity is embedded in its conciliar practice. After the demise of the practice during the high tide of the Middle Ages, both prior to and during the Reformation, the notion of authentic conciliarity reentered the ecclesial scene. Martin Luther was surely aware of the so-called "conciliar movement," the Council of Constance (1414–18) and the radical conciliar confession that was issued there on April 6, 1415, which became renowned as the *Haec sancta synodus* ("This holy synod") declaration.

Luther repeatedly asked for a free council, yet all his efforts turned futile.[22] For example, in 1520 he insisted on a general council, so as to boldly discuss the charges he made against current penitentiary practices. He may also have expected to convince the prelates and the pope of the accuracy of his theories. In his treatise "Appeal to a Free Christian Council" (1520), the Reformer expounded the idea that a general council regarding matters pertaining to the Christian faith would surpass even the authority of

---

18. "'Catholicity' also means authenticity, that is to say, authenticity of belief and practice in the Church. . . . So from New Testament times onward, we find that when some weighty matter is to be decided, this is done by summoning a council and ascertaining the consensus of the Church" (Macquarrie, *Principles of Christian Theology*, 407).

19. Cf. Harmon, *Towards Baptist Catholicity*, 71–110, 151–77.

20. McClendon, *Witness*, 335.

21. In this regard the report of the Baptist-Catholic conversations (2006–10) is very instructive; see BWA and Catholic Church, "Word of God."

22. See "Disputatio de potestate concilii" (1536) in Luther, *Martin Luther: Lateinisch-Deutsche Studienausgabe*, 3:682–85; and the treatise "Von den Konzilien und Kirchen" (1539) in Luther, *Martin Luther: Ausgewählte Schriften*, 5:182–221.

the pope.²³ Yes, the powers of the pope were strictly bound to the voice of the plenary council (as the *Haec sancta synodus* declaration declared one century earlier).²⁴

In the same treatise, Luther explained that the free council equals the gathered church assembling to discuss pressing ecclesial issues.²⁵ In his later treatise "The Right and Power of the Christian Assembly or Church to Judge all Doctrine and to Appoint Teachers to Install and to Dismiss Them" (1523), Luther declared that Christ's mandate of judging doctrine is not invested in bishops, scholars, and prelates who dictate councils but in "everyone and all Christians together."²⁶ Clergy or nonclergy may teach, but nevertheless "the sheep should judge if they actually teach the voice of Christ or the voice of a stranger."²⁷ After all, the word of God is entrusted to every Christian. Every Christian is taught from God, and consequently every Christian is to be called an anointed priest.²⁸

God had appointed the church as royal priesthood, and all its priests were equal, Luther unfolded. "We are all equal" was his dictum.²⁹ Accordingly, he propounded a drastic reduction of the church and its faith. By

---

23. "Auch ist es offenbar, daß ein christliches allgemeines Konzil, besonders in Sachen des christlichen Glaubens, über dem Papst steht" ("Appellation oder Berufung an ein christliches freies Konzil von dem Papst Leo und seinem unrechten Frevel, erneuert und repetiert" (1520), in Luther, *Martin Luther: Ausgewählte Schriften*, 3:71).

24. "And that everyone of whatever state or dignity, even papal, is bound to obey (*cui quilibet cuiuscumque status vel dignitatis etiam si papalis exsistat obedire tenetur*)" (Bakker, "'We Are All Equal,'" 359).

25. "Deshalb appelliere ich und berufe mich mit dieser Schrift auf ein zukünftiges freies, sicheres Konzil für mich und für alle, die mir anhängen und zukünftig anhängen werden" ("Appellation oder Berufung," in Luther, *Martin Luther: Ausgewählte Schriften*, 3:74–75).

26. "Daß eine christliche Versammlung oder Gemeinde Recht und Macht habe, alle Lehre zu urteilen und Lehrer zu berufen, ein- und abzusetzen" (1523), in Luther, *Martin Luther: Ausgewählte Schriften*, 5:9.

27. "Bischof, Papst, Gelehrte und jedermann hat die Vollmacht zu lehren, aber die Schafe sollen urteilen, ob sie die Stimme Christi oder die Stimme der Fremden lehren" (Luther, in *Martin Luther: Ausgewählte Schriften*, 5:10).

28. Luther, *Martin Luther: Ausgewählte Schriften*, 5:13; "De captivitate Babylonica ecclesiae" (1520), §§17–18, in Luther, *Martin Luther: Lateinisch-Deutsche Studienausgabe*, 3:350.

29. "Omnes sumus aequales"; cf. the language "omnes sumus aequales, sacerdotes et laici" ("De captivitate," §§5–6, in Luther, *Martin Luther: Lateinisch-Deutsche Studienausgabe*, 3:248); and "omnes nos aequaliter esse sacerdotes" and "nos omnes esse aequaliter sacerdotes, quotquot baptisati sumus, sicut revera sumus" ("De captivitate," §§12–13, Luther, *Martin Luther: Lateinisch-Deutsche Studienausgabe*, 3:350, 356).

definition, Protestants represented a reductionist mode of thinking. Protestants, most literally, downscaled the traditional amount of Bible text, creeds, beliefs, rituals, and rites. Christianity should do with less than the Catholic Church prescribes and stick to merely five *solas*. For that matter, the church could do without dominant clergy. For "whosoever had Christ, had all that Christ was, and everything that Christ did," Luther writes.[30] The church comprises a congregation of equals, whose basic task it is to preach and teach the word of God.[31] For that reason, the priesthood of equals purports to make decisions concerning matters of spiritual direction by communal consent.[32]

Glaubensgespräch and Conciliarity: Zwingli

During the Magisterial Reform in Zürich, no formal appeal whatsoever was made to the Catholic Church for a free council. However, Huldrych Zwingli's influence as a humanist on the Swiss Reformation seems to have been decisive.[33] He had his students read the Scripture in the original languages and had them translate and discuss the text. These so-called "prophecyings" officially started in June 1525 but formally had their antecedents in earlier days.[34] Among his students and other bodies that learned from Zwingli's open humanist inquisitiveness were Conrad Grebel and many others who turned against their teacher later and became Anabaptists. They learned from Zwingli that church and state need to have a common vehicle of civic dispute (Latin *disputatio*; German: *Glaubensgespräch*). The disputation was a free council with adequate opportunity for communal debate and discussion (*"ein freies Konzil"*[35]). It was not new but yet had vital importance for the city of Zurich during the third decennium of the

---

30. "Qui Christianus est, Christum habet, qui Christum habet, omnia, quae Christi sunt habet, omnia potens" ("De captivitate," §§ 21–22, in Luther, *Martin Luther: Lateinisch-Deutsche Studienausgabe*, 3:358).

31. "Consensu communitatis" ("De captivitate," §§13, 17, 24, 26, in Luther, *Martin Luther: Lateinisch-Deutsche Studienausgabe*, 3:349, 357).

32. "De captivitate," §§14–15, in Luther, *Martin Luther: Lateinisch-Deutsche Studienausgabe*, 3:356.

33. Erasmus's influence on Zwingli was significant. See Rogge, *Zwingli und Erasmus*.

34. The prophesying started on a regular basis on June 19, 1525, at 8:00 a.m. See Locher, *Zwinglische Reformation*, 161–63, and Hauser, *Prophet und Bischof*, 132–47.

35. Farner, *Lehre von Kirche*, 92–93.

sixteenth century.³⁶ It is well established that Zwingli's theology displays a strong dialogic format.³⁷

Initially, for Zwingli the *Glaubensgespräch* was a vital instrument to invite every believer to participate in matters of ecclesial interest. Every Christian might have an understanding of the meaning of Scripture and subsequently participate in disputations regarding the religious state of affairs in the city. In his treatise "The Clarity and Certainty of the Word of God" (1522), Zwingli explained how the word of God, by its clarity and certainty, may capture the soul of the faithful. The word is free and does not need to be regulated and arranged by ecclesial institutions and explanations. People may read and hear, then decide for themselves, Zwingli maintained.³⁸

Accordingly, every individual listening to Scripture could refrain from philosophy and theology and still be directed to sound spiritual discernment. In an autobiographical note, Zwingli lucidly clarified his conviction by personal experience. When almost eight years earlier Zwingli committed himself to the Scripture, critical learning prevented him from obtaining a clear understanding of the word of God. Prompted by Scripture itself, he decided to lay all theological instruments aside, to plainly study the word and pray for understanding and enlightenment. He wished to learn about the will of God unconditionally, from the word itself: "*Gottes Willen unmittelbar aus seinem eigenen, eindeutigen Wort lernen.*"³⁹ This is exactly the attitude the Reformer passed on to his students and to many more, also to the radical Reformers who spread throughout the South of Germany and advocated this vision on Scripture and church polity. They accused their former teacher of letting the congregation down ("*die Preisgabe der Gemeinde*") as a conciliar means to come to proper discernment.⁴⁰ After all, Zwingli still insisted on hierarchical ecclesial (and magisterial) structures.

---

36. See Witteveen, "Leven van Huldrych Zwingli," 35–36.

37. Wandel, "Zwingli and Reformed Practice," 271.

38. "Die Klarheit und Gewißheit des Wortes Gottes" (1522), in Zwingli, *Huldrych Zwingli Schriften*, 1:124–54.

39. "Die Klarheit und Gewißheit des Wortes Gottes" (1522), in Zwingli, *Huldrych Zwingli Schriften*, 1:149.

40. Bakker, "'We Are All Equal,'" 367.

Sticking to the "Old Custom": Hubmaier

Instructive in this regard is the close connection between the Reformers Balthasar Hubmaier and Zwingli. In the early twenties Hubmaier was still on speaking terms with Zwingli. Both reflected on many issues regarding the Swiss Reformation in private conversations. A year before his turn to faith-baptism, Hubmaier issued in Waldshut the well-known "Eighteen Dissertations Concerning the Entire Christian Life and of What It Consists" (1524).[41] The text specifically calls for a council and, for that reason, adds eighteen theses for public discussion. In the cover letter introducing the theses, Hubmaier wrote:

> Beloved men and brethren: it is an old custom that comes to us from the times of the apostles, that when evil things befall concerning the faith, all men who wish to speak the word of God, and are of a Christian way of thinking, should assemble to search the Scriptures.... Such an assembly has been called the synod, or chapter, or brotherhood... and at the next meeting of the chapter which will be held at Waldshut, you may confer with me fraternally and peaceably. Now in order that we may not consume time unnecessarily with human vanities... bring your Bibles.[42]

The "old custom" referred to by Hubmaier here concerns the practice of conciliar decision of local and regional churches. It gained fresh impetus from the earliest Reformation days on to the emergence of Anabaptist and Baptist life. The Council of Constance and similar innovations of Luther, Zwingli, and Hubmaier altogether point into this direction. This is the conciliar spirit that Baptists have learned to appreciate and which they have developed into their congregational theology. This is the dialogical vision of a "disputatio" of priests who are equal and who are called to prophecy in the church according to the word of God. This is the conciliar principle, the idea of communal (congregational) *Glaubensgespräch*, that Luther as well as Zwingli somehow betrayed.

Baptists Serving the Church Catholic

The Reformation idea of conciliar discernment, only poorly reintroduced by Luther and Zwingli, exercised profound influence on radical parties in

---

41. Lumpkin, *Baptist Confessions of Faith*, 19–23.
42. Lumpkin, *Baptist Confessions of Faith*, 19–20.

Germany, Swiss, and the Lowlands, also on early Baptists, who are considered "birds of the same feather" in this regard. They carry (and cherish) this as a sort of crown jewel in their congregational legacy. Baptist churches consider themselves discerning churches, Bible-reading churches with communal hermeneutics. However, gleaning low-hanging fruit from early Reformation times, we learn that the church is not a democracy. The sphere of worship, watch-care, and prophecy has no immediate concerns with the sphere of politics and playing tricks whatsoever. Congregationalism is not like running your own business in the church, as if it were an extension of the world. The conciliar principle can easily lead to disunity rather than unity, as we (unfortunately) see happen in Baptist circles of all times; but congregationalism is about the rule of Christ and about equipping Christians to voice the mind of Christ on behalf of the whole congregation.

Baptists are privileged to have the care for congregational responsibility deeply rooted in their spiritual genes. Yet, it seems hard to carefully listen to more voices than those present in the local church. Respective of every church's calling to catholicity, we conclude this chapter with saying that this Baptist jewelry is not prone to detach us from other churches but critically defines us as accountable to other churches as well. Whereas Baptist churches are inclined to limit attention to the square meters of their own church life, their original predisposition tends to look wider and longer. Baptist churches can be of value to the church catholic. They may significantly contribute to the practice of congregational discernment within the worldwide church, since they are keen in upholding the voice of the simple folk who walk in the footsteps of Christ.

Bibliography

Bakker, Henk. "'We Are All Equal' (*Omnes sumus aequales*): A Critical Assessment of Early Protestant Ministerial Thinking." *Perspectives in Religious Studies* 44 (2017) 353–76.

Bakker, Henk, et al. "Introduction: Cyprian's Stature and Influence." In *Cyprian of Carthage: Studies in His Life, Language, and Thought*, edited by Henk Bakker et al., 1–27. Late Antique History and Religion 3. Leuven: Peeters, 2010.

Barth, Karl. *Kirchliche Dogmatik* IV/1. Studienausgabe 23. Zürich: Theologisch Zürich, 1986.

Berkhof, Louis. *Systematic Theology*. 1939. Reprint, Grand Rapids: Eerdmans, 1984.

Brent, Allen. *Cyprian and Roman Carthage*. Cambridge: Cambridge University Press, 2010.

BWA, and Catholic Church. "The Word of God in the Life of the Church: A Report of International Conversations between the Catholic Church and the Baptist World Alliance 2006–2010." *American Baptist Quarterly* 31 (2012) 28–122.

Denzinger, H., and A. Schönmetzer, eds. *Enchiridion symbolorum definitionum et declarationum de rebus fidei et morum*. 36th ed. Rome: Herder, 1976.

Doornenbal, Robert. *Crossroads: An Exploration of the Emerging-Missional Conversation with Special Focus on "Missional Leadership" and Its Challenges for Theological Education*. Delft, Netherlands: Eburon, 2012.

Erickson, Millard J. *Christian Theology*. 3rd ed. Grand Rapids: Baker Academic, 2013.

Farner, Alfred. *Die Lehre von Kirche und Staat bei Zwingli*. Reihe Libelli 318. 1930. Reprint, Darmstadt, Germany: Wissenschaftlich, 1973.

Harmon, Steven R. *Towards Baptist Catholicity: Essays on Tradition and the Baptist Vision*. Studies in Baptist History and Thought 27. Milton Keynes, UK: Paternoster, 2006.

Hauser, Martin. *Prophet und Bischof: Huldrych Zwinglis Amtsverständnis im Rahmen der Züricher Reformation*. Ökumenische Beihefte 21. Freiburg, Switzerland: Universitätsverlag Freiburg Schweiz, 1994.

Hodge, Charles. *Systematic Theology*. 3 vols. 1873. Grand Rapids: Eerdmans, 1986.

Locher, Gottfried W. *Die Zwinglische Reformation im Rahmen der europäischen Kirchengeschichte*. Göttingen: Vandenhoeck & Ruprecht, 1979.

Lumpkin, William L. *Baptist Confessions of Faith*. 1959. Reprint, Valley Forge, PA: Judson, 1969.

Luther, Martin. *Martin Luther: Ausgewählte Schriften*. 6 vols. Edited by Karin Bornkamm and Gerhard Ebeling. Frankfurt am Main: Insel, 1982.

———. *Martin Luther: Lateinisch-Deutsche Studienausgabe*. 3 vols. Edited by Günther Wartenberg and Michael Beyer. Leipzig: Evangelisch, 2009.

Macquarrie, John. *Principles of Christian Theology*. Rev. ed. London: SCM, 1966.

McClendon, James Wm., Jr. *Witness*. Vol. 3 of *Systematic Theology*. Nashville: Abingdon, 2000.

Rogge, Joachim. *Zwingli und Erasmus: Die Friedensgedanken des jungen Zwingli*. Arbeiten zur Theologie 11. Stuttgart: Calwer, 1962.

Schoedel, William R. *Ignatius of Antioch: A Commentary on the Letters of Ignatius of Antioch*. Hermeneia. Philadelphia: Fortress, 1985.

Van den Brink, J. N. Bakhuizen. *S. Caecilii Cypriani episcopi Carthaginiensis martyris scripta quaedam*. Scriptores christiani primaevi 1. The Hague: Bakker, 1961.

Wandel, Lee Palmer. "Zwingli and Reformed Practice." In *Educating People of Faith: Exploring the History of Jewish and Christian Communities*, edited by John van Enge, 270–93. Grand Rapids: Eerdmans, 2004.

WCC. *The Church: Towards a Common Vision*. Faith and Order 214. Geneva: WCC, 2013.

Witteveen, K. M. "Het leven van Huldrych Zwingli" [The Life of Huldrych Zwingli]. In *Zwingli in vierderlei perspectief*, edited by W. Balke et al., 7–39. Utrecht, Netherlands: De Banier, 1984.

Zwingli, Huldrych. *Huldrych Zwingli Schriften*. 4 vols. Edited by Thomas Brunnschweiler and Samuel Luntz. Zürich: Theologisch Zürich, 1995.

5

Gathering Churches

Jan Martijn Abrahamse

THE FIRST BAPTIST JOHN Smyth once wrote: "But to his Discipl[e]s Christ promiseth his presence to the worldes end, even to two or three gathered together into his name: Mat. 18.20 & 28. 20."[1] Baptists, like most free churches, tend to describe their ecclesiology in terms of their central act: gathering (Latin *congregatio*) to worship God in the name of Christ. Gathering is not only a short time interruption of its diaspora[2] but, on a deeper level, an understanding of the nature of the church itself. Gathering, hence, contains and names the Baptist theology of the church. However, to be fair: for most Baptists today, religion has become a private affair. Living in a highly mobile and individualized society, long-term and exclusive commitments to one community have become untenable.[3] Gathering today, therefore, is not the same as it once was. In some ways an ecclesiology of gathering itself seems to have become an act against the tides once more, be it on a different level. What does it mean to understand the church as "gathering" in a fragmented society with fragmented "selves"? Where do we find cohesion? And what kind of cohesion is that, that we individuals can be church? This chapter, therefore, aims to bring an adjournment of

---

1. Smyth, "Paralleles, Censures, Observations," 410.
2. Cf. Ellis, *Gathering*, 3.
3. See Klaver, "We Are the World?," 420–30.

the Baptist understanding of gathering by retrieving its meaning for our contemporary fragmented context.

Gathering in an Age of Fragmentation

The changes in Baptist church life reveal how much we live in a fragmented world. Contemporary society is characterized by its social and moral disintegration.[4] Fragmentation commonly refers to the religious pluralism prevalent in Western society that is deficient of providing a coherent and unifying story.[5] This fragmentation, obviously, pressures community life both in society as a whole and in the multiple groups and associations that we have: labor unions, political parties, music associations, sport clubs, etc.—they all face dropping numbers. Baptist theologian Harvey Cox already observed these massive social shifts in his theological bestseller *The Secular City* (1965), when he described the process of urbanization as "a structure of common life in which diversity and the disintegration are paramount. It means a type of impersonality in which functional relationships multiply. It means that a degree of tolerance and anonymity replace traditional moral sanctions and long-term acquaintanceships."[6] The diversity of city life has become a template for modern life and the self-evident social settings that are now characterized by anonymity and mobility.[7]

The dangers of such disintegration are pronounced by Charles Taylor, as he writes that Western societies are on the brink of losing all cohesion and, consequently, will find themselves in a state of internal strife, heightened oppositions, caught by a mentality of getting your rights and power.[8] "Fragmentation," according to Taylor, "arises when people come to see themselves more and more atomistically, otherwise put, as less and less bound to their fellow citizens in common projects and allegiances."[9] Elsewhere, Taylor explains the current problem of authenticity as in the

---

4. See Wilson, *Living Faithfully*, 24–38.

5. Cf. Davie, *Sociology of Religion*, 155, and Boutellier et al., *Bindingsloos of bandeloos*, 8–10.

6. Cox, *Secular City*, 4.

7. Cox, *Secular City*, 38–59.

8. See Taylor, *Malaise of Modernity*, 110–21. Brad Gregory explained these phenomena against the background of the influences of the Reformation. See *Unintended Reformation*, esp. 180–234.

9. Taylor, *Malaise of Modernity*, 120.

reductive tendency of limiting the self to itself as source of self-realization and dissecting the self from all social ties ("social atomism").[10] Individual freedom has become a reason in and of itself that increasingly fails to foster community. The emancipation of the individual also brought further fragmentation and, sometimes, conflict.[11] And, our fragmented society finds its counterpart in a fragmented self.[12] Like our societies at large, our individual selves lack coherence.[13] Our life is divided in all kinds of activities and connections: work, hobbies, family, friends, social media, and leisure, which lack a coherent teleological framework. In other words, identity has become egocentric, a radical anthropocentrism due to a lack of a shared story that unites and commits us to shared goal or *telos*.[14] Our mobility and "city life" made this possible. In such a climate Cox's tolerance quickly has become indifference.[15] So, what does gathering mean, when everything falls apart in segments?

Our understanding—and even more important—our practice of gathering today as Baptist churches stumbles on our fragmented lives, separating Sunday from the rest of the week, our spirituality from our finances, and our communal life from our individual lives, prohibiting us from actually coming together as a community. Gathering, hence, lost its intelligibility: we've become pieces who lack coherency.

Gathering Belief: A Separatist Tradition

When we consider the Baptist heritage, and especially its roots in the English Separatist tradition, partition seems more essential than union. A central element in the congregationalist understanding of what makes a group of people a church is the church covenant. The earliest references to gathering churches are within the early Elizabethan years, when certain Protestants separated themselves to continue—often in secret—a Protestant free liturgy.[16] Yet, not much is known about the theological convic-

---

10. Taylor, *Secular Age*, 41–42.
11. See Paas, "Missionary Ecclesiology."
12. Taylor, *Secular Age*, 381.
13. See MacIntyre, *After Virtue*, 204–26.
14. See MacIntyre, *After Virtue*, 216.
15. See Ten Hooven, "Lege tolerantie."
16. See the classic study by White, *English Separatist Tradition*, 29–31.

tions that motivated these "circumstantial separatists."[17] The first developed theological defense of gathered churches is written by Robert Browne (c. 1550–1633) who grew weary with the hesitant attitude of his fellow Puritan and broke away, living in and out of prison, hiding in Middelburg in the Netherlands, finally to succumb to the authorities.[18] In his footsteps, later Separatists, such as Henry Barrow, Francis Johnson, John Robinson, and also John Smyth, followed.[19] In his autobiographical apology *A True and Short Declaration* (1583), in which Browne explains the course of his actions, he writes: "the kingdom off God Was not to be begun by whole parishes, but rather off the worthiest, Were thei neuer so fewe."[20] Out of disappointment with the lack of reformation of English parishes, Browne left the institutional structures for the private meetings. Pivotal behind this move was his theological conviction that Christ's authority is first communally received.[21] "Gathering the worthy"—made visible by way of covenanting together[22]—hence, was a direct application of discipline in accordance with Matt 18:15-20. In keeping with this text ("tell it to the church" [Matt. 18:17]), Browne argued against Presbyterians like Thomas Cartwright that the gathering of believers, precisely by being separated from evil, receive the constitutive power to be a church together, "*even to binde men on earth, and to loose them on earth, that they may be bound or loosed in heaven.*"[23] The disciplinary "power of the keys"—associated with the act of covenanting—"binds" people to Christ and to each other. Gathering, accordingly, has a Christological significance. It manifests the ruling presence of Christ: "Indeed one person will not make a church, for the church must needes be a number, *but where two or three are gathered in the name of Christ, there is he in the middes of them.*"[24] A church, consequently, is not planted by mere "belief" alone but, emphatically, by belief expressed in the visible obedience to Christ in a local community. Browne's heavy emphasis on discipline, the third mark of the true church, convinced him of the constitutive role of

17. Collinson, *Elizabethan Puritan Movement*, 89, 85–91, 131–36.
18. See Abrahamse, *Ordained Ministry*.
19. Cf. Abrahamse, "Is Smyth Also."
20. Browne, "True and Short Declaration," 404.
21. Browne, "True and Short Declaration," 399.
22. See Fiddes, "Covenant and Inheritance."
23. Browne, "Answere to Master Cartwright," 442 (emphasis added). Cf. Johnson, *Short Treatise*.
24. Browne, "Answere to Master Cartwright," 443 (emphasis added).

gathering believers in response to Christ's calling. For precisely the same reason, Browne denounced the national church. Civil measures based on coercion do not suit the rule of Christ, since his rule, as again explained in Matt 18:15-17, demands brotherly correction, repentance, and faith. Civil means, such as payments and imprisonment, cannot make recompense for spiritual trespasses.

Gathering in the Baptist vision, like in the broader English Separatist tradition, manifests the communal essence of Christian faith and practice. Not the singular bishop, not the parish structures as such, but the local coming together of people under the lordship of Jesus makes "church." Concrete participation in a visible and tangible community, therefore, is at the center of being church in the Baptist way. However, it also reveals a weakness at the roots of the Separatist tradition: sometimes the emphasis is placed more on "breaking off ties" with the world than on bringing together people in the world. To put it differently, the purpose (*telos*) of gathering is more about keeping discipline than about bringing people into community (*koinonia*) with Christ; more about preservation, than restoration.[25]

Gathering as Mission: Rereading Matt 18

To review our understanding of gathering we need to reread the central text in Browne's defense of the gathered church: Matt 18:15-20. The first thing to notice is that Matthew turns the tables on us by making not the perpetrator but the sufferer responsible: "If your brother or sister sins, go and point out their fault, just between the two of you" (Matt 18:15; cf. 5:23). Pointing out the fault (Greek ἔλεγξον), here, should not be seen as (civil) judgment but explained as brotherly correction, as Browne already noted in opposition to the ecclesial courts. Rather than publicly shaming the offender, Jesus admonishes the victim to the costly endeavor of "winning over" or "winning back" this lost person (Gr. ἐκέρδησας; cf. 1 Cor. 9:19ff).[26] Eventually the whole community is called upon to win this person back for the community: "If they still refuse to listen, tell it to the church" (Matt 18:17). The church is like a search party looking how to bring back the lost sheep (cf. Matt 18:12). Again, the connotation here is not judgment but

---

25. Cf. Klaver, "We Are the World?," 427: "A radical distinction and antithetical stand between the church and world runs the risk of a negative outlook on the world and confines the work and presence of God primarily in and through the church."

26. France, *Matthew*, 693. Cf. Schlier, "κερδαίνω."

restoration (Matt 5:12–14; cf. Deut 19:15).[27] "Tell the church," hence, is an expression of communal care and responsibility to seek and support each other that underlines the essence of the church as gathering.

Matthew 18 is about the collective responsibility not to abandon each other, as Stanley Hauerwas comments on this verse.[28] The tolerance celebrated in Western societies, therefore, is not enough. Gathering here means to refuse to be indifferent toward each other but to care. James McClendon's coinage "watch care" is therefore an apt description of what happens in this text.[29] Even the final line, "treat them as you would a pagan or a tax collector" (Matt 18:17), should be read as pastoral advice, rather than a judicial verdict.[30] The difference between gathering and living in fragmentation here is willingness to be accountable. So, the much cherished verses—"truly I tell you that if two of you on earth agree about anything they ask for, it will be done for them by my Father in heaven. For where two of three gather in my name, there am I with them" (Matt 18:19–20; cf. 1 Cor 5:3–5)—are essentially the language of prayer.[31] "Binding and loosing" is the ecclesial call to gather people into the liberating reality of forgiveness and reconciliation. Gathering in the name of Jesus essentially means that grace transcends our wrongdoings.[32] Hence, unanimous prayer here is not the prayer of people who agree but people who find each other in the forgiveness of Jesus. That is where Jesus commits himself (cf. Matt 18:5, 19). Matthew 18 is not about living immaculately but living a reconciling life under Christ's care.

Our rereading of Matt 18 recalibrates a one-sided Separatist understanding of gathering. The emphasis should not be so much on the separation of evil, but rather on the winning over of sinners. Holiness is about reconciling care, about gathering people into Christ's eschatological presence. That means a life that brings together not only our own fragmented lives under Christ's discipline but also wayward people into a company of mutual caring discipline. Reading this text in a fragmented society consequently requires training ourselves in the skills of living a coherent life: overcoming our indifference towards others by treating them as family. "Being church," then, is gathering the pieces, by making them members—that

---

27. See Roitto, "Reintegrative Shaming," and France, *Matthew*, 693.
28. See Hauerwas, *Matthew*, 166.
29. See McClendon, *Ethics*, 216–18, 227–30.
30. France, *Matthew*, 693.
31. See Evans, *Matthew*, 335.
32. Cf. Volf, *After Our Likeness*, 146–47.

is, participants—in Christ's reconciling space. To understand the church as gathering means, therefore, that it anticipates God's reconciliation of all things (2 Cor 5:18–21).[33]

Gathering Together: Towards a Common Vision

Our recalibration of gathering fits well with *TCTCV*. Although the terminology of gathering appears only once to denote the church,[34] its chosen denominator "communion" (Greek *koinonia*) is consistent with the Baptist notion of the church.[35] As such, it describes the church as part of the "dynamic history of God's restoring *koinonia*" to bring people back into communion with God and each other.[36] In this it joins and continues Christ's mission.[37] In chapter 2 the terminology of *koinonia* receives further explication. Most significant is that community is God's initiative: God brings together people to participate and partake of his restoring reconciliation through the church as community.[38] The gifts of the Spirit, therefore, "place obligations of responsibility and mutual accountability on every individual and local community and on the Church as a whole at every level of its life."[39] Holiness, referred to in section 22, receives a missionary interpretation: "part of the holiness of the Church is its ministry of continually calling people to repentance, renewal and reform." Gathering, hence, is the mission of the church. By bringing people together, the church brings people back to God: "It is God's design to gather humanity and all of creation into communion under the lordship of Christ."[40] This is a wonderful formulation that captures the restoring power of gathering well; both in respect to the nature of the church as well as in relation to its being in a fragmented world. It gathers cultural diversity.[41] That is why being church is not the sum of

---

33. Cf. Abrahamse, "Zwakkelingen en dwazen."
34. WCC, *TCTCV*, §54.
35. As others already noted; see Hatch, "*Koinonia* as Ecumenical Opening," and Searle, "Moving towards Ecumenism."
36. WCC, *TCTCV*, §1.
37. WCC, *TCTCV*, §4.
38. WCC, *TCTCV*, §13.
39. WCC, *TCTCV*, §18.
40. WCC, *TCTCV*, §25.
41. WCC, *TCTCV*, §28.

believers gathering but communion with God that transcends its locality and time into the catholic whole.[42]

TCTCV shows how much gathering and restoration belong together. Regrettably, the preeminent text of Matt 18 that pictures this restoring act so tangibly in the midst of an actual gathering is absent. Maybe this is because the focus of *TCTCV* is more on a universal church than the local gathering, where Baptists commonly tend to place their attention. For Baptists the church is first and foremost local since it is there where Christ's reconciling presence is realized by actual people gathering in the name of Jesus (cf. Matt. 18:20). However, its major strength is its missionary focus, which does amplify what we found in our rereading of this text. The holiness of the church is missionary; the church is God's initiative seeking to gather people under Christ's reconciling care and rule.

Gathering the Pieces: Obedience, Resistance, and Restoration

So, what does this all mean for a Baptist vision on being church? Gathering is first and foremost a response, a visible and tangible act of obedience and testimony to Christ. Gathering is not perceived as a self-initiated decision but as a submissive response to Christ's call that he is Lord. Therefore, gathering is by itself the first act of communal worship.[43] Being church is not about individuals seeking God but about God's bringing together of wayward people into his community of reconciliation. Gathering means "God's sovereign call to gather as believers under his direct reign in this local gathering."[44] Gathering is bringing our individual lives to the gathered saints as confession.[45] Gathering under the lordship of Jesus is recognizing Christ as our horizon of meaning, our *telos*. We don't make our lives. Our life is Christ. Choice is only significant and therefore worthwhile in light of God's choosing and gathering of us as his disciples. Hence, the validation of voluntarism in congregational ecclesiology is discipleship. Following Christ is, as Dietrich Bonhoeffer showed, directly connected to obedience: "Only the obedient believes, and the believer obeys."[46] This is also the common

42. WCC, *TCTCV*, §§23, 31.
43. Ellis, *Gathering*.
44. Sell, *Saints*, 2.
45. See Volf, *After Our Likeness*.
46. Bonhoeffer, *Cost of Discipleship*, 69.

thread in John Bunyan's *Pilgrim's Progress*. As Christian says to Faithful when Talkative leaves them on their pilgrimage: "He had rather leave your company, than reform his life."[47] He represents Christians who have the talk but not the walk and lack the Puritan emphasis on the reformation of manners. Nevertheless, as *TCTCV* teaches us: communal obedience to Christ must not be detached from God's mission in the world. Of course, this attitude of isolation is closely related to the sectarian component within the Baptist tradition: namely, the sometimes slumbering, sometimes boisterous inclination to separate from existing patterns of social life and society. Such a narrow focus on Christ can easily result in a negligence towards the world and its concerns but also towards other traditions, denominations, and churches; or what you might call a lack of ecumenical concern, fueled by the fear of contamination.

Second, the missionary direction of gathering is supported by its more "nonconformist" implications: resistance. For the obedience to Christ invokes conflict with the powers that be, as the Separatists and early Baptists well knew. Gathering was literally illegal in Browne's days. More recently, Martin Luther King Jr. and Dorothy Day lived the same resistance against different forces. It follows out of the recognition of Christ's lordship; for if Christ is King, then all other powers, rulers, and institutions are secondary, precisely since, as Baptists are convinced, true gathering comes through Christ's restoring forgiveness. Curtis Freeman rightly emphasizes this aspect of Baptist history and theology when describing this gathering tradition as *Contesting Catholicity*.[48] Today this resistance might (again) take a different shape, however. In a context where the freedom to gather has become one of the basics of Western life, gathering has become an act that contests our individualistic tendencies. Gathering on a Sunday is not so much defying the power of the state but more the urge to stay in bed, or the temptation to put together your own religion like an IKEA closet. Gathering testifies that for Christians tolerance of others is simply not enough, for they are called to reconciling care. It is the refusal to surrender our lives to the "gods" of the here and now.[49] Harvey Cox once defined the church as "cultural exorcist."[50] Though I would not go so far, since the church itself is too much part and parcel of its surrounding culture, the church is a place

---

47. Bunyan, *Pilgrim's Progress*, 67.
48. See Freeman, *Contesting Catholicity*.
49. See Smith, *You Are What You Love*, and Paul, *Slag om hart*.
50. See Cox, *Secular City*, 149–63.

where idolatry can be unmasked and, by discipling/liturgical training, dismantled.

Third, gathering means that faith is communal. The emphasis on community sometimes leads to democratic ideals and egalitarianism, theologically supported by the idea of priesthood of all believers. Yet, gathering as community of Christ also binds us to the communion of faith of all ages and places. Essentially, community is thus a gift made possible by Christ's binding and unifying presence. We don't make community; we are invited to join into God's fellowship, as *TCTCV* rightly accentuates. While local communities are indeed tangible expressions of Christ's friendship and fellowship, this locality can also be a threat. It is precisely on this point that many gathering churches suffer from internal conflicts. Like Browne's congregation disbanded in Middelburg, and Smyth's in Amsterdam, many free churches today—within the broad spectrum of Baptist, evangelical, and Pentecostal churches—face the problem of their limitations. For the freedom of structures does not save from individual preferences and opinions. A gathering church has sometimes "freed" itself from the very traditions that enriched and supported its continual existence, and in so doing sawed off the branch on which it sat. It lacks the resources to allow the community to rise above its own situation. The ecumenical encounter once again shows the strength of structures that help to make local gatherings aware of the catholic church—that is, the whole church. Community as a gift for discipleship: to be part of a community of transformation in which the individual self is disciplined in what it means to have Christ as Lord of all creation. Gathering is a catholic act of the broadening of community that has local roots but is never limited to its locality. For, as Smyth wrote: "Christ promiseth his presence to the worldes end."[51]

Bibliography

Abrahamse, Jan Martijn. "'Is Smyth Also among the Brownists?' Confronting John Smyth with His Predecessor Robert Browne." *Baptist Quarterly* 46 (2015) 1–10.

———. *Ordained Ministry in Free Church Perspective: Retrieving Robert Browne (c. 1550-1633) for Contemporary Ecclesiology*. Studies in Reformed Theology 41. Boston: Brill, 2020.

———. "Zwakkelingen en dwazen: Het ambt van biechtvader of -moeder in een schuldige tijd." *Inspirare: Tijdschrift voor evangelische en charismatische theologie* 1 (2019) 13–21.

---

51. Smyth, "Paralleles, Censures, Observations," 410.

Bonhoeffer, Dietrich. *The Cost of Discipleship*. Translated by R. H. Fuller, with some revision by Irmgard Booth. New York: Macmillan, 1937.

Boutellier, Hans, et al. *Bindingsloos of bandeloos: Normen, waarden en individualisering*. The Hague: Sociaal en Cultureel Planbureau, 2004.

Browne, Robert. "An Answere to Master Cartwright." In *The Writings of Robert Harrison and Robert Browne*, edited by Albert Peel and Leland H. Carlson, 430–506. Elizabethan Nonconformist Texts 2. London: Allen & Unwin, 1953.

———. "A True and Short Declaration." In *The Writings of Robert Harrison and Robert Browne*, edited by Albert Peel and Leland H. Carlson, 396–429. Elizabethan Nonconformist Texts 2. London: Allen & Unwin, 1953.

Bunyan, John. *The Pilgrim's Progress*. Edited by Cynthia Wall. Norton Critical. London: Norton, 2009.

Collinson, Patrick. *The Elizabethan Puritan Movement*. Oxford, UK: Clarendon, 1967.

Cox, Harvey. *The Secular City: Secularization and Urbanization in Theological Perspective*. London: SCM, 1965.

Davie, Grace. *The Sociology of Religion*. BSA New Horizons in Sociology. London: Sage, 2007.

Ellis, Christopher J. *Gathering: A Theology and Spirituality of Worship in Free Church Tradition*. London: SCM, 2004.

Evans, Craig A. *Matthew*. New Cambridge Bible Commentary. Cambridge: Cambridge University Press, 2012.

Fiddes, Paul S. "Covenant and the Inheritance of Separatism." In *The Fourth Strand of the Reformation: The Covenant Ecclesiology of Anabaptists, English Separatists, and the Early General Baptists*, edited by Paul S. Fiddes, 63–91. Centre for Baptist History and Heritage Studies 17. Oxford, UK: Regent's Park College Press, 2018.

France, R. T. *Matthew*. New International Commentary on the New Testament. Grand Rapids: Eerdmans, 2007.

Freeman, Curtis W. *Contesting Catholicity: Theology for Other Baptists*. Waco, TX: Baylor University Press, 2014.

Gregory, Brad. *The Unintended Reformation: How a Religious Revolution Secularized Society*. Cambridge: Belknap, 2012.

Hatch, Derek C. "*Koinonia* as Ecumenical Opening for Baptist." *Ecumenical Review* 71 (2019) 175–88.

Hauerwas, Stanley. *Matthew*. Brazos Theological Commentary on the Bible. Grand Rapids: Brazos, 2005.

Johnson, Francis. *A Short Treatise Concerning the Exposition of Those Words, Tell the Church, &c. Mat. 18 17*. Amsterdam: Thorp, 1611.

Klaver, Miranda. "We Are the World? Identity Politics and Congregational Transformation of Dutch Baptists." *American Baptist Quarterly* 31 (2012) 420–30.

MacIntyre, Alasdair. *After Virtue: A Study in Moral Theory*. 3rd ed. Notre Dame, IN: University of Notre Dame Press, 2007.

McClendon, James Wm., Jr. *Ethics*. Vol. 1 of *Systematic Theology*. Rev. ed. Nashville: Abingdon, 2002.

Paas, Stefan. "Missionary Ecclesiology in an Age of Individualization." *Calvin Theological Journal* 48 (2013) 91–106.

Paul, Herman. *De slag om het hart: Over secularisatie van verlangen*. Utrecht, Netherlands: Boekencentrum, 2017.

Roitto, Rikard. "Reintegrative Shaming and a Prayer Ritual of Reintegration in Matthew 18:15–20." *Svensk exegetisk årsbok* 79 (2014) 108–9.

Schlier, Heinrich. "κερδαίνω." In *Theological Dictionary of the New Testament*, edited by Gerhard Kittel, translated by Geoffrey W. Bromiley, 3:672–73. Grand Rapids: Eerdmans, 1965.

Searle, Joshua T. "Moving towards an Ecumenism of *Koinonia*: A Critical Response to 'The Church: Towards a Common Vision' from a Baptistic Perspective." *Journal of European Baptist Studies* 15 (2015) 17–27.

Sell, Alan P. F. *Saints: Visible, Orderly and Catholic: The Congregational Idea of the Church*. Allison Park, PA: Pickwick, 1986.

Smith, James K. A. *You Are What You Love: The Spiritual Power of Habit*. Grand Rapids: Brazos, 2016.

Smyth, John. "Paralleles, Censures, Observations." In *The Works of John Smyth*, edited by W. T. Whitley, 2:327–546. Cambridge: Cambridge University Press, 1915.

Taylor, Charles. *The Malaise of Modernity*. CBC Massey Lectures. Toronto: Anansi, 1991.

———. *A Secular Age*. Cambridge: Belknap, 2007.

Ten Hooven, Marcel. "De lege tolerantie—inleiding: Op zoek naar een nieuwe inhoud voor verdraagzaamheid." In *De lege tolerantie: Over vrijheid en vrijblijvendheid in Nederland*, edited by Marcel ten Hooven, 11–36. Amsterdam: Boom, 2001.

Volf, Miroslav. *After Our Likeness: The Church as the Image of the Trinity*. Sacra Doctrina. Grand Rapids: Eerdmans, 1998.

WCC. *The Church: Towards a Common Vision*. Faith and Order 214. Geneva: WCC, 2013.

White, B. R. *The English Separatist Tradition: From the Marian Martyrs to the Pilgrim Fathers*. Oxford Theological Monographs. Oxford, UK: Oxford University Press, 1971.

Wilson, Jonathan R. *Living Faithfully in a Fragmented World: Lessons for the Church from MacIntyre's "After Virtue."* Christian Mission and Modern Culture. Harrisburg, PA: Trinity, 1997.

6

Befriending Churches

Lina Toth (Andronoviene)

Some friends play at friendship but a true friend sticks closer than one's nearest kin. (Prov 18:24)

No one has greater love than this, to lay down one's life for one's friends. (John 15:13)

Look, . . . a friend of tax-collectors and sinners! (Matt 11:19)

TCTCV OBSERVES THAT IN order to appreciate the multifaceted nature of church expressions, various images need to be employed: "people of God, body of Christ, temple of the Holy Spirit, vine, flock, bride, household, soldiers, friends and so forth."[1] This chapter considers the last of the suggested images—that of a community of friends, and the practice of friendship that this image necessitates.

Christian theology has frequently displayed an ambivalent relationship to the idea of friendship. This ambivalence stands in contrast to the great significance attributed to friendship in the classical world of Greece and Rome, as exemplified in Plato's and Aristotle's interest in *philia*,[2] where friendship was assumed to be a central, if not the most important, feature of a good, happy life. Yet with the arrival of Christianity, the practice of

---

1. WCC, *TCTCV*, 7.
2. Bolotin, *Plato's Dialogue on Friendship*; Aristotle, *Nicomachean Ethics*, bks 8 and 9.

friendship became suspect as morally inferior in comparison to perfect love—*agape*—of one's neighbor. At the heart of this superiority of *agape* was the assumed preferential nature of friendship, and therefore favoring of some people (who were friends) over some others (who were not).[3]

Today, friendship is frequently treated as nothing more than an accessory to leisure—a nice thing to have, but hardly anything essential.[4] It is further impoverished by the lack of time due to high demands of the work life as well as people's mobility, which often precludes the nurture that lasting friendships require. The fear arising from the problems shaking the institution of family in the Western world certainly adds further strains to the practice of friendship. When all of this takes place in a highly individualistic, rather than relational, framework of personal identity, friendship becomes simply an "extra," however nice and helpful.

At the same time, however, Western societies are facing what has been widely described as the "epidemic of loneliness,"[5] and there has been a renewed interest in friendship, both in philosophy and in culture at large.[6] What is still largely missing, however, is a recognition of the importance of the theology and practice of friendship for the life and witness of those who make up the church of Jesus Christ.[7] As this chapter will argue, the intentional nature of Baptist communities is an invitation to consider Christian life through the lens of a theology of friendship.

I start with a personal story. As long as I remember, my Lithuanian grandmother always insisted on using a very particular word for her Baptist community, *drauguomenė*—which could be literally translated as "friend-hood." She was recommended a more modern and much more widespread word, *bendruomenė*—"common-hood" or community—but in her daily prayers, she would continue to pray for the "friend-hood," often going over the names of each of these friends. She kept doing that until the last days of her 102-year-long life.

---

3. Andronoviene, "I Have Called You," 118–19.

4. On the diminishing quality of friendship in current times, see Anderson, *Losing Friends*.

5. *Week* Staff, "Epidemic of Loneliness"; Easton, "How Should We Tackle."

6. E.g., Derrida, *Politics of Friendship*; Pahl, *On Friendship*; Hruschka, *Friendship*; Crane et al., *Friends*.

7. This is not to say, however, that there have been no attempts whatsoever; see, for instance, Carmichael, *Friendship*; Meilaender, *Friendship*; Wadell, *Becoming Friends*; Burrell, *Friendship*.

Her word of choice offers an important theological reminder: congregations could be understood, and understand themselves, as communities of friends. In a Baptist theology, such communities are those of gathered disciples who have responded to the call of Jesus through conversion, covenanting together to follow him and to discern God's will together.[8] Indeed, we see a thread of friendship in the life of Jesus himself. We have stories of his intimate friendships such as with the "beloved disciple" or with Lazarus, Mary, and Martha. We also witness Jesus addressing his disciples as friends, after three years spent together under his leadership. Yet we also find out that Jesus was mockingly called a friend of sinners and tax collectors. All three modes of friendship are important—indeed, vital—for the Christian practice today.[9]

Friendship as a Personal Practice

We start with the most widespread understanding of friendship as a practice experienced personally and individually. Even if adults may not have time for friendships, parents usually greatly care about the friends their children have, because they know too well that "through friendships we gain a sense of who we are and what the world is like—of the universe of the everyday."[10] At the same time, just like romantic love, friendship is often portrayed in an idealized fashion: a myth of a perfect friend suddenly appearing[11] is somewhat similar to the appearance of the knight on a white horse.[12] One of the ways to help ground the practice is to consider the key virtues involved in the growth of healthy personal friendships. I propose to start the list with commitment, particularity, mutuality, and vulnerability.[13]

---

8. See, e.g., Fiddes, *Tracks and Traces*, 21–47.

9. An astute eye may recognize in this ordering the pattern for thinking about Christian ethics by a Baptist theologian, James Wm. McClendon. His starting point is the bodily element, or personal life, followed by the focus on the "community of care," or the social expression of ethics. Third follows the realm of the "anastatic," or resurrection ethics, which colors and aligns the other two strands with the vision of the newness of life through Christ (McClendon, *Systematic Theology*, 1). For a concise description, see McClendon, *Systematic Theology*, 2:109.

10. McCarthy, *Good Life*, 35.

11. E.g., O'Connor, *Friendships between Women*, 181.

12. On the comparison between romantic love and friendship, see Andronoviene, *Transforming the Struggles*, 201–23.

13. "Virtues" are understood here as certain skills, or personal and communal

Commitment is often understood in terms of readiness to give one's time and attention to a friend. It grows together with the practice, when friends discover each other's trustworthiness and faithfulness—not as a cold rational calculation and testing but as a process of an ongoing growth of lives together, conscious as well as unconscious. Here, however, comes an interesting point. Although friends may be those whom we like and with whom we naturally become friends, there is another dimension of friendship in the conscious choosing—and committing—to make and keep a friend, even in relationships that started without any attraction or even with antipathy.

One of the aspects of commitment is that it necessarily limits the number of people one can be committed to in this way: genuine friendships are necessarily particular. Here again comes the common reproach of friendship being too limited and too preferential. Yet, in Mother Mary Francis's words, "how can we have a universal love except by particularities?"[14] It is out of committing to befriend the first, the second, and the third person that one can begin to grasp how to befriend the fourth, the fifth, and the sixth, who perhaps seem more difficult to love at the start. What is important, as we shall see later, is to keep the door open for new friendships yet to be born.[15]

Friendship is also inherently mutual; it "grows best in the soil of reciprocity."[16] Yet such reciprocity is not necessarily straightforward. Although people often befriend those with similar interests and capabilities, friendships can also develop between very unlikely friends differing in age, status, or outlook. As I shall argue later, this is the basis of the understanding of the church as a community of Jesus's friends. For some, giving may turn out to be the more challenging part of mutuality, yet for others it will be their ability to accept the gifts of friendship that will be the test of its genuineness. Without knowing reciprocal, mutual love, it is unlikely that we will be able to eventually love those who will not reciprocate it: strangers and enemies.

---

qualities needed for the successful participation in a practice such as that of friendship. Such an approach follows the methodology of Alasdair MacIntyre; see his seminal *After Virtue*.

14. Francis, *But I Have Called*, 18.
15. Francis, *But I Have Called*, 20–21.
16. Humphrey, *Ecstasy and Intimacy*, 161.

Mutuality leads to another virtue of a genuine friendship: namely, vulnerability. It is a crucial virtue at the start of a new friendship, when we risk having our offer of friendship or our need snubbed. It is also imperative later, as friendship develops and the amount of trust put in another person risks great sorrow if betrayed. It is precisely such risk that can be too much to bear, with the result of various mechanisms of protection being built against the possibility of making oneself open to the impact of the other. Perhaps the most significant of such mechanisms is an imitation of friendship that does not allow the other to reciprocate: "We get the unpleasant feeling that [neighborly] love is being turned into a weapon with which to protect the self against the possibility of rejection."[17]

Commitment, particularity, reciprocity, and vulnerability: these virtues, or qualities, are key to healthy personal friendships. Of course, the list can be continued by adding trust, respect, or patience.[18] Moreover, the virtue list is just as relevant to the communal expression of friendship. How then can the practice of friendship be enlarged to include the life of an intentional community that embodies the commitment to follow Jesus?

Friendship as a Communal Practice

In the words of Jesus to his disciples, "I have called you friends, because I have made known to you everything that I have heard from my Father" (John 15:15). The twelve as a group were in no way "natural" or personal friends: it is difficult to think of outlooks more different than that of a tax collector and a zealot. Yet their being gathered together presupposed a certain common purpose, which required walking together, eating together, living together, and getting to know each other so well that they had to become either enemies or friends. Because of that common purpose, they were to "embody a kind of friendship not otherwise available."[19]

---

17. Maileander, *Friendship*, 45.

18. Francis would suggest three such virtues and the progression from the first to the second to the third: esteem, respect, and affection (Francis, *But I Have Called*, 16ff). Cf. Aelred of Rievaulx: "There are four qualities which must be tested in a friend: loyalty, right intention, discretion, and patience, that you may entrust yourself to him securely" (Aelred of Rievaulx, *Spiritual Friendship*, 3:61). James McClendon, reflecting on friendship as a practice in MacIntyrean terms, offers loyalty, patience, sympathy, and fidelity (McClendon, *Systematic Theology*, 1:178).

19. Clapp, *Peculiar People*, 204.

It must be noted that the church is not the only place in which such friendships are born. As sociologists and social psychologists have noted, a certain goal can bind unlikely people in friendship in context-specific relationships such as those formed at work[20] or groups united by a political goal.[21] Yet theologically, the church is called to be "the pattern of friendship for the world. . . . We ought to be the ones to whom other people could look for the clear picture of how real friendships work: this is the way it functions; this is what it does, this is what it produces in people."[22]

At this point, it is worthwhile to consider the relationship between the practice of friendship and the convictions we carry, both as individuals and communities. In contrast to opinions or preferences, convictions are understood here as the drives behind our motivations: in a very real way they make us who we are.[23] If we undergo a radical change of convictions, we become a significantly different person, and if holders of significantly different convictions arrive at a mutual understanding of the issue in question, they both—or both groups—will have been considerably changed in the process. Indeed, it is in this context that a profound change of convictions can be called "conversion."

It is also important to note that convictions do not necessarily match our professed theology. Instead, they become visible in the things and practices we choose to spend time or money on, and the loyalties and interests these choices reflect. Humans have an incredible capacity to deceive themselves (and others), and here is where friendship has a key role to play. Without friends who are able to speak the truth, "one becomes the victim of one's hopes and fears, of wishful thinking and fantasy. . . . Unless we are very careful, we tend not to see things as they are, but as our fantasies predispose us to see them. And we can only be rescued from this by a certain kind of friendship."[24]

---

20. O'Connor, *Friendships between Women*, 161.

21. Meilaender, *Friendship*, 73.

22. Francis, *But I Have Called*, 13.

23. Convictional theology has arisen out of the work of a Baptist theologian, James McClendon, and has gained a significant attraction by a number of Baptist schools and theologians. The key works exploring convictions are McClendon and Smith, *Convictions*, and McClendon's three-volume systematic theology: *Ethics*, *Doctrine*, and *Witness*. For an overview of the development of convictional theology, see Freeman, "Introduction:; Parushev, "Convictions and the Shape"; Andronoviene, *Transforming the Struggles*, 115–18.

24. MacIntyre, "Illusion of Self-Sufficiency," 120.

Indeed, as Baptist scholar Sean Winter argues, Baptist hermeneutics can be viewed as a practice of a "community of friends" who are gathered around Scripture, striving to read the world through its lenses. In their "diversity, disagreement, and even conflict over the meaning of scripture," they are to build one another by offering a witness to what, by the grace of God, has been revealed to each.[25] As they engage in communal discernment (Matt 18:15–20), this may lead to repentance, a change of perspective, but also possibly—and sadly—the parting of ways.

Such convictional struggles among the friends of Jesus serve as reminders of how difficult loving friends may sometimes be. Yet there seems to be no other way but to learn to be friends because of the One who befriended us all first and who invites us to extend our friendship beyond our own circle.

Friendship as a Missional Practice

At this point, another virtue, or characteristic, comes to the fore: that of hospitality. Inhospitable friendship is not friendship but its caricature, and that is especially true in the case of befriending strangers. Hospitality is one of the central virtues in the Scriptures, and certainly a feature of the communities of Jesus as far as the New Testament is concerned. Yet it is also something that is easily overlooked in the life of a contemporary church busy with "doing" mission. Extending friendship to the other means facing our fear of those who are different; our suspicion that we might be taken advantage of or manipulated; our uneasiness with the (very likely) possibility that as we make room for that which is foreign, it is going to change our current patterns and indeed our very selves. "When friendship brings an offer of hospitality, it is an intrusion upon our safe and smooth-running world."[26]

The possibility and the fear of such an intrusion are acutely felt at the present time, in an increasingly multicultural society marked by such challenges as migration and refugee crises and religious violence. The reaction of the churches is a litmus test of this third, missional mode of friendship, and therefore the test of the convictions of these communities of faith.

The practice of public worship may be a good starting point of exploring our convictions concerning friendship and hospitality. The gathering of

25. Winter, "Persuading Friends," 269.
26. McCarthy, *Good Life*, 37.

the community of Jesus's friends is not to be focussed on *attracting* strangers, but it should have a welcoming door—literally and metaphorically—for all who may come.[27] Assessing the welcome—or its absence—is likely to lead us to consider such ideas as liturgical inculturation[28] or missional worship.[29]

Importantly, many of the strangers entering our worship will do so because of an already existing relationship with someone who is "in": "Friendship is the most basic reason outsiders come into the gravitational field of Christian churches and communities."[30] More to that, what will speak most is the implicit, yet strongly, if subconsciously, felt reality of a certain ethos: an atmosphere, a communal attitude expressed in language as well as in nonverbal cues.[31]

Missional friendship guards the Christian community from becoming insular and self-serving. At the same time, the practice of friendship understood missionally dismisses such strategies as "friendship evangelism," whereby one might want to become friends with another person *so that* the latter then would become open (or feel obliged?) to hear the gospel. Instead, it asks for noninstrumental, open-ended relationships that respect the freedom of the other, including the freedom to believe and worship differently (or not at all). In the Baptist tradition, this has often been expressed as a concern for and the conviction of the freedom of conscience, from Thomas Helwys's appeal for religious freedom for "heretics, Turks, Jews or whatsoever"[32] in the seventeenth century, to Baptist World Alliance General Secretary J. H. Rushbrooke reiterating a declaration against racial persecution issued by the 1934 Baptist World Congress in Berlin and offering the "hand of sincere friendship" to the British Jewish community in 1935.[33]

Abbot Aelred of Rievaulx speaks of "true and eternal friendship, which begins in this life and is perfected in the next, which here belongs to

---

27. Kreider and Kreider, *Worship and Mission*, 221.
28. Chupungco, *Liturgical Inculturation*.
29. Meyers, *Missional Worship, Worshipful Mission*.
30. Kreider and Kreider, *Worship and Mission*, 223.
31. Kreider and Kreider, *Worship and Mission*, 237.
32. Helwys, *Short Declaration of Mystery*, 53.

33. Rushbrooke, "Evils of Arrogant Nationalism," 30, as quoted in Spitzer, *Baptists, Jews, and Holocaust*, 3. Spitzer's work is an extended study of the Baptist relationships with the Jews during the Holocaust era.

the few where few are good, but there belongs to all where all are good."[34] In Aelred's vision, "this friendship, to which here we admit but few, will be outpoured upon all and by all outpoured upon God, and God shall be all in all."[35] The moments we are able to experience with very particular people are indeed the signs of the very presence of God and of the promise of the fullness of life. The hope for the future, then, is not the extinction of such relationships, but their healing, transformation, and expansion through the costly journey of learning to be a church of the friends of Jesus.

Not everybody would agree that the relationships between and beyond the members of a believing community are best termed as friendship, but I have taken a view that the practice of friendship is an inseparable element not only of our personal life but also of Christian discipleship and mission. More than that, friendship can be seen as one of the central practices of the church set in a culture that yearns for connection but often is unable to practice healthy bonds of love. Indeed, the church "should be a befriending community that not only welcomes all who come to it but also offers them a place where the grammar of intimacy and friendship can be learned."[36] In the process of such learning, both personal and communal transformations can take place. Furthermore, the nature of friendship to which Jesus calls his disciples is of a radically hospitable nature. It asks us to open up ourselves to others beyond our personal attractions and preferences, and even beyond our communal loyalties. It urges us towards the missional practice of friendship, both within and without the confines of the buildings in which we gather, and calls us to the risk of being called friends of the despised and disregarded.

Bibliography

Aelred of Rievaulx. *Spiritual Friendship*. Edited by Marsha L. Dutton. Translated by Lawrence C. Braceland. Cistercian Fathers 5. Collegeville, MN: Cistercian, 2010.
Anderson, Digby C. *Losing Friends*. London: Social Affairs Unit, 2001.
Andronoviene, Lina. "'I Have Called You Friends': On a Theology of Friendship." In *Ethical Thinking at the Crossroads of European Reasoning*, edited by Parush R. Parushev et al., 115–29. Prague: International Baptist Theological Seminary Press, 2007.
———. *Transforming the Struggles of Tamars: Single Women and Baptistic Communities*. Eugene, OR: Pickwick, 2014.

---

34. Aelred of Rievaulx, *Spiritual Friendship*, 3:80.
35. Aelred of Rievaulx, *Spiritual Friendship*, 3:134.
36. Wadell, *Becoming Friends*, 53.

Aristotle. *The Nicomachean Ethics*. Edited and translated by H. Rackham. Loeb Classical Library 73. Cambridge, MA: Harvard University Press, 1990.

Bolotin, David. *Plato's Dialogue on Friendship: An Interpretation of the Lysis, with a New Translation*. Ithaca, NY: Cornell University Press, 1979.

Burrell, David B. *Friendship and Ways to Truth*. Notre Dame, IN: University of Notre Dame Press, 2000.

Carmichael, E. D. H. *Friendship: Interpreting Christian Love*. London: T. & T. Clark International, 2004.

Chupungco, Anscar J. *Liturgical Inculturation: Sacramentals, Religiosity, and Catechesis*. Collegeville, MN: Liturgical, 1992.

Clapp, Rodney. *A Peculiar People: The Church as Culture in a Post-Christian Society*. Downers Grove, IL: InterVarsity, 1996.

Crane, David, et al., prods. *Friends*. Burbank, CA: Warner Brothers, 1994–2004. https://www.warnerbros.com/tv/friends-complete-series-collection/.

Derrida, Jacques. *The Politics of Friendship*. Translated by George Collins. London: Verso, 2005.

Easton, Mark. "How Should We Tackle the Loneliness Epidemic?" *BBC News*, February 11, 2018. https://www.bbc.co.uk/news/uk-42887932.

Fiddes, Paul S. *Tracks and Traces: Baptist Identity in Church and Theology*. Carlisle, UK: Paternoster, 2003.

Francis, Mary. *But I Have Called You Friends: Reflections on the Art of Christian Friendship*. San Francisco: Ignatius, 2006.

Freeman, Curtis W. "Introduction: A Theology for Radical Believers and Other Baptists." In *Systematic Theology: Ethics*, by James Wm. McClendon Jr., 1:vii–xxxviii. Waco, TX: Baylor University Press, 2012.

Helwys, Thomas. *A Short Declaration of the Mystery of Iniquity (1611/1612)*. Edited by Richard Groves. Macon, GA: Mercer University Press, 1998.

Hruschka, Daniel J. *Friendship: Development, Ecology, and Evolution of a Relationship*. Berkeley: University of California Press, 2010.

Humphrey, Edith M. *Ecstasy and Intimacy: When the Holy Spirit Meets the Human Spirit*. Grand Rapids: Eerdmans, 2006.

Kreider, Alan, and Eleanor Kreider. *Worship and Mission after Christendom*. Harrisonburg, VA: Herald, 2011.

MacIntyre, Alasdair. *After Virtue*. 2nd ed. Notre Dame, IN: University of Notre Dame Press, 1984.

———. "The Illusion of Self-Sufficiency." Interview by Alex Voorhoeve. *Conversations on Ethics*, edited by Alex Voorhoeve, 111–34. Oxford, UK: Oxford University Press, 2009.

McCarthy, David Matzko. *The Good Life: Genuine Christianity for the Middle Class*. Christian Practice of Everyday Life. Grand Rapids: Brazos, 2004.

McClendon, James Wm., Jr. *Systematic Theology*. 3 vols. Nashville: Abingdon, 1994–2000.

———, and James A. Smith. *Convictions: Diffusing Religious Relativism*. Rev. ed. Valley Forge, PA: Trinity International, 1994.

Meilaender, Gilbert C. *Friendship: A Study in Theological Ethics*. Notre Dame, IN: University of Notre Dame Press, 1981.

Meyers, Ruth A. *Missional Worship, Worshipful Mission: Gathering as God's People, Going Out in God's Name*. Grand Rapids: Eerdmans, 2014.

O'Connor, Pat. *Friendships between Women: A Critical Review*. London: Harverster Wheatsheaf, 1992.

Pahl, Ray. *On Friendship*. Cambridge: Polity, 2000.

Parushev, Parush R. "Convictions and the Shape of Moral Reasoning." In *Ethical Thinking at the Crossroads of European Reasoning*, edited by Parush R. Parushev et al., 27–45. Prague: International Baptist Theological Seminary Press, 2007.

Rushbrooke, J. H. "The Evils of Arrogant Nationalism." *Jewish Chronicle*, April 4, 1935, 30.

Spitzer, Lee B. *Baptists, Jews, and the Holocaust: The Hand of Sincere Friendship*. Valley Forge, PA: Judson, 2017.

Wadell, Paul J. *Becoming Friends: Worship, Justice and the Practice of Christian Friendship*. Grand Rapids: Brazos, 2002.

WCC. *The Church: Towards a Common Vision*. Faith and Order 214. Geneva: WCC, 2013.

Week Staff. "An Epidemic of Loneliness." *Week*, January 6, 2019. https://theweek.com/articles/815518/epidemic-loneliness.

Winter, Sean. "Persuading Friends: Friendship and Testimony in Baptist Interpretative Communities." In *The "Plainly Revealed" Word of God? Baptist Hermeneutics in Theory and Practice*, edited by Helen Dare and Simon Woodman, 253–70. Macon, GA: Mercer University Press, 2011.

7

Proclaiming Churches

Ruth Gouldbourne

At the heart of the Church's vocation in the world is the proclamation of the Kingdom of God inaugurated in Jesus the Lord, crucified and risen. Through its internal life of eucharistic worship, thanksgiving, intercessory prayer, through planning for mission and evangelism, through a daily lifestyle of solidarity with the poor, through advocacy even to confrontation with the powers that oppress human being, the churches are trying to fulfil this evangelistic vocation.[1]

To this assertion about the heart of the church, a Baptist will say "yes." Indeed, a Baptist may say "yes, amen, hallelujah!" Such a statement not only allows for but insists on an identity that is outwardly focused, shaped by convictions about the announcement of change, and based on the presence of the risen Christ in the midst of believers. But this said, is there anything in Baptist conviction and practice that makes a distinctive contribution? This essay will suggest that in our particular practices of preaching, evangelism, and sacraments, Baptists bring insights and gifts that contribute to the wholeness of this vision of the church's vocation.

Before starting to explore these, it will be useful to outline a little of the context from which I am writing and the understanding of Baptist identity that informs my reflection. I write as part of the Baptist Union of

---

1. WCC, *TCTCV*, §4.

Great Britain (BUGB), standing within a wider tradition shaped by a commitment to exploring being church as a community of believers, brought together by God's call and responding through God's action of grace in personal commitment, signified in believers' baptism. Such a church is both a believers' church—that is, it is those who have made a personal confession—and a disciples' church, a community seeking ways to live out faithfully a response to the call of God, both in gatherings for worship and in everyday life and choices.

The BUGB has as its "Declaration of Principle"[2] a series of statements that form a basis on which churches of like mind can associate together. This declaration is neither creed nor confession but an agreed basis to allow those who disagree on certain issues to still recognize a kinship to affirm one another's way of faithful living. I highlight this both because it shapes the context within which I am writing and because it is a document that I will refer to. It is not a statement that is "authoritative" in the way that bases of faith are for membership of a community, but rather one that describes and summarizes an agreed position that, over the years, has been understood to express a particular understanding of Baptist identity—the one that has shaped me and from which I will be writing.

The statement cited at the beginning of this essay expresses an understanding of the vocation of the church, the call of Christ on the life and practice of the church as being to proclaim the kingdom of God, and further describes that kingdom as inaugurated—and therefore having its being and meaning determined—by the crucified and risen Lord. I suggest that this proclamation takes place through preaching, through evangelism, and through the sacraments; that it is a proclamation to church, to world, and to the powers; and that a Baptist understanding of church illuminates these different facets in distinctive ways. In preaching, that is, proclamation

---

2. Baptist Union of Great Britain, "Declaration of Principle":

    The Basis of the Baptist Union is:
    1. That our Lord and Saviour Jesus Christ, God manifest in the flesh, is the sole and absolute authority in all matters pertaining to faith and practice, as revealed in the Holy Scriptures, and that each Church has liberty, under the guidance of the Holy Spirit, to interpret and administer His laws.
    2. That Christian Baptism is the immersion in water into the Name of the Father, the Son, and the Holy Spirit, of those who have professed repentance towards God and faith in our Lord Jesus Christ who "died for our sins according to the Scriptures; was buried, and rose again the third day."
    3. That it is the duty of every disciple to bear personal witness to the Gospel of Jesus Christ, and to take part in the evangelisation of the world.

to the church, we attend to the call of the risen Christ as witnessed to by the Scriptures. In evangelism, the announcement to those who do not yet profess faith, we offer the call and claim of the risen Christ; and in the sacraments, with the particular emphases of our tradition, we attend to enacting the kingdom of the risen Christ in opposition to the powers that oppress.

Central to the conviction expressed in these practices is the faith that when two or three gather in his name, the risen Christ is in the midst (Matt 18:20). For Baptists, from our earliest confessions, this conviction that a gathering in the name of Christ is wholly church (though not fully the church) has been central; such a local gathering needs no other authority nor structure to be the church present and active. Thus, in reflecting on proclamation, expressed through preaching, through evangelism, and through sacraments, it is of this context that Baptists first and centrally think: the local community of believers gathered in the name of Christ, by the call of Christ. This does not of course preclude larger gatherings or even structures. But it does not depend on them; the presence of the risen Christ among the people of Christ is the church. And therefore it is a place of and context for the proclamation of the kingdom of God. As communities of disciple-believers, it is also our conviction that this proclamation is the privilege and call of each person within the community, fulfilled in different ways.

Preaching

In many Baptist church buildings, it is clear that central to any gathering for worship is preaching; the space is shaped so that the preacher can be heard and seen. When a congregation is gathered in worship, traditionally, emphasis has been on hearing and reading the Scriptures and attending to the word as proclaimed through preaching. There are risks inherent in such a position. Historically, we know the damage that can occur when the emphasis has been more on the written word and less on the risen Lord, but this is not a necessary development. As the "Declaration of Principle" explains, our conviction is that "our Lord and Saviour Jesus Christ, God manifest in the flesh, is the sole and absolute authority in all matters pertaining to faith and practice, as revealed in the Holy Scriptures"; thus, Scripture points to, directs attention to, and gives content to an understanding of our risen Lord. The proclamation in the preaching is not of Scripture per se but of Jesus Christ crucified and risen, and present among his people. Preaching therefore is not lecturing or teaching, nor moral homily, nor self-help exhortation. It is the proclamation of the risen Christ and his call on the lives of individuals, of communities, and finally on the whole of creation.

Preaching is a church-based practice. That is, it usually takes place within the context of a gathered community meeting for worship. It can (and often does) have an evangelistic aspect, but even then, the intention of preaching is to proclaim the presence of the risen Christ among the people and to discern and attend to his call to discipleship. Preaching can also have a teaching element, as we seek to understand the Scriptures and their way of pointing to the risen One, and as we seek to understand the context in which we are called to be disciples. Thus, preaching has two horizons: the risen Christ as witnessed to in the Scriptures and the context in which we are called to follow the risen Christ in our individual contexts and our historical setting.

But there is more. Preaching is also proclamation: an announcement that enacts that which it announces. As people gather in the name of the risen Christ, depending on his promise, it is in the conviction that he is present in their midst. Thus, preaching is not simply an announcement of what will or even should be. It is proclaiming the present Christ, and therefore the announcement of the kingdom in ways that enable the believers gathered around the word to know their place within the kingdom and discover how to live it as a concrete reality in their particular historical context. Depending on promises such as "The kingdom of God is among you" and "Do not be afraid, it is the Father's good presence to give you the kingdom," as well as the challenge "seek first the kingdom of God" and "strive for the kingdom," preaching proclaims to the church its identity, not as the kingdom but as one of the places where the kingdom is present and gives content to that claim. Thus preaching, in attending to the presence of the risen Christ among the believers, will call them to obedience and trust, repentance, and hope. Such preaching will also help believers to see their context and time in the light of the kingdom, to pay attention to ways in which the risen One is present in the circumstances not only of their individual lives but of the life of communities: as promise and as challenge, as the gift of abundant life and as the one who challenges—and calls them to challenge—injustice and sin.

Preaching, in this setting, enables the congregation to learn to see the kingdom of Christ and therefore to be able to live as if it is present until it is present. While we may never identify the kingdom with the church, it is within the church that the preaching of the kingdom, the exploring of its nature, the uncovering of its identity in the risen Christ, and its claims on individual activity and identity have a particular place.

Evangelism

Evangelism—the call to those who do not name Christ as Savior and Lord to do so—has long been a part of Baptist identity. Oncken's assertion "*Jeder Baptist ein Missionar*" (Every Baptist a missionary)[3] has been true not only for Baptists within the German communities but around the world. With our convictions about believer baptism and about faith as a gift to be appropriated by each individual, the place of the call to conversion has been central to our identity. Just as with our capacity to misshape our convictions about Scripture so that we end up as bibliolaters, so we have been able to distort our convictions about evangelism into something too simplistic and rigid, requiring people simply to say certain words and insisting that only certain kinds of responses are true or permissible. However, this is not how it has to be within our tradition, and when we are true to our deep roots and radical convictions, evangelism is the proclamation of the kingdom of the risen One to those who have not yet responded to his call.

For Baptists, this practice emerges from two convictions: first, that conversion is necessary, for the kingdom is not "natural" but something for which we are chosen and which we choose; and second, that response to such a call is possible, because grace is already at work. Thus, evangelistic proclamation is required, because otherwise the news of the kingdom is not known. But it is not coercive, nor does it depend on our skill, determination, or ability, because the response is enabled by grace, and therefore the shape of response cannot be something we determine.

In practical terms, evangelism can take many shapes. Like preaching, it can be a verbal proclamation of the gospel, complete with challenge and invitation, structured in such a way that people are given a context in which to enact a response, often publicly. This form of evangelism is (all too often) the primary or indeed only way in which we have thought of evangelism, and thus we have run the risk of narrowing the nature of the kingdom and of the possible responses. It can become too narrow, because it runs

---

3. For more on Johann Gerhard Oncken (1800–1884), who has often been referred to as the European Baptist "pioneer" and as the "father" of the continental Baptists, see Randall, *Communities of Conviction*, 49–70.

the danger, if it is our only practice, of limiting our understanding of the kingdom to an individualistic identity; focussing only on "salvation," as understood in terms of rescuing from condemnation to hell; and limiting the kingdom to a heaven beyond death and, in our lifetime, the path towards it. While salvation from death and its sting is clearly part of the good news that we proclaim, limiting it to such is a loss of depth and richness.

When we work from our fundamental convictions, evangelism can also take the shape of, for example, political activism: calling on structures, and working within them, to proclaim the values and demands of the kingdom's nature. In such a proclamation, we are dependent on attending to the call of the risen Christ—that is, recognizing that Jesus was crucified according to structures and laws of the day, by a combination of religious and imperial decisions, and that in the resurrection, what we encounter is the refusal of the kingdom of the risen One to be determined by power and force. In identifying with those who were powerless and oppressed, and in losing his life along with them, Jesus uncovered the world's denial of the kingdom. And in raising him from the dead, God vindicated him and denied the power of the world to defeat the kingdom. Thus, proclamation of the kingdom to the world, evangelism, will also involve challenging the structures that resist the kingdom, because we know that, in the face of risen Love, they have no power and cannot stand.

While our Baptist convictions about the separation of church and state mean that we do not look for a "Christian nation," yet still we seek political, social, and economic structures that allow for and support flourishing lives, just societies, and free community. The proclamation of the kingdom to the world through evangelism is part of this and is worked out, in part, through solidarity with those who live as victims of the world as it resists the kingdom. One way, historically, for Baptists, that this has been expressed has often been rooted in convictions about religious freedom. At our very beginnings we were shaped by a recognition that if the response of faith to the gracious calling of God is indeed a free gift of God, then it cannot be constrained by legislation. This conviction led to a call not for freedom for those who were convinced of Baptist principles but rather for freedom for all.[4] As with the practice of evangelism of individuals through proclamation discussed above, there have been times when this conviction and practice

---

4. "For men's religion to God is between God and themselves. The king shall not answer for it. Neither may the king be judge between God and man. Let them be heretics, Turks, Jews, or whatsoever, it appertains not to the earthly power to punish them in the least measure" (Helwys, *Short Declaration of Mystery*, 53).

have curdled into something unhealthy and oppressive—a need to be so separate from our wider societies, for example, that we have been led into condemnation of and isolation from others. But in our flourishing, we have held to convictions about freedom and the importance of conscience that have enabled us—indeed, compelled us—to challenge structures that have diminished abundant lives, restricted freedom, and dehumanized people.

However, we have never regarded this as an end in itself. The kingdom may be expressed through justice and freedom, but the call of Christ always includes individual response. Thus, even when we have embraced an understanding of evangelism as having a social and political aspect, we have resisted the possibility of reducing it only to this. The central confession is that Jesus is Lord. And while this has more than individual content, it certainly has that. With the practice of baptism of believers as such a central mark of identity, Baptists will always include individual response as a significant part of evangelism, and any evangelism that does not confront individuals with the claims of Christ and the possibility of individual response will be seen as lacking.

This recognition of the persistence of the call of the risen Christ to individuals and the challenge of individual response, together with our rejection of an identification of church and community, has meant that we have at times been seen as proselytizing. Our convictions about the nature of the church as a community of believer-disciples and our conviction about faith as a free gift of God can set us at odds with other communities of faith whose understanding draws more on community covenant, or historically on *cuius regio, eius religio* (whose realm, his religion), or on other forms of church life that link social and political community with church identity. This has always been and remains an area where Baptists, and others who share a similar history and set of convictions, often embodied in a theology of believer baptism, offer a challenge to ecumenical consensus; the same words can be interpreted in opposing ways and can lead to tensions and mistrust.

Sacraments

The mention of baptism moves us appropriately to considering the proclamation of the sacraments and their role in the announcing of the kingdom to the powers that oppress. Historically, Baptists bring together strands of Calvinism and Zwinglianism, and this is seen most particularly in the practice of what we have normally called the ordinances of baptism and Lord's Supper. We have drawn largely on Zwinglian theology of sign, or memorialism; that in the water, we announce and vow our discipleship, and in sharing bread and wine, we are reminded of the death and resurrection of Christ. Our danger has been a reductionism which has regarded these actions as merely symbols, visual mnemonics, with no meaning beyond our own thoughts and feelings, dependent on our faith. However, I suggest that if we dare to trust our convictions about the presence of the risen Christ, we will discover that these practices are proclamations—and more than that, they are proclamations to the powers that oppress.

The way in which we carry out baptism makes it proclamatory. The heightened emotion of the full immersion of a believer, usually involving the testimony or storytelling by the candidate, as well as the drama of the affirmations of faith and of the determination to follow the risen Christ, means that, while we may not say the creed when we gather to worship, we enact it in the confession of faith and the representation of death, burial, and resurrection, which identifies us with Jesus's death, burial, and resurrection.

Similarly, while our celebration of the Lord's Supper does not have the drama of the liturgy of some other traditions, in the way we tell the story and our serving of one another, rather than approaching an altar, we enact a proclamation of our convictions about the supper as fellowship meal in the presence of the risen Lord. Both of these enactments, I suggest, proclaim the kingdom not simply at a human level but to the powers, the suprahuman structures of the world that oppose God and challenge the kingdom of God. In this discussion I am drawing on the work of Walter Wink in his definitions and discussion of the powers as more than the aggregate of human activity and as having an identity and presence more than the people through which they are embodied.[5]

Thus, while in evangelism it is the role of the faith community to challenge people within structures to act in ways that are just and life-affirming, in the sacraments a new kind of world is enacted and given embodiment in ways that challenge the hidden structures and systems that dominate and shape people's lives. We make no claims about the nature of water, bread, or wine: that they are of their nature bearers of grace, apart from the actions within which they are used. The presence of the grace, or better, of the risen Lord, is not located primarily in the water, wine, or bread but in the

---

5. See, for example, the discussion in Wink, *Unmasking the Powers*, 1–8.

gathered community. The importance of the bread and wine and water is not in their separateness but precisely in their normality, and encountered in the presence of the risen Christ, they point us to him.

In the practice of baptism by full immersion, on the basis of an individual's confession of faith within and before the community, we are shaped as confessors and identified as followers of the risen Christ. We knowingly and with the support of our community adopt and are adopted into an identity which is at odds with and shaped by different stories than what the powers tell us. Baptism is on our profession of faith; the one being baptised confesses Jesus as Lord and identifies with that Lord in death and resurrection. This confession entails the confession that nobody—and nothing—else is Lord. In confessing Jesus, not Caesar, as Lord, the earliest believers were stepping aside not only from the political realities of their day but also from the symbolic power of the empire that dominated life in all its expressions.

Today, our confession in baptism sets us apart from the powers that shape our context. To be baptized as a believer is both to proclaim and to hear proclamation made about us of another kingdom, another life, another Lord, and this proclamation is not only to those present in the room but to the powers that dominate and shape the world. We can attempt to identify these powers whose power we see: for example, the market, militarism and the myth of redemptive violence, individualism and self-determining autonomy. In baptism, we proclaim another kingdom to these powers. To the market, we proclaim the worth of an individual not in economic terms but as one for whom Christ died. To the power of militarism, we proclaim victory won not through violence but self-giving love. To the myth of redemptive violence,[6] we speak of resurrection; to the power of individualism, we speak of community; and to self-determining autonomy, we speak of following One who is our Lord. Such a proclamation shapes the ones who are taking part in the practice; to do this with integrity and commitment, either as candidate or as receiving communion, is to find ourselves asking questions and therefore challenging habits of submission to the powers. But it is more than that. In such practices we challenge the power of the powers, by demonstrating, proclaiming another world, that of the kingdom, and insofar as the powers have autonomous existence, that existence is called into question by such a proclamation.

---

6. See, for example, Wink, *Engaging the Powers*, 33–36.

The same is true of our practice of the Lord's Supper. The norm of our practice, though it may take different forms, is that the members of the congregation are served by deacons or serve one another, rather than the elements dispensed by priestly action. Instead, the emphasis is on community celebration. It is often the case that the story of the Last Supper is told to the congregation, rather than included within a prayer—that is, the person leading the meal tells or proclaims to the congregation the story of the Lord's sharing a meal with friends and of his command that his friends should continue the practice. This, rather than telling the story within the prayer of thanksgiving, expresses the Baptist conviction that this is a community meal, which is a sign of the cross and resurrection, rather than an offering of a sacrifice. By proclaiming the story, we are again not only proclaiming it to those present but also to the powers that control or are represented by those present. In the same way as at baptism, to a power of hoarding, we announce sharing; to a power of domination, we announce freedom to participate; and to a power of isolation, we announce community.

Conclusion

It is the church's calling to proclaim the kingdom, not to be the kingdom nor yet to build the kingdom. The kingdom is the work of God, made present through the death and resurrection of the Lord. In preaching, in evangelism, and in sacrament, the church announces this kingdom. For Baptists, as we explore our ongoing tradition and listen to our deepest call, we have gifts to offer to the whole church in this vocation.

Bibliography

Baptist Union of Great Britain. "Declaration of Principle." Baptists Together, 1873. https://www.baptist.org.uk/Groups/220595/Declaration_of_Principle.aspx.

Helwys, Thomas. *A Short Declaration of the Mystery of Iniquity*. Edited by Richard Groves. Macon, GA: Mercer University Press, 1998.

Randall, Ian M. *Communities of Conviction: Baptist Beginnings in Europe*. Schwarzenfeld, Germany: Neufeld, 2009.

WCC. *The Church: Towards a Common Vision*. Faith and Order 214. Geneva: WCC, 2013.

Wink, Walter. *Engaging the Powers: Discernment and Resistance in a World of Domination*. Minneapolis: Augsburg, 1992.

———. *Unmasking the Powers: The Invisible Powers That Determine Human Existence*. Philadelphia: Fortress, 1986.

8

Equipping Churches

Uwe Swarat

ONE OF THE CORE practices of Baptists may be called equipping. It means that Baptist believers serve one another to grow in faith, love, and hope and to build up the church, especially in the local context. As the New Testament says, Jesus Christ has equipped each Christian with a spiritual gift, with which he or she can and should serve the others (1 Cor 12:7ff), "so that the church may be built up" (1 Cor 14:5). These gifts and duties constitute the equal authority of each believer. For this concept Baptists usually take from Scripture and tradition the phrase "priesthood of all believers." To the gifts of Christ to the church belong also varieties of service (1 Cor 12:5) or ministries, which Christ gives, as Eph. 4:11ff says, "to equip the saints for the work of ministry, for building up the body of Christ." So, the mutual equipping of the church members is encouraged through special, Christ-given ministries. This raises the question whether according to the mind of Christ the church should have an official, hierarchical priesthood, as Catholic and Orthodox teachers believe, or if the church should be arranged according to the universal priesthood of the believers.

As this is a crucial question in ecumenical dialogues, we will explain in the following the Baptist understanding of the priesthood of all believers. In the first step, we will introduce this concept as one of the Baptist distinctive principles; in the second, we will present Martin Luther's doctrine of the priesthood of all believers, which has been the historical paradigm for the corresponding Baptist concept; in the third, we will approach the question of how the priesthood of all believers relates to the ministry of pastors and elders; and in the fourth and last step, we will look at how the priesthood of all believers is treated in *TCTCV*.

The Priesthood of All Believers as a Baptist Distinctive

The expression of "Baptist principles" or "Baptist distinctives" arose among Baptists towards the end of the nineteenth century.[1] A generally agreed listing of these distinctive principles has never existed, because they should never override the Baptist confessions. The listing of distinctives should demonstrate the historically rooted profile of the Baptists among the plurality of Christian denominations. W. M. S. West has stressed that Baptists hold in common with all Christians the fundamental beliefs of the Christian faith. And: "Baptist Principles are particular interpretations, understandings and emphases of that one great Christian faith."[2]

The priesthood of all believers is often specified as one of these Baptist distinctive principles.[3] Some actually consider this concept as "the keystone truth for Baptists,"[4] as "central to Baptist thought,"[5] or as "a core principle of Baptist doctrine."[6] Already the first confession of Baptists in history, the "Short Confession of Faith in XX Articles" by John Smyth (1609), though not using the phrase "priesthood of all believers," gives expression to this concept in article 13:

> That the church of Christ has power delegated to themselves of announcing the word, administering the sacraments, appointing

---

1. E.g., Williams, *Principles and Practices*; Pendleton, *Distinctive Principles of Baptists*; cf. Garrett, *Baptist Theology*, 531ff.

2. West, *Baptist Principles*, 5.

3. E.g., BWA, *We Baptists*, 28ff; Bund Evangelish-Freikirchlicher Gemeinden, "Was wir glauben"; Canadian Baptists of Ontario and Quebec, "What Do Baptists Believe?" Cf. West, *Baptist Principles*; Shurden, *Proclaiming the Baptist Vision*; Wright, *Challenge to Change*, 13–35; Wright, *Free Church, Free State*, 40–43; Norman, *More Than Just Name*, 45ff, 132–34, 144–46; Norman, *Baptist Way*, 94–99; Tooze, *Baptist Principles*, 129–52; and Pinson, "Baptists."

4. Truett, "Baptist Message," 113.

5. Shurden, *Proclaiming the Baptist Vision*, 2ff.

6. Blevins, "Priesthood of All Believers."

ministers, disclaiming them, and also excommunicating; but the last appeal is to the brethren or body of the church.[7]

In his own writings, Smyth states that the believers through Christ are made spiritual priests to offer spiritual sacrifices. They have all power of the priesthood immediately from Christ by virtue of the covenant God makes with them. Therefore, even if a congregation has no ordained persons among it, it nevertheless has power to preach, administer the Holy Communion, excommunicate, and absolve.[8] The Methodist historian Cyril Eastwood has found: "The doctrine of the priesthood of believers is not incidental but central in Baptist Theology."[9] It explains the Baptist doctrine of the church and the ministry, the Baptist position in relation to the state, and Baptist teaching on Holy Communion.

Martin Luther's Concept of the Priesthood of All Believers as Adopted by Baptists

In an ecumenical perspective it is notable that Baptists adopted this doctrine—most likely mediated through Puritan teachings—from Martin Luther and have put it into practice, perhaps more consistently than some Lutheran churches did.[10] In any case, this doctrine, among some others, forms a close bond between Baptists and the Lutheran reformation.[11]

Luther taught that not only persons consecrated by bishops are priests but all Christians.[12] For him this is a result not only of the clear witness of Holy Scripture (1 Pet 2:4–10; Rev 1:6; 5:10; 20:6) but also of the nature of the church as a communion of saints, i.e., a congregation of true believers.

---

7. Lumpkin, *Baptist Confessions of Faith*, 91–95.

8. Smyth, *Works of John Smyth*, 2:737, cited in Eastwood, *Priesthood of All Believers*, 155.

9. Eastwood, *Priesthood of All Believers*, 160.

10. Bakker, "'We Are All Equal.'"

11. See George, "Reformation Roots," and Swarat, "What Baptists Have Learned."

12. Luther presented his concept of the priesthood of all believers several times, e.g., "An den christlichen Adel deutscher Nation von des christlichen Standes Besserung" (1520), in Luther, *Deutsch-Deutsche Studienausgabe*, 3:1–135; "De captivitate Babylonica ecclesiae" (1520), in Luther, *Lateinisch-Deutsche Studienausgabe*, 3:173–375; "De instituendis ministris ecclesiae" (1523), in Luther, *Lateinisch-Deutsche Studienausgabe*, 3:575–647. I shall try to briefly summarize his remarks with the help of Wendebourg, "Kirche," 409ff; Goertz, *Allgemeines Priestertum*; and Althaus, *Theologie Martin Luthers*, 270–75, 279–83.

Each and every believer is a priest: man or woman, young or old, lord and lady or servant and maid, scholar or layperson. This is founded in their faith, through which they participate in the priesthood of Jesus Christ. Their ordination to the priesthood is nothing else than their baptism. Through faith and baptism every Christian may "confidently approach the throne of grace" (Heb 4:16) without any mediation of a priest except of Christ himself; every Christian has direct access to and immediate communion with God. There is no need for a proxy apart from Jesus Christ. No one can believe in place of another one. There is no place for a hierarchy (holy authority) that mediates between God and the people of God.

Included in this priestly status of every Christian is an obligation, according to Luther, namely the task of serving others as a priest. Being a priest means acting as a representative for others before God, offering sacrifices to God, and proclaiming the word of God to others. In this sense, Jesus Christ became priest for us all, and in this sense all Christians should sacrifice themselves for others, pray for them, and tell God's word to them. Every Christian thus metaphorically becomes a priest for others. Included in this priesthood of all believers is the spiritual authority and fundamental right of every Christian to preach, to baptize, to administer the Lord's Supper, to listen to the confession of others, and to judge all doctrine and spirits. Luther makes what in the Catholic Church is reserved for the ordained priests to a right and a commission for all Christians.

Baptists used to take both aspects seriously—the privilege of being a priest personally and the obligation of being a priest for others—laying the stress sometimes on the first, sometimes on the second. The gift of direct access to God for every single Christian includes the right to read and interpret the Bible for themselves and to follow their own conscience. This understanding has sometimes been called "soul competency"[13] or "soul freedom."[14] It follows from this that the church *has* no priesthood but *is* a priesthood. All church members partake in the ministry of the church—equipped by the Holy Spirit with manifold gifts.[15] There is a fundamental spiritual equality between the church members. Therefore, a local church is governed neither by a bishop nor by an elder or a group of elders but by the

---

13. Most prominently by Mullins, *Axioms of Religion*. Timothy George said, in contrast, that soul competency is the natural capacity of all human beings for God and has nothing to do with the priesthood of all believers (George, "Priesthood of All Believers").

14. Shurden, *Baptist Identity*, 23–32; cf. Shurden, *Doctrine of the Priesthood*.

15. Cf. Rees, "Worship of All Believers."

church members themselves (Congregationalism instead of Episcopalianism and Presbyterianism).

The Priesthood of All Believers and the Ministry of Pastors and Elders

If all Christians are priests and are endowed with the same authority and spiritual powers as the priests, bishops, and popes in the Roman Catholic church then inevitably the question arises, why is there an ordained ministry in Baptist churches at all? Is the ordination of some Christians not a contradiction to the priesthood of all believers? This question has not always been put clearly enough among Baptists. Often they have been satisfied with stating that Baptists have both: an ordained ministry and the priesthood of all believers.[16] On that background it became possible for the Southern Baptists at their Convention in June 1988 in San Antonio, Texas, to adopt a resolution that declared the "priesthood of the believer" as a marginal, mistakable, and misapplied doctrine, and resolved that it in no way contradicts the role, responsibility, and authority of the pastor.[17] This resolution discloses a severe lack of clarity about the relationship between the ministry of a pastor and the universal priesthood of the believers.[18]

On this matter it cannot hurt to listen again to Luther. Luther argues that there should be particular ministries in the congregation of priests, in order to avoid chaos, should all members of the congregation want to preach or lead the Lord's Supper at the same time. This point of good order is important not only for practical reasons but also for a specific theological reason, that is, for the sake of the universal priesthood of believers itself. The equality of all believers in their spiritual authority would be harmed if individual believers should claim their rights for themselves without a calling through the congregation. The congregation must therefore call an appropriate person to represent the others in their name in preaching, administering the sacraments, and listening to confession. Whoever is thus

16. See Shurden, "Priesthood of All Believers."

17. The wording of the resolution in McBeth, *Sourcebook for Baptist Heritage*, 521ff.

18. A few months later, in November 1988, the Baptist General Convention of Texas in Austin sought to counteract the San Antonio resolution by its own, declaring "that we vigorously undergird the biblical teaching of the priesthood of the believer in Baptist life in local church, associational, and state convention activities" (McBeth, *Sourcebook for Baptist Heritage*, 522). However, the relationship between the ministry of a pastor and the universal priesthood of the believers remains open in this resolution as well.

called gains no advantage before the congregation, but is rather a servant of the congregation in their common commission from God. To be an appointed minister or pastor does not bestow a status different from the universal priesthood but grants a function that allows the church to fulfill her ministry. Luther's understanding of ministry thus arises directly from the concept of the universal priesthood of believers.

This is an understanding that Baptists can easily share. The calling of elders or pastors is a necessary consequence of the universal priesthood. This means that setting apart recognized leaders (not necessarily to ordain them formally) belongs to the *esse* (the essence) of the church. And the role of these ministers in the congregation is to be first among equals. The priesthood of all believers is both the source and the limit of the authority of pastors and elders. The ordination of ministers does not convey a way of being that laypersons don't have but installs a person to a specific function in the church. Recently some Baptist theologians have proposed a sacramental understanding of ordination.[19] But a sacrament in Protestant thinking is a means of salvation or of saving grace, instituted by Jesus Christ, to unite the believers with Christ's death on the cross and his resurrection and in fellowship with one another. Therefore, baptism and the Lord's table may well be understood as sacraments, but not ordination. And to teach ordination as a sacramental transfer of an ontological status different to the status of laypersons means to introduce Roman Catholic sacerdotalism into an evangelical denomination. This is a wrong path.

In one respect, however, Baptists should go beyond Luther's theology of ministry: that is, in the relation of the ordained ministries to the abundance of charismata testified to in the New Testament. An ordained minister not only relieves other church members from certain duties, he or she also encourages and equips the others to practice their respective spiritual gifts, as Eph 4:11ff puts it: "And he (that is Jesus Christ) gave the apostles, the prophets, the evangelists, the shepherds and teachers, to equip the saints for the work of ministry." Ordained ministers and the other saints form a community of service. A ministry that makes the congregation passive has misunderstood its task.

---

19. Colwell, "Sacramental Nature of Ordination"; Holmes, "Towards a Baptist Theology"; Goodliff, *Ministry, Sacrament and Representation*; Brewer, "Baptist View"; Bakker, "Roaring Side of Ministry."

The Priesthood of All Believers in *TCTCV*

TCTCV names faith, sacraments, and ministry as the essential elements of communion. Its section about the ministry within the church starts with the distressing but realistic statement that there exist serious differences relating to the priesthood of the ordained, because some churches consider ordained ministers as priests and others do not. Regrettably the text does not say why others do not. It is because they believe in the universal priesthood of believers. This seems to me the biggest obstacle on the path to unity among the churches. If the churches could agree about the ontological equality between ordained ministers and the other church members and that the priesthood of all believers is both the source and the limitation of the ordained ministry, then we could more easily get through the other difficulties relating to the ministry within the church. The convergence text states these other difficulties in the following paragraphs: the necessity of the threefold ministry of bishop, presbyter, and deacon; the apostolic succession of ordained ministry; the way in which authority is recognized and exercised in the church; the authority of ecumenical councils and a universal ministry of unity.[20] The text rightly says that "it must continue to be an urgent priority for the churches to discover how they [i.e., the differences relating to the priesthood of only some Christians or of all] can be overcome."[21] It seems that still a long way lies before us.

Bibliography

Althaus, Paul. *Die Theologie Martin Luthers*. 5th ed. Gütersloh: Gütersloher Verlagshaus Gerd Mohn, 1980.

Bakker, Henk. "The Roaring Side of the Ministry: A Turn to Sacramentalism." *Perspectives in Religious Studies* 38 (2011) 403–26.

———. "'We Are All Equal' (*Omnes sumus aequales*): A Critical Assessment of Early Protestant Ministerial Thinking." *Perspectives in Religious Studies* 44 (2017) 353–76.

Blevins, Carolyn D. "The Priesthood of All Believers." Baptist History, 2001. http://www.baptisthistory.org/baptistorigins/priesthood.html.

Brewer, Brian C. "A Baptist View of Ordained Ministry: Just a Function, or a Way of Being?" In *Papers of the Study and Research Division of the Baptist World Alliance 2005–2010*, 249–77. Baptist Faith and Witness 4. Falls Church, VA: BWA, 2011.

Bund Evangelish-Freikirchlicher Gemeinden (Union of Evangelical Free Churches [Baptists in Germany]). "Was wir glauben." Baptisten, n.d. https://www.baptisten.de/der-befg/wir-ueber-uns/was-wir-glauben/#c2931.

20. See Swarat, "Einheit und Trennung."
21. WCC, *TCTCV*, §45.

BWA. *We Baptists*. Franklin, TN: Study and Research Division of the BWA, 1999.
Canadian Baptists of Ontario and Quebec. "What Do Baptists Believe?" Canadian Baptists of Ontario and Quebec, n.d. https://baptist.ca/about/what-do-baptists-believe/.
Colwell, John E. "The Sacramental Nature of Ordination: An Attempt to Re-Engage a Catholic Understanding and Practice." In *Baptist Sacramentalism*, edited by A. R. Cross and P. E. Thompson, 228–46. Carlisle, UK: Paternoster, 2003.
Eastwood, C. Cyril. *The Priesthood of All Believers: An Examination of the Doctrine from the Reformation to the Present Day*. Minneapolis: Augsburg, 1960.
Garrett, James Leo, Jr. *Baptist Theology: A Four-Century Study*. Macon, GA: Mercer University Press, 2009.
George, Timothy. "The Priesthood of All Believers." In *The People of God: Essays on the Believers' Church*, edited by Paul Basden and David S. Dockery, 85–96. Nashville: Broadman & Holman,1991.
———. "The Reformation Roots of the Baptist Tradition." *Perichoresis* 1 (2003) 65–81.
Goertz, Harald. *Allgemeines Priestertum und ordiniertes Amt bei Luther*. Marburger theologische Studien. Marburg, Germany: Elwert, 1997.
Goodliff, Paul. *Ministry, Sacrament and Representation: Ministry and Ordination in Contemporary Baptist Theology, and the Rise of Sacramentalism*. Oxford, UK: Regent's Park College Press, 2010.
Holmes, Stephen R. "Towards a Baptist Theology of Ordained Ministry." In *Baptist Sacramentalism*, edited by A. R. Cross and P. E. Thompson, 247–62. Carlisle, UK: Paternoster, 2003.
Lumpkin, William L. *Baptist Confessions of Faith*. 2nd rev. ed. Revised by Bill J. Leonard. Valley Forge, PA: Judson, 2011.
Luther, Martin. *Deutsch-Deutsche Studienausgabe*. 3 vols. Leipzig: Evangelisch, 2016.
———. *Lateinisch-Deutsche Studienausgabe*. 3 vols. Leipzig: Evangelisch, 2009.
McBeth, H. Leon. *A Sourcebook for Baptist Heritage*. Nashville: Broadman & Holman, 1990.
Mullins, Edgar Y. *The Axioms of Religion: A New Interpretation of the Baptist Faith*. Edited by C. D. Weaver. Macon, GA: Mercer University Press, 2010.
Norman, R. Stanton. *The Baptist Way: Distinctives of a Baptist Church*. Nashville: Broadman & Holman, 2005.
———. *More Than Just a Name: Preserving our Baptist Identity*. Nashville: Broadman & Holman, 2001.
Pendleton, J. M. *Distinctive Principles of Baptists*. Philadelphia: American Baptist Publication Society, 1882.
Pinson, William M., Jr. "Baptists: The Priesthood of *the Believer* or of *Believers*?" Baptist Distinctives, n.d. https://www.baptistdistinctives.org/resources/articles/the-priesthood-of-the-believer-or-of-believers/.
Rees, Frank D. "The Worship of All Believers." In *Papers of the Study and Research Division of the Baptist World Alliance 2000–2005*, 26–40. Baptist Faith & Witness 3. Falls Church, VA: BWA, 2005.
Shurden, Walter B. *The Baptist Identity: Four Fragile Freedoms*. Macon, GA: Mercer University Press, 1993.
———. *The Doctrine of the Priesthood of Believers*. Nashville: Convention, 1987.
———. "The Priesthood of All Believers and Pastoral Authority in Baptist Thought." In *The Priesthood of All Believers: Proclaiming the Baptist Vision*, edited by Walter B. Shurden, 1:131–54. Macon, GA: Mercer University Press, 1993.

———, ed. *Proclaiming the Baptist Vision*. Vol. 1 of *The Priesthood of All Believers*. Macon, GA: Mercer University Press, 1993.

Smyth, John. *The Works of John Smyth*. 2 vols. Edited by W. T. Whitley. Cambridge: Cambridge University Press, 1915.

Swarat, Uwe. "Einheit und Trennung in der Kirche Jesu Christi: Eine freikirchlich-evangelische Perspektive." *Catholica* 73 (2019) 35–52.

———. "What Baptists Have Learned and Still Can Learn from Luther in the Doctrines of Justification and of the Church." *Baptistic Theologies* 8 (2016) 1–15.

Tooze, George H. *Baptist Principles with Practical Applications and Questions for Discussion*. Macon, GA: Mercer University Press, 2013.

Truett, George W. "The Baptist Message and Mission for the World Today." In *The Life of Baptists in the Life of the World: 80 Years of the Baptist World Alliance*, edited by Walter B. Shurden, 107–27. Address to the Baptist World Congress, Atlanta, 1939. Nashville: Baptist Sunday School Board,1985.

WCC. *The Church: Towards a Common Vision*. Faith and Order 214. Geneva: WCC, 2013.

Wendebourg, Dorothea. "Kirche." In *Luther Handbuch*, edited by Albrecht Beutel, 403–14. Handbucher Theologie. Tübingen, Germ.: Mohr Siebeck, 2005.

West, W. M. S. *Baptist Principles*. London: Baptist Church House, 1963.

Williams, Charles. *The Principles and Practices of the Baptists: A Book for Inquirers*. London: Baptist Tract Society, 1879.

Wright, Nigel G. *Challenge to Change: A Radical Agenda for Baptists*. Eastbourne, UK: Kingsway, 1991.

———. *Free Church, Free State: The Positive Baptist Vision*. Milton Keynes, UK: Paternoster, 2005.

9

Baptizing Churches

Anthony R. Cross

CENTRAL TO BAPTIST LIFE and thought is God in Trinity.[1] The locus of authority for Baptists is similarly God, for we are his people. The importance of Scripture lies in its being God's revelation of himself and his ways. This is not to suggest that Baptists agree on their exegesis and exposition of texts, but it does mean that Scripture is normative: people can be trusted to interpret Scripture aright, in the context of community and under the guidance of the Spirit. While valuing the counsel of other Christians, Baptists are not tied to their decisions, for their devotion is to the Bible and the triune God whose word it is. Recognizing this helps other Christians understand why New Testament baptism is determinative for Baptists.

Baptists exhibit many common emphases and considerable diversity, and when it comes to the question of baptism, this diversity is equally evident.[2] If other Christian traditions are to understand Baptists, they need to understand this variety. There is no hierarchy or body that can legislate in matters of doctrine or practice. The ideal is, however, always that together and individually Baptists seek the mind of Christ, recognizing his ultimate authority and the centrality of the Bible as the revelation of his will.

---

1. Haymes et al., *On Being the Church*.
2. Cross, *Baptism and the Baptists*, 455.

Baptism

Christian baptism's origin is the risen Christ's commission to "Go and make disciples of all nations, baptizing . . . and teaching them" (Matt 28:19–20), which was clearly followed by the apostolic church in which it was integral to the *kerygma*. All who repented and accepted Christ were baptized immediately (e.g., Acts 8:36–8; 16:31–3) and were assured of the forgiveness of their sins and the gift of the Spirit (Acts 2:38, 41; 1 Cor 12:13). New Testament baptism is conversion-baptism, and new converts were then discipled in the faith both in doctrine and ethics (Rom 6:3–4). "Baptism . . . should mark the beginning of a life-long 'catechumenate' rather than the conclusion of a preliminary and 'qualifying' catechumenate."[3] This shows that baptism is not individual but personal, bringing the convert into a relationship with the triune God and also with all others in that same relationship.[4] In New Testament times there were *no* unbaptized believers (1 Cor 12:13), and the church was the community of the baptized. Recognition of this explains why the New Testament writers appealed to baptism as the basis for community exhortation, admonition, and instruction (Rom 6:1–11; Eph 5:25–27).

The word that gives us baptism/baptize comes from the Greek "to dip, to plunge," which is why baptism is by immersion, expressing the death and resurrection of Jesus (Acts 8:38; Matt 3:16). The physical going down into the water, being immersed, then being raised from it, provides baptism with its powerful symbolism, which Paul uses to show us that "all of us who were baptized into Christ Jesus were baptized into his death" and were "buried with him through baptism into death in order that, just as Christ was raised from the dead . . . we too may live a new life" (Rom 6:3–4). This ties in with New Testament baptism being the occasion where the forgiveness of sins is first experienced (Acts 2:38) and is washing us clean (Acts 22:16; 1 Cor 6:11; Eph 5:26) by the Spirit (Titus 3:5). Baptism is integral in the process of becoming a Christian,[5] which effects an ontological change from being "in Adam" to "in Christ" (1 Cor 15:22), from being "our own" to "Christ's," and this means the beginning of a new life in relationship

---

3. Colwell, *Promise and Presence*, 132.
4. Beasley-Murray, *Baptism in New Testament*, 91.
5. Stein, "Baptism in Luke–Acts."

with God.[6] In Rom 6:3–8, Paul speaks of this in terms of union with Christ "through baptism" (6:4).

Many Baptists, however, have difficulty accepting baptism as an essential part of becoming a Christian, and they do so because of their tendency to spiritualize conversion. Reacting against ritualism, they have often rejected the biblical fact that God uses his creation to mediate his grace and love.[7] A relationship with God that is totally spiritualized is not found in Scripture. In fact, to deny that God employs material means to convey his grace to humanity is to succumb to a modern form of Gnosticism.[8]

Baptists have always understood baptism as an ordinance (i.e., ordained by Christ), and because it is a dominical ordinance and the God-ordained response to the preaching of the gospel (Acts 2:38), it is not optional. It is important, however, to admit that nowhere in the New Testament is baptism ever called an ordinance—in the same way, it is never called a sacrament. It is only over the last two hundred years that many Baptists have insisted that baptism is an ordinance and *not* a sacrament. Yet baptism in the New Testament is so much more than a symbol; it is an *effective* symbol, and as such is a sacrament, a divinely appointed *means of grace*. New Testament baptism is faith-baptism, and this is clearly shown in the fact that the full range of the gifts of salvation attributed to faith in the New Testament are also attributed to baptism: forgiveness (cf. Rom 4:5–7 with Acts 2:38); justification (cf. Rom 3:28 with 1 Cor 6:11); union with Christ (cf. Eph 3:17 with Gal 3:27); being crucified with Christ (cf. Gal 2:20 with Rom 6:2–11); death and resurrection (cf. Rom 8:12–13 with Col 2:12); sonship (cf. John 1:12 with Gal 3:26–27); the Holy Spirit (cf. Gal 3:2–5, 14 with 1 Cor 12:13); entry into the church (cf. Gal 3:6–7 with 3:27); regeneration and life (cf. John 3:14–16; 20:31 with 3:5; Titus 3:5); the kingdom and eternal life (cf. Mark 10:15; John 3:14–16 with 1 Cor 6:9–11); and salvation (Rom 1:16; John 3:16 with 1 Pet 3:21).[9]

However, this is *not* to suggest baptism acts *ex opere operato*—as personal faith is *always* implicit, otherwise the action is meaningless. Any suggestion of the mechanical operation of baptism is excluded in 1 Pet 3:21: "baptism now saves you" because it is "not the removal of dirt" but "the pledge/prayer of a good conscience towards God." In fact, "It saves . . . *by*

---

6. Stackhouse, *Gospel-Driven Church*, 144.
7. Fiddes, *Tracks and Traces*, 107–24.
8. Freeman, "'To Feed Upon,'" 204.
9. Cross, *Recovering the Evangelical Sacrament*, 51–72.

the resurrection of Jesus Christ." Elsewhere, Paul tells us that we are "saved . . . through the washing of rebirth and renewal/regeneration by the Holy Spirit" who is poured out through Christ so that "having been justified by his grace, we might become heirs having the hope of eternal life" (Titus 3:5–7; cf. John 3:3, 5).

The view that baptism is only an ordinance overlooks the fact that the first Baptists understood baptism and the Lord's Supper as sacraments,[10] that there has been a continuous tradition of sacramentalism across four centuries,[11] and that it is as strong today as it has probably ever been.[12] As Philip Thompson puts it, "Earlier Baptists did not understand the sacraments in terms of the symbolic minimalism that so characterizes contemporary accounts. Rather, there was definite and saving effect in the rites by the presence of the Lord held forth in each."[13]

Increasingly, Baptist scholars refer to the "realist language" of passages, including Acts 2:38, Rom 6:2–11, and Col 2:11–12. On Rom 6:3–4, Colwell observes that "baptism is the means through which the Spirit mediates this inclusion in Christ . . . the sacramental realism of biblical language can only be avoided through extreme special pleading."[14] Stanley Fowler identifies John 3:3, 5; Titus 3:5; Eph 5:26; and 1 Cor 12:13 as baptismal:

> It looks as if these texts are saying that baptism is instrumental in the experience of salvation, i.e., that spiritual rebirth, cleansing from sin, and union with Christ and his church are effects of baptism. That this is the apparent meaning of the texts is evident from the common Baptist attempt to evade this conclusion by interpreting these passages in a non-baptismal sense.[15]

It is clear, then, that God's gift in faith and baptism is one,[16] namely, salvation in Christ—it is faith-baptism. This is why Peter can say "baptism . . . now saves you" (1 Pet 3:21), because he is using baptism metaphorically. But what kind of metaphor? It is a synecdoche,[17] a figure of speech in which the name of an attribute of something is substituted for the thing itself.

---

10. See Cross, "Sacrament of Baptism."
11. Fowler, *More Than a Symbol*.
12. See Cross and Thompson, *Baptist Sacramentalism* (5 vols.).
13. Thompson, "New Question," 66–67.
14. Colwell, *Promise and Presence*, 121.
15. Fowler, *More Than a Symbol*, 65. Cf. 156–95.
16. Beasley-Murray, "Authority and Justification," 65.
17. Cross, *Recovering the Evangelical Sacrament*, 72–83.

In this case, becoming a Christian is represented by part of that process, namely baptism. The simplest form of synecdoche is a single word. Other synecdoche with which Baptists have no problem are the "blood" and the "cross" of Christ.

Recognizing baptism as a synecdoche allows us to understand how Peter can say "baptism . . . now saves you" and why Paul includes baptism as one of the seven unities of the faith in Eph 4:5 and in 1 Cor 12:13 says "For in the one Spirit we were all baptized into one body." It helps us understand the accounts of conversions in Acts and frees us from trying to determine which is the normative order of becoming a Christian. There is not one, because the Spirit comes to people differently and brings them into God's kingdom by a process that can be long and protracted or swift, even sudden. The need to keep trying to determine the sequence of these events is obviated once we stop seeing conversion in sudden, punctiliar terms rather than as a process. Robert Stein explains, "In the experience of becoming a Christian, five integrally related components took place at the same time, usually on the same day: repentance, faith, confession, receiving the gift of the Holy Spirit, and baptism," and this applies to New Testament teaching as a whole.[18] What matters is that people come to new life in Christ. R. E. O. White cautions that "we may speak of Paul's sacramentalism, provided we remember that to his mind efficacy belongs not to the ceremony of baptism as such but to the action of God, by the Spirit, within the soul of the convert who at this time and in this way is making his response to the grace offered him in the gospel." No dualism exists here "because for Paul baptism is always, and only, faith-baptism: given that, Paul is emphatically a sacramentalist."[19] Nevertheless, "in the doctrine of the Sacraments the act of God and the act of man must neither be confounded nor be separated."[20] God's grace is always prevenient, because "within the sacraments, as in Christ himself, the human and the divine occur together albeit that the divine, here as elsewhere, has priority."[21] The human response in faith-baptism is necessary because it is the locus of the Spirit's operation; it is a "divine-human encounter."[22]

---

18. Stein, "Baptism in Luke–Acts," 51–52, and Stein, "Baptism and Becoming a Christian."
19. White, *Biblical Doctrine of Initiation*, 226.
20. Beasley-Murray, *Baptism in New Testament*, 275.
21. Colwell, *Promise and Presence*, 116.
22. Fiddes, *Tracks and Traces*, 128.

Problems of Terminology

But what about those for whom the word *sacrament* is problematic? For Ukrainian Baptists it is synonymous with Orthodox theology; for Norwegian Baptists it is Lutheran theology; for South Korean Baptists it is a mixture of Catholic, Lutheran, and Reformed theological associations.

The first thing to state is that the definition of every theological word or concept always comes from the author and their context. Second, those who oppose sacrament need to realize that many definitions of sacrament have been offered and defended for over two thousand years,[23] and the one Baptists are most at home with is a "means of grace."[24] Third, not all those who have held to a sacramental understanding of baptism—or the Lord's supper—have used the word. Historically, Baptists have used a range of terms to explicate God's work in baptism and communion.[25] In 1801, James Hinton reminds us that in the ordinances Christ has "promised to enrich [us] with his presence." Further, in baptism and the Lord's Supper we "publicly own his authority, and commemorate the great events of his death and resurrection" in the expectation that our souls might be "established and increased in vital godliness" and that "sinners also may be converted unto God."[26]

Second, for Colwell, "baptism is a sacrament; it is a means of grace; it is a human event through which a divine event is promised to occur."[27] For those who demur from using sacramental language and theology, he explains that "we are not saved *by* faith any more than we are saved *by* the sacraments; we are saved *by* God *through* faith and *through* the sacraments—and these instrumental means of salvation ought not to be opposed as rivals or alternatives."[28]

Third, in the 1640s, Thomas Lambe asserts that the "baptism of believers is the instrumental means by which the Church . . . comes to be a

---

23. Cross, *Recovering the Evangelical Sacrament*, 188. See also 35–37, 180–88.
24. See Cross and Thompson, *Baptist Sacramentalism* 3.
25. See Cross, "Introduction."
26. Ryland and Hinton, *Difficulties and Supports*, 39–40.
27. Colwell, *Promise and Presence*, 133.
28. Colwell, *Promise and Presence*, 130.

Church,"[29] and in 1773 Hugh Evans declares how God "is pleased to make use of instruments to effect his own purposes."[30]

Fourth, writing in 1707, William Mitchill carefully argues that the grace "exhibited" or "conferred" by the sacraments does not reside in any power they have, "neither doth the Efficacy of a Sacrament depend upon the Piety or Intention of him that doth administer it, but upon the Work of the Spirit, and the Word of Institution, which contains, together with a Precept authorizing the use thereof, a Promise of benefit to the worthy Receivers." These worthy recipients are "those who actually profess Repentance towards God, Faith in and Obedience to our dear Lord Jesus Christ."[31]

What these pastor-theologians have done is to provide a nomenclature that acknowledges that God actually works in and through believers' baptism without recourse to the term "sacrament" that so many find problematic. Specific terms do not need to be used at all, as the New Testament baptismal language and imagery says everything that can—and should—be said, but in "means of grace," "instrument/instrumentality," and the language of efficacy there is plenty of historical precedent and rich theology in the Baptist tradition to assist the contemporary Baptist recovery of a more evangelical baptismal theology and practice.

Baptism in Ecumenical Debate

Baptism has figured prominently in ecumenical discussions, culminating in *Baptism, Eucharist and Ministry (BEM)*[32] and, most recently, in *TCTCV*. These discussions have undergone methodological shifts from comparative studies to those seeking convergence. Since *BEM* the ecumenical discussion of baptism has continued, exploring and developing its proposals, with emphasis falling on the mutual recognition of baptism, a common baptism, equivalent alternatives, or recognition of a common pattern of initiation.

Progress towards exploring the acceptance of a common pattern of initiation is reflected in Paul Fiddes's work, in which he suggests:

> Rather than urging an equivalence of infant baptism with believer-baptism, it might be possible to recognize whole *patterns of*

---

29. Lambe, *Confutation of Infants Baptisme*, 35, 38.
30. Evans, *Able Minister*, 4.
31. Mitchill, "William Mitchill's 'Jachin & Boaz' 1707," 159–60.
32. WCC, *Baptism, Eucharist and Ministry*.

> *initiation* as being equivalent. Baptism, at whatever age, could be seen as only part of a journey of Christian beginnings, a journey with its starting point in the prevenient grace of God and ending with an 'owned' faith of a Christian disciple. . . . Along the way there will be various kinds of opportunities for receiving children into the fellowship of the church (whether by baptism or by the blessing of infants) and for growth into faith in Christ. Baptism would stand as a focus for the whole journey of beginning the Christian life, whether it came earlier or later in the process as a whole.[33]

Fiddes looks for a moment in the various initiation rites when the baptismal candidate exercises their own faith in Christ. If this cannot be located in the event of baptism, as in infant baptism, then initiation has to be stretched in some way in order to accommodate it. In the Western churches this is traditionally done in confirmation, "but whether or not it takes this particular form, Baptists will expect personal faith (arising from divine grace) to be a part of Christian *beginnings*."[34]

However, many Baptists, out of theological conscience, are unable to pursue such proposals. Further, these avenues do not adequately address Eph 4:5's "one baptism," other than by forcing together mutually exclusive baptisms.[35] Ephesians 4:4–6 sets out seven essential loci of oneness for the people of God, and baptism's inclusion shows that it, like the other six, cannot just be negotiated away, no matter how laudable the motives.

Christopher Ellis argues that for Baptists the basis of unity does not lie in a common baptism, with its acceptance of infant baptism,

> but in the saving work of the Triune God manifested in recognizing the Spirit's work in others and thereby as fellow believers. This highlights the value Baptists place on ecclesiology over the due administration of the sacraments; the church is comprised of believers.[36]

For the first Baptists, baptism was not a means of exclusion, for they identified themselves with historic Christianity,[37] frequently sought fellowship

---

33. Fiddes, "Baptism of Believers," 78–79.
34. Fiddes, "Baptism and the Process," 49.
35. See Cross, *Recovering the Evangelical Statement*, 1–24, on multiple baptisms and the inadequacy of settling for this.
36. Ellis, "Baptism of Disciples," 348.
37. Harmon, *Towards Baptist Catholicity*.

and worshiped with Paedobaptists,[38] and set themselves within the catholic/universal church.[39] Rather, baptism was a means of preserving a pure church comprised of genuine Christians, and this is why baptism was applied only to believers old enough to profess their own faith in Christ. It was not till later that baptism began to act as a way of keeping the non-baptized out of the church.

There is here historical precedent among Baptists for an alternative approach to the oneness of the church. It is nowhere clearer than in John Ryland's writings, when Ryland argues, "Surely, they who have fellowship with the Father and with his Son; who were loved with the same everlasting love, bought with the same precious blood; who are led by the same Spirit, and inhabited by him as his temple . . . must have fellowship one with another."[40] When he addressed union with other Christians, he saw something as of greater importance than right doctrine. In fact, he focused on "the greater articles of faith on which we agree," contending that these "should have more influence to unite us, than any smaller points on which good men can disagree, should have to divide us."[41] He relegated to "smaller points" those doctrines over which Christians disagreed because Christian fellowship did not rise or fall with right doctrine. This catholicity is grounded in communion with Christ:

> It appears to me *so much the nature of the new creature . . . for true believers to have intimate communion with each other*, that nothing but clear precept or precedent for debarring a mistaken brother from the Lord's table, could induce me to refuse those whom Christ had evidently received, and who could be admitted without any injury to my own exercise of the rights of conscience, or without endangering any privilege of my own.[42]

Ryland sets out the basis for his catholicity:

> Especially in proportion as we enter into the Spirit of his Gospel, our Union with him will produce Attachment to each other. The [cross] is the great rallying Point for the true Catholic Church. Do

---

38. Cross, *Baptism and the Baptists*, 91–96.

39. E.g., "Second London Confession (1677)," in Lumpkin, *Baptist Confessions of Faith*, 283–84.

40. Ryland, "Communion of Saints," 2:282. I am indebted for this to Lon Graham's PhD research in "All Who Love."

41. Ryland, "Communion of Saints," 2:281.

42. Ryland, "Letter to Paedobaptist Church."

you worship God in the Spirit, rejoice in Christ Jesus, & place no Confidence in the flesh? This will more closely unite true Saints in one Communion, than any outward Denomination. Whether you wear my uniform, or of my Regiment, you are really of my side.[43]

The freedom of conscience and religious liberty Baptists cherish for themselves, they equally advocate and defend for others. On this contentious matter of baptism, it not inconceivable for Christians to recognize that those who interpret God's word differently are not beyond the pale, and therefore we neither need to break fellowship with them nor try to force them into accepting our perception and understanding of the things of God. Such an approach seeks mutual respect, though there is a step further that could be taken.

Reform—The Way Forward

This further step is the wholesale reform of baptism. Baptists have been known for the inadequacy of their theology of baptism, and, from a Baptist perspective, though not exclusively so, infant baptism is a theological development of the scriptural conversion-baptism/faith-baptism. An increasing number of Baptists have called for the reform of Baptist baptismal theology and practice,[44] and there are a growing number of pedobaptist traditions that have called for the reform of their theology and practice or even disagree with or have actually abandoned infant sprinkling. This suggestion gains added impetus from the recognition that churches are living in post-Christian, multifaith, secularized societies reminiscent of the setting of the New Testament and ante-Nicene churches. The church universal is always *semper reformandum*, and this should apply no less to baptism than to other aspects of her life and doctrine.

Bibliography

Beasley-Murray George R. "The Authority and Justification for Believers' Baptism." *Review and Expositor* 77 (1980) 63–70.
———. *Baptism in the New Testament*. Exeter, UK: Paternoster, 1972.

---

43. Ryland, "Sermon Notes." Again, I am indebted to Lon Graham for this.

44. See Beasley-Murray, *Baptism in New Testament*, 387–95; and Cross, *Recovering the Evangelical Statement*, passim.

Colwell, John E. *Promise and Presence: An Exploration of Sacramental Theology*. Milton Keynes, UK: Paternoster, 2005.

Cross, Anthony R. *Baptism and the Baptists: Theology and Practice in Twentieth-Century Britain*. Eugene, OR: Wipf & Stock, 2017.

———. "Introduction: Sacraments by Any Other Name." In *Baptist Sacramentalism 4*, edited by Anthony Cross and Philip E. Thompson. Eugene, OR: Cascade, forthcoming.

———. *Recovering the Evangelical Sacrament: Baptisma Semper Reformandum*. Eugene, OR: Pickwick, 2013.

———. "The Sacrament of Baptism among the First Baptists." In *Ecclesia semper reformanda est: A Festschrift on Ecclesiology in Honour of Stanley K. Fowler*, edited by David G. Barker et al., 189–211. Kitchener, Canada: Joshua, 2016.

Cross, Anthony R., and Philip E. Thompson, eds. *Baptist Sacramentalism 1*. Waynesboro, GA: Paternoster, 2003.

———, eds. *Baptist Sacramentalism 2*. Milton Keynes, UK: Paternoster, 2008.

———, eds. *Baptist Sacramentalism 3*. Eugene, OR: Cascade, 2020.

———, eds. *Baptist Sacramentalism 5*. Eugene, OR: Cascade, forthcoming.

Ellis, Christopher J. "The Baptism of Disciples and the Nature of the Church." In *Dimensions of Baptism: Biblical and Theological Studies*, edited by Stanley E. Porter and Anthony R. Cross, 333–53. Sheffield, UK: Sheffield Academic, 2002.

Evans, Hugh. *The Able Minister*. Bristol, UK: Pine, 1773.

Fiddes, Paul S. "Baptism and the Process of Christian Initiation." *Ecumenical Review* 54 (2002) 48–65.

———. "The Baptism of Believers." In *Baptism Today: Understanding, Practice, Ecumenical Implication*, edited by T. F. Best, 73–80. Collegeville, MN: Liturgical, 2008.

———. *Tracks and Traces: Baptist Identity in Church and Theology*. Carlisle, UK: Paternoster, 2003.

Fowler, Stanley K. *More Than a Symbol: The British Baptist Recovery of Baptismal Sacramentalism*. Carlisle, UK: Paternoster, 2002.

Freeman, Curtis W. "'To Feed Upon by Faith': Nourishment from the Lord's Table." In *Baptist Sacramentalism 1*, edited by Anthony R. Cross and Philip E. Thompson, 194–210. Waynesboro, GA: Paternoster, 2003.

Graham, Lon A. "'All Who Love Our Blessed Redeemer:' The Catholicity of John Ryland Jr." PhD diss., International Baptist Theological Study Centre, Amsterdam, 2021.

Harmon, Steven R. *Towards Baptist Catholicity: Essays on Tradition and the Baptist Vision*. Studies in Baptist History and Thought 27. Milton Keynes, UK: Paternoster, 2006.

Haymes, Brian, et al. *On Being the Church: Revisioning Baptist Identity*. Milton Keynes, UK: Paternoster, 2008.

Lambe, Thomas. *A Confutation of Infants Baptisme*. London: N.p., 1643.

Lumpkin, William L. *Baptist Confessions of Faith*. 2nd rev. ed. Revised by Bill J. Leonard. Valley Forge, PA: Judson, 2011.

Mitchill, William. "William Mitchill's 'Jachin & Boaz' 1707." Introduction by W. E. Blomfeld. *Transactions of the Baptist Historical Society* 3 (1913) 154–75.

Ryland, John. "The Communion of Saints." In *Pastoral Memorials*, edited by Jonathan E. Ryland, 2:277–84. London: Holdsworth, 1826–28.

———. "Letter to the Paedobaptist Church at Broadmead." In *Pastoral Memorials*, edited by Jonathan E. Ryland, 2:20. London: Holdsworth, 1826–28.

———. "Sermon Notes: Isaiah 11:10." In *Original Manuscript Sermons (c. 1771–1823),* vol. 1 of *Old Testament,* unpaginated. In Bristol Baptist College Archives, Bristol, UK.

Ryland, John, and James Hinton. *The Difficulties and Supports of a Gospel Minister; and The Duties Incumbent on a Christian Church.* Bristol, UK: Harris and Bryan, 1801.

Stackhouse, Ian. *The Gospel-Driven Church: Retrieving Classical Ministries for Contemporary Revivalism.* Milton Keynes, UK: Paternoster, 2004.

Stein, Robert H. "Baptism and Becoming a Christian." *Southern Baptist Journal of Theology* 2 (1998) 6–17.

———. "Baptism in Luke–Acts." In *Believer's Baptism: Sign of the New Covenant in Christ,* edited by Thomas A. Schreiner and Shawn D. Wright, 35–66. Nashville: B. & H. Academic, 2006.

Thompson, Philip E. "A New Question in Baptist History: Seeking a Catholic Spirit Among Early Baptists." *Pro Ecclesia* 8 (1999) 51–72.

WCC. *Baptism, Eucharist and Ministry.* Geneva: WCC, 1982.

White, R.E.O. *The Biblical Doctrine of Initiation.* London: Hodder & Stoughton, 1960.

10

Discipling Churches

Marion L. S. Carson

A Story from the Streets of Glasgow

THE WORLD COUNCIL OF Churches' Faith and Order Commission's stated aim is to "proclaim the oneness of the Church of Jesus Christ and to call the churches to visible unity in one faith and eucharistic fellowship, expressed in common worship and in common life in Christ, through witness and service to the world so that the world may believe."[1] The call for visible unity has a missional purpose: the world has to be able to observe unity amongst believers if it is going to consider the message it brings to be credible.

The importance of this was brought home to me one evening on the streets of Glasgow, in Scotland. Each Friday night a group of us from our Baptist congregation would go into the streets of Glasgow, offering hot drinks and cakes to the women who were working in prostitution. Our aim was to get to know them, to listen, and to tell them of God's love. We did not set out to convert or rescue (although we had to learn ways of helping when they expressed a desire to leave prostitution) but to share the love of God by building up relationships with them. We soon discovered that we were not the only Christian group reaching out to the women. In fact, groups from other denominations and parachurch organizations were doing exactly the

---

1. WCC, *TCTCV*, 2.

same thing as us, every night of the week. Some, like ourselves, came from the evangelical stable, but Roman Catholic organizations and more liberal Protestants were also active.

Gradually, the women began to trust us and confide in us. I remember one particular night when we stopped to talk to a woman who was sitting on the pavement. She accepted a cup of coffee and a cake, and we began to chat. She told us that she had been out working the night before and that two ladies had stopped to talk to her, just as we were doing now. Like us, they had offered her a warm drink and spent time with her, listening to her relate her longing to see her children who were living with foster parents. They had prayed with her and given her a gift of a "miraculous medal," which she handled reverently. Tears came to her eyes as she showed it to us. Then she looked up at us and said, "But you don't like these people, do you?"

The girl's remark filled me with dismay. She had noticed lack of communication and cooperation amongst the various groups and had assumed that their basis was hostility. This was hardly surprising given that Glasgow is a city riven by entrenched sectarian animosity between Protestants and Catholics. In fact, our failure to communicate or work together was born out of apathy and even ignorance on our part rather than hostility. In this instance, however, the reason was irrelevant—our lack of visible unity was undermining our mission. It revealed a gaping hole in our missional strategy—how could we take the love of Christ to these women while failing to demonstrate that we loved our fellow believers?

It is with this experience in mind that I welcome *TCTCV*, whose purpose is to provide an occasion for churches to "reflect upon their own understanding of the Lord's will so as to grow towards greater unity" for the purposes of mission.[2] I believe that its call for visible unity is crucial for the church as a whole, and I hope that it will be widely read and discussed throughout the Christian community.

From the outset, the authors make it clear that the rationale for the link between unity and mission is to be found in Scripture. In particular, Christ's prayer in John 17 provides the basis of their argument, references to it forming a kind of *inclusio* to the document as a whole. It is because Christ himself prayed for unity in mission that we must work towards this goal. The document is thus an "invitation to the leaders, theologians and faithful of all churches to seek the unity for which Jesus prayed (cf. John

---

2. WCC, *TCTCV*, 2.

17:21) on the night before he offered his life for the salvation of the world (cf. Eph. 5:25; Gal. 1:4, 2:20; Rom. 8:32)."[3]

There can be no doubt that the appeal to Scripture must be central to ecumenical dialogue.[4] As the authors note, "Since all Christians share the conviction that Scripture is normative, this biblical witness provides an irreplaceable source for acquiring greater agreement about the Church."[5] However, while I appreciate that the nature of this document precludes in-depth exegesis, it is, from a biblical studies perspective, rather frustrating that the prayer is merely referred to without mention of its literary context and at least some analysis to support the argument. Indeed, the quote given above is an example of the tendency throughout the document to cite verses as proof texts, with no exploration of their contexts or implications. As Michael Kinnamon notes, there is a need for the ecumenical movement to "wrestle" with Scripture at a deeper level than proof texting and for us to listen to and learn from one another as we do so.[6] With this in mind, I offer in this chapter a brief exploration of Jesus's prayer, asking what it can teach us with regard to the relationship between mission and unity, in the hope that it might stimulate further discussion. In order to do so, I will adopt a missional hermeneutical approach, asking what the prayer might have to say about the *missio Dei* and believers' part in it.[7]

The Prayer in John 17

In the so-called "farewell discourses" (John 13–16), Jesus has told his disciples that he will be leaving them soon and warned them that they will be persecuted. He has also reassured them that they need not be afraid, because he has conquered the world. He has told them of the unity between himself and the Father and promised them the gift of the Holy Spirit. He has urged them to stay close to him (as close as the vine is to its branches) and commanded them to love one another. Now, in chapter 17, we listen

---

3. WCC, *TCTCV*, 6.

4. On the place of the Bible in the ecumenical movement, see Flesseman-Van Leer, *Bible*.

5. WCC, *TCTCV*, 7.

6. Kinnamon, "Scripture and Mission."

7. Barram, "Bible, Mission, and Social Location"; Bauckham, *Bible and Mission*; Wright, "Bible and Christian Mission." On missional hermeneutics in John's Gospel, see in particular Gorman, *Abide and Go*.

in as he prays. He asks that he may be glorified in his time of suffering, so that the Father may be glorified. That is, he asks that God's purposes may be fulfilled in his sufferings, death, and resurrection. He then prays for his disciples—those who have believed that Jesus has come from God and who have been given the revelation of God's name. First, he asks specifically that they may be one as he and the Father are one (v. 11). Then, he asks for their protection as they carry on the work of taking God's word to the world. Now that he is about to leave them, they will come under intense pressure from persecution and the work of the evil one (v. 15). Lastly, he asks that they be sanctified in the truth of the word that they have received (v. 19). In other words, his prayer is that they will increasingly be able to apprehend what it means to be consecrated disciples of Christ, separate from the world, yet present and serving in it.[8] In verse 20, the prayer broadens out to encompass those who will become believers because of the disciples' message. Jesus also prays for unity among them, so that "the world may believe that you have sent me," and says that he has given them his "glory" to enable them to be in unity, again for the sake of mission.[9]

John 17 in Missional Perspective

In its literary context, the prayer has a twofold function—it is a record of Jesus's intercession for his disciples, and a revelation of God's will for those who listen in.[10] It is clear that the disciples, and those who come after them, have been assigned the task of keeping and passing on the word of truth (17:20), testifying to the fact of God's love. Equally clear is that if the task of mission is to be accomplished, unity amongst believers is necessary. But what does Jesus mean by unity, and how does he think it can be achieved?

The unity of which Jesus speaks has a theological basis. It is because the Father and Son are one that Jesus's followers can and should be one (v. 21). Believers are invited to become one with Christ, and in so doing they

---

8. Thompson, *John*, 355.

9. I am taking the view that John's view of mission concerns the world as a whole (3:16), and not merely those who are "elect who are called to faith" (*pace* Käsemann, *Testament of Jesus*, 65.) On mission in John's Gospel, see especially Köstenberger, *Missions of Jesus*. Cf. also Peterson, *John's Use of Ezekiel*, 165–86: Jesus's thinking is in line with the prophetic tradition expressed in Ezekiel—that unity amongst God's people is necessary for the world as a whole to believe, and not simply the elect within Israel.

10. "Because there is an audience, the prayer is just as much revelation as it is intercession" (Brown, *Gospel According to John*, 748).

enter into the relationship between Father and Son, enabled by the gift of the Holy Spirit. Unity, then, should be the normal state of affairs for Jesus's followers. This is the way things should be—intimacy and love within the Godhead, flowing from the Godhead to believers, flowing amongst believers, and outwards towards to the world. As Newbigin writes, this is a spiritual unity "which not merely reflects but actually participates in the unity of God—the unity of love and obedience which binds the Son to the Father (cf. 15:9–10)."[11] According to Newbigin, evidence of love and obedience in the lives of believers is the "visible unity" for which Jesus prays:

> The prayer of Jesus is for a unity which is real participation of believers in the love and obedience which unites Jesus with the Father, a participation which is as invisible as the flow of sap which unites the branches with the vine, and which at the same time is as visible as the unity of branch and vine—as visible as the love and obedience of Jesus.[12]

It is this spiritual unity that will cause the world to come to know God. But how does Jesus think this unity is to be achieved? First, there is the fact that Jesus makes the request, and since his will and the Father's are one, God will surely answer his prayer. Second, when Jesus sends them out, he gives them the gift of the Holy Spirit (20:21–23), who will guide them in all truth (16:13). Third, here in the prayer Jesus says that they have already been given the gift of glory (*doxa*)—so that they may be in unity and so that the world may know that Jesus was sent be God and loves those who follow him (v. 23). However, it is not immediately obvious what this gift of *doxa* entails. Several suggestions have been made. According to Köstenberger, it refers to the empowering to carry out the mission task.[13] It may also refer to the honor and reputation that will come to them in the future when they share in the honor which will be given to Jesus.[14] Talbert suggests it refers to the gift of the Holy Spirit that will enable them to live life together.[15] There is truth in all of these suggestions. However, since the emphasis in this prayer is on the relationship between Son, Father, and believers, and on the mission to show God's love to the world, I am inclined to the view that *doxa* here refers to the actual participation of believers in the relationship

11. Newbigin, *Light Has Come*, 234.
12. Newbigin, *Light Has Come*, 235.
13. Köstenberger, *Missions of Jesus*, 498.
14. Thompson, *John*, 357.
15. Talbert, *Reading John*, 237.

between the Father and the Son, which is enabled by the gift of the Holy Spirit. The unity that that entails is a "sharing in the glory of oneness like that existing between father and son."[16] As Schnackenburg puts it, this *doxa* "points toward the fullness of divine life," making present now that which will be fully realized only in the heavenly or future world. The more powerfully the divine life is present in believers, "the more fully unity is achieved among them."[17] It is this transformative relationship (which Michael Gorman terms "missional *theosis*"[18]) that will convince the "world" that what they are saying is actually true.

The *doxa* of the close relationship between believers, Jesus, and the Father is God's extraordinary gift to us, and it is on this basis that we can be in unity in the first place. However, the gift is not given merely for our own edification. It is a gift that must be used (not just looked at and admired), and it has a specific purpose—mission. It is this glory—the participation of believers in God's work and the love that ensues from that—that unbelievers should be able to see if the message is to be credible and elicit a response—whether it be acceptance or hostile rejection and persecution.

The Responsibility of Missional Unity

It is clear from a missional reading of this text that believers have been given the privilege of a close relationship to the Godhead. However, it is equally clear that this privilege entails certain responsibilities. First, we have a responsibility to resist the forces that seek to divide us. We have seen that mission and unity are intimately linked in John 17 and that God has given us extraordinary gifts to enable us to join in the *missio Dei*.[19] But Jesus also speaks of the threat that will come from the evil one as the disciples take the word of truth into the world. If unity is God's desire for his people and necessary for the *missio Dei*, it follows that the forces of evil will do everything in their power to work against it. Significantly, these themes of mission, unity, gift and threat are brought together in the Revised Common Lectionary (year A) readings for the seventh Sunday of Easter. John 17 is to be read alongside Luke's account of Jesus's ascension and the promise

16. Kruse, *Gospel According to John*, 341; cf. Moloney, *Glory Not Dishonor*, 121.
17. Schnackenburg, *Gospel According to St. John*, 3:192.
18. Gorman, *Abide and Go*, ch. 2.
19. On the idea of the *missio Dei* in ecumenism, see Bosch, *Transforming Mission*, 389–93.

that they will receive power from the Holy Spirit (Acts 1:6–14) and Peter's call to resist the devil (1 Pet 4:12–14; 5:6–11). In Acts as in John, the gift of the Holy Spirit is for the sake of mission. The intimate relationship with Christ, which will continue even after he is gone, will empower them to be witnesses "in Jerusalem, and in all Judea and Samaria, and to the ends of the earth (Acts 1:8)." As Scott Bader-Saye remarks, "Reading Acts alongside John we may surmise that the Spirit empowers us not only for proclamation but for unity."[20] While it is true that God's purposes will not be thwarted, we cannot be complacent, for our adversary the devil is "like a roaring lion prowling around seeking to devour us" (1 Pet 5:8).[21] When God's spirit of glory rests on his people (1 Pet 4:4), his people need to be sober and alert, for the powers of evil will want to disrupt its work. It falls to us to recognize this and to play our part in ensuring that God's will is done.

The second responsibility is corporate prayer. In John 17 and elsewhere, Jesus prays out of intimacy with his Father. If Jesus himself prays, then so should his followers in their gift of intimacy with Father, Son, and Spirit. In response to, and using our gift of *doxa*, we can and must meet together to pray, joining in with his prayer for us (cf. Acts 1:14). We can ask for greater understanding of the truth and pray for help to work towards the kind of unity he requires of us. We can pray that God will protect his church from the evil one. As Jesus asks that we be sanctified in truth (John 17:19), so we too can pray together that we increase in holiness as a people set apart—and that our hearts be changed to be in alignment with his will. We can consecrate ourselves for his purposes, willing to give up our lives, our precious shibboleths, and anything that is of human origin rather than from God himself. We can ask together that he help us to understand more of what it means to fulfil the commandment to "love one another."

The third responsibility is to live lives of obedience and love as participators in the work of the Godhead. We cannot rest on our laurels; we must work together in and for visible unity. Sharing in Christ's glory means that, like the Good Shepherd, we look after the sheep: going after the strays, caring for the sick, binding up the wounds (John 10).[22] It is not merely a matter of evangelism but of working together to reach out to the poor and marginalized, demonstrating unity in a way that makes sense to those whom we serve. In my experience, the common aim of taking God's love

---

20. Bader-Saye, "Long Division."
21. *Pace* Bultmann, *Gospel of John*, 513.
22. Michaels, *Gospel of John*, 525.

to others serves to unite believers from different traditions in ways that discussions of doctrine and practice (indispensable as they are) do not. In the face of stark human need we have to prioritize, and as we respond, theological differences must take second place. If we let our disagreements divide us and prevent us from working together, our missional activity will be compromised—as I discovered on the streets of Glasgow all those years ago.

This does not mean the erasure of difference: it is inevitable and indeed essential that we have varying points of view, for without them we stultify and fail to grow. What we do need, however, is humility and willingness of heart to work together, in the truth of our shared faith in Christ, in spite of our disagreements. This is another aspect of *doxa*, which must entail self-sacrifice and suffering on our part, as it did for Christ himself.[23] The self-sacrifice in this case will include the humble recognition that our human theological understanding is necessarily incomplete, and that we can learn from those with whom we disagree. Not everyone will concur with this view, of course, and where the will to collaborate is not present, we can, at the very least, strive to "live at peace with everyone" (Rom 14:18).

Conclusion

This brief exploration of John 17 shows that the invitation extended by the authors of *TCTCV* "to seek the unity for which Jesus prayed" is one that cannot, must not be declined. Unity must therefore not merely be an aspiration, an ideal—it is something for which we have been equipped and something for which we must take active responsibility. "By this shall they know that you are my disciples," Jesus said, "if you love one another, as I have loved you" (13:34–35; 15:12, 17).

As I look back to that night in Glasgow, it still grieves me that our lack of love for other believers was so evident. Or rather, it grieves me that the woman could see no difference between us and the divided world in which she lived.[24] But I am also grateful for the experience, for it brought home to me the need for visible unity. From our study of John 17 we can see that it starts with a recognition of how essential it is for mission and our responsibility to work towards it. It starts with consciously reaching out to each other, adopting what Miroslav Volf terms an "openness" towards churches and

---

23. Barrett, *Gospel According to St. John*, 513.
24. Cf. Keener, *Gospel of John*, 1061.

traditions other than our own.[25] It involves a willingness to pray together, seeking to know more of the meaning of the word of truth. We might also add studying Scripture together—learning from our different hermeneutical stances and traditions. These things are undoubtedly transformative in our lives. However, I doubt if the women on the streets of Glasgow would be impressed if we told them that this was going on amongst Christians. They need to see unity, not just hear about it. Without the visible unity of collaboration in mission, such behind-the-scenes expressions of spiritual harmony run the risk of being self-serving and ineffective.

For many, if not most of us, taking active responsibility in these ways will be risky. It will mean putting aside entrenched ideas as to the relationships between churches, and opening ourselves up to new experiences and ideas. It may even mean misunderstanding and hostility from people in our own communities. However, sacrificial living is central to the *missio Dei* and we must play our part. If Christ was willing to lay down his life for the sake of the world and to allow us to share in his glory, this is surely a small price to pay.

Bibliography

Bader-Saye, Scott. "Long Division: Acts 1:6–14; John 17:1–11." *Christian Century* (Apr. 24, 2002). https://www.christiancentury.org/article/2002-04/long-division.
Barram, M. "The Bible, Mission, and Social Location: Toward a Missional Hermeneutic." *Interpretation* 61 (2007) 42–58.
Barrett, C. K. *The Gospel According to St. John*. 2nd ed. London: SPCK, 1978.
Bauckham, Richard. *The Bible and Mission: Christian Witness in a Postmodern World*. Grand Rapids: Baker Academic, 2004.
Bosch, David J. *Transforming Mission: Paradigm Shifts in Theology of Mission*. Maryknoll, NY: Orbis, 1991.
Brown, Raymond E. *The Gospel According to John xiii–xxi*. Anchor Bible. New Haven, CT: Yale University Press, 1970.
Bultmann, Rudolf. *The Gospel of John: A Commentary*. Translated by G. R. Beasley-Murray et al. Eugene, OR: Wipf & Stock, 2014.
Flesseman-Van Leer, Ellen. *The Bible: Its Authority and Interpretation in the Ecumenical Movement*. Faith and Order 99. Geneva: WCC, 1983.
Gorman, Michael J. *Abide and Go: Missional Theosis in the Gospel of John*. Eugene, OR: Cascade, 2018.
Käsemann, Ernst. *The Testament of Jesus: A Study of the Gospel of John in the Light of Chapter 17*. Translated by Gerhard Krodel. London: SCM, 1968.
Keener, Craig. *The Gospel of John: A Commentary*. Grand Rapids: Baker, 2010.

---

25. According to Volf, the "openness of every church towards all other churches" is an "indispensable condition of ecclesiality" (Volf, *After Our Likeness*, 156).

Kinnamon, Michael. "Scripture and Mission." In *Unity in Mission: Theological Reflection on the Pilgrimage of Mission*, edited by Mitzi J. Budde and Don Thorsen, 24–32. Mahwah, NJ: Paulist, 2006.

Köstenberger, Andreas J. *The Missions of Jesus and the Disciples According to the Fourth Gospel: With Implications for the Purpose of the Gospel's Purpose and the Mission of the Contemporary Church*. Grand Rapids: Eerdmans, 1998.

Kruse, Colin G. *The Gospel According to John: An Introduction and Commentary*. Rev. ed. Downers Grove, IL: InterVarsity, 2017.

Michaels, J. Ramsey. *The Gospel of John*. Grand Rapids: Eerdmans, 2010.

Moloney, Francis J. *Glory Not Dishonor: Reading John 13–21*. Minneapolis: Augsburg Fortress, 1998.

Newbigin, Leslie. *The Light Has Come: An Exposition of the Fourth Gospel*. Grand Rapids: Eerdmans, 1982.

Peterson, Brian Niel. *John's Use of Ezekiel: Understanding the Unique Perspective of the Fourth Gospel*. Minneapolis: Augsburg Fortress, 2015.

Schnackenburg, Rudolf. *The Gospel According to St. John*. 3 vols. New York: Crossroad, 1982.

Talbert, Charles H. *Reading John: A Literary and Theological Commentary on the Fourth Gospel and the Johannine Epistles*. Macon, GA: Smith & Helwys, 1992.

Thompson, Marianne Maye. *John*. New Testament Library. Louisville: Westminster John Knox, 2015.

Volf, Miroslav. *After Our Likeness: The Church as the Image of the Trinity*. Grand Rapids: Eerdmans, 1986.

WCC. *The Church: Towards a Common Vision*. Faith and Order 214. Geneva: WCC, 2013.

Wright, N. T. "The Bible and Christian Mission." In *Scripture and Its Interpretation: A Global, Ecumenical Introduction to the Bible*, 345–55. Grand Rapids: Baker, 2017.

11

Caring Churches

Frank Rees

SINCE THE INCEPTION OF the movement now known as Baptists, the term *pastor* has had some usage, and the idea of care and oversight of the community has been a vital part of their organization. In this essay, we will draw upon some of the historic Baptist understandings of this ministry. We will then describe a distinctive modern concept of pastoral care and compare it with ecumenical discussions of ministry. These three sources provide the basis for describing a more rounded Baptist understanding of the ministry of pastoral care and oversight.

Pastors and Pastoral Care in Baptist History

In 1610 Thomas Helwys and his followers issued a Short Confession of faith, in which article 23 indicates the ministries God has ordained for the church: "the ministers of the Gospel, the doctrines of the holy Word, the use of the holy sacraments, the oversight of the poor, and the ministers of the same offices." Importantly, the paragraph goes on to refer to "the exercise of brotherly admonition and correction" and "separating of the impenitent."[1]

It is clear from the succeeding paragraph that while there is a diversity of gifts among the members of the church, "the administration of the said

---

1. "Short Confession of Faith" (1610), in Lumpkin, *Baptist Confessions of Faith*, 100–113.

offices or duties partaineth only to those who are ordained thereto, and not to every particular common person."[2] Here we have a clear indication of the "office" of pastoral oversight and care. It is also important to note, however, that the duties and offices of those so ordained included the role of "admonition and correction"—to the point, where necessary, of exclusion or separation of those who will not be so corrected. This element of pastoral discipline was a significant feature of Baptist tradition, held by the community at large and exercised on its behalf by the ordained minister.

The confessions of the early English Baptist associations provide a similar understanding of the role of ordained ministers. The London Confession of 1644 asserts that "every Church has power given them from Christ for their better well-being, to choose to themselves meet persons into the office of Pastors, teachers, Elders, Deacons . . . for the feeding, governing, serving, and building up of his Church."[3] These pastors are to administer the ordinances. It is also stated that no one else has power to "impose" these offices. In contrast to the earlier Short Confession, the London Confession makes it clear that the power "to receive in and cast out" any member pertains to the whole congregation "and not one particular person, either member or Officer."[4]

The Second London Confession, made by "the Elders and Brethren of many congregations" in 1677, offers further insight into the early Baptist understanding of the ministries of pastors and overseers, here named Bishops. Chapter 26 concerns the church, with paragraph 8 explaining that a particular church consists of its members and officers. The paragraph then details that the members are to choose and set apart these officers in accordance with Christ's own choosing:

> for the peculiar Administration of Ordinances, and Execution of Power, or Duty, which he intrusts them with, or calls them to, to be continued to the end of the World, are Bishops or Elders and Deacons.[5]

---

2. "Short Confession of Faith" (1610), in Lumpkin, *Baptist Confessions of Faith*, 106–7.

3. "London Confession" (1644), in Lumpkin, *Baptist Confessions of Faith*, 166.

4. "London Confession" (1644), in Lumpkin, *Baptist Confessions of Faith*, 168.

5. "Second London Confession" (1677), in Lumpkin, *Baptist Confessions of Faith*, 287.

These bishops or elders are to be constant in attending to the service of Christ in his churches: "in the Ministry of the Word, and Prayer, with the watching for their Souls, as they that must give an account to him."[6]

From these early indications, then, it is clear that for its formative decades and into the following centuries, the Baptist vision of the church recognized the importance of the gathered life, centered around the ministries of word and sacrament or ordinances. Within this life of discipleship in community, the "officers" were responsible for these vital ministries. Thus, for most of this period, ordination was to the ministry of word and sacraments, though the term *sacraments* was avoided by many. As a result, such ordination was referred to as "the pastoral ministry" or "the gospel ministry."

Within this Baptist tradition, then, pastoral duties were understood within the broader Christian concept of "the cure of souls." There may be some specific concern for the poor and infirmed, as well as the ministry of prayer, exercised generally through a daily period of personal devotion. The constant study of the Bible, both for personal edification and in preparation for the ministry of the word, was another pastoral duty. Another element was visitation of church members, for encouragement or nurture in faith and discipleship. Some administration of the local church's affairs would be the pastor's responsibility, in partnership with the deacons. In the last century, however, a quite distinctive perspective on pastoral ministry developed, with the movement towards specific ideas of *pastoral care*.

"Pastoral Care": A Modern Development

During the middle part of the twentieth century there developed a distinctive emphasis in the understanding of a pastor's work, particularly in Western countries. This development took the form of a stress upon pastoral care and included for a time the idea of pastoral counseling. It was not a uniquely Baptist development but has been very influential in Baptist church life.

The following definition of this concept of pastoral care was offered by William A. Clebsch and Charles R. Jaekle.

> Pastoral Care consists of helping acts done by representative Christian persons, directed towards the healing, sustaining,

---

6. "Second London Confession" (1677), in Lumpkin, *Baptist Confessions of Faith*, 287.

guiding and reconciling of troubled persons, whose troubles arise in the context of ultimate meanings and concerns.[7]

The definition neatly indicates many elements. Pastoral care is not merely speaking with people but may include other activities. It is undertaken by "representative Christian persons," possibly ordained ministers but not explicitly limited to them. Finally, we see one of the most important elements, and perhaps limitations, of this movement is the focus upon "troubled persons." This modern movement in pastoral care has reflected a therapeutic model, broadly reflecting a medical model of care. The focus is upon "troubled people," those with worries, problems, needs—and pastoral care is somewhat like a service to be delivered by appropriate persons to those in need. Although the definition uses the plural word "persons," in many respects this movement in pastoral care has reflected a highly individualized focus. In common with pastoral counseling and psychotherapy more broadly, such pastoral care aimed at enhancing the well-being of its recipients, their personal growth towards "ultimate meanings and concerns."

In a later development, perhaps to return the focus of pastoral care towards a more ecclesial or overtly spiritual emphasis, Stephen Pattison offered a directly similar and yet contrasting description of pastoral care:

> Pastoral care is that activity, undertaken especially by representative Christian persons, directed towards the elimination and relief of sin and sorrow and the presentation of all people perfect in Christ to God.[8]

Other writers provide a more nuanced and richer understanding of this concept of pastoral care. Howard Clinebell's classic work identified five key elements: healing, sustaining, guiding, reconciling, and nurturing.[9] These can be seen to correlate well with Clebsch and Jaekle's definition.

In a critical development of these ideas, Emmanuel Y. Lartey has offered an intercultural and more communal approach to pastoral care. After a survey of various concepts and definitions of pastoral care, Lartey

---

7. Clebsch and Jaekle, *Pastoral Care in Historical Perspective*, 4. Clebsch and Jaekle note that their first three activities of pastoral care are derived from the foundational work of Hiltner, *Preface to Pastoral Theology*.

8. Pattison, *Critique of Pastoral Care*, 13.

9. Clinebell, *Basic Types of Pastoral Care*, 1966 and 1984. A significantly updated and revised edition, incorporating substantial shifts towards an intercultural focus, was issued by McKeever in 2011.

summarizes briefly what he calls models of pastoral care. These can be readily identified and understood through the labels given:

> Pastoral care as *therapy*—broadly based upon a counseling model
> Pastoral care as *ministry*—involving the classical elements of preaching, teaching, service, community building, and administration
> Pastoral care as *social action*—where a prophetic element is at the fore
> Pastoral care as *empowerment*—emphasizing nurture of the potential of the community or context, through "educational and dialogical" facilitation
> Pastoral care as *personal interaction*—with a focus on enabling relationships and personal development[10]

Lartey quite properly asks what it is that makes them Christian ministry. He refers to Frank Wright, who suggests that the task of the pastor is "to keep alive the mystery of God in the human situation."[11] Further dimensions of pastoral care are explored, including a concept of nurture, similar to what Clinebell calls "growth counseling."[12] Finally, reflecting his interest in an intercultural approach to pastoral care, Lartey adds *liberating* and *empowering*, as well as an exploration of the spirituality of pastoral care. In this model, pastoral care moves beyond an individualist focus towards a more integrated communal and spiritual perspective.

This modern concept and practice of pastoral care has had a very considerable influence upon contemporary understandings of the work of a Christian minister and a commensurate influence upon courses of ministerial training. We now turn to recent ecumenical documents concerning the nature of the church and its ministry, where we find almost no reference at all to these ideas of pastoral care.

Ecumenical Discussion of the Church and Ministry

In what can be considered the foundational document for recent ecumenical dialogue about the church, *Baptism, Eucharist and Ministry*, ministry is "service to which the whole people of God is called." There are also specific ministries of authority and responsibility generally understood as "ordained

---

10. Lartey, *In Living Color*, ch. 3.
11. Wright, *Pastoral Nature of Ministry*, especially ch. 1; Lartey, *In Living Color*, 61.
12. Lartey, *In Living Color*, 66.

ministry."[13] The primary responsibility of these persons is "to assemble and build up the body of Christ by proclaiming and teaching the Word of God, by celebrating the sacraments, and by guiding the life of the community in its worship, its mission and its caring ministry."[14] Three particular guidelines are offered for the exercise of ordained ministry: that it must be personally present, collegial, and communal.[15] The most direct reference to pastoral care is found in the paragraph describing the work of presbyters, the term used for local congregational ministers: "They are preachers and teachers of the faith, exercise pastoral care, and bear responsibility for the discipline of the congregation to the end that the world may believe and that the entire membership of the Church may be renewed, strengthened and equipped in ministry."[16] It is clear that the nature of pastoral care described above may be accommodated within this broad statement of ministry, despite its being given virtually no specific mention.

A later Faith and Order paper on *The Nature and Purpose of the Church* has a shorter but more specific section on the nature of ministers in the local church. Paragraph 85 states that ordained ministers have a "special responsibility for the ministry of Word and sacrament. They have a ministry of pastoral care and are leaders in mission." What this means is indicated earlier: they "serve in the building up of the community, in equipping the saints, and in strengthening the Church's witness in the world"—and are not to neglect the support and encouragement of the community.

In this document there is significant reference to the ministry as oversight, *episcope*. This form of ministry seeks to express and promote the visible unity of the body, involves "a faithful feeding of the flock." There is a helpful recognition that this function of ministry is not only found in those churches that name an order of ministry as bishops. Rather, in some branches of the church this ministry of oversight takes synodal forms, and the document calls for the different parts of the church to recognize each other's forms of episcope.[17]

A positive example of ecumenical dialogue working towards mutual recognition of different forms of episcope can be seen in the report of conversations between the Anglican Communion and the Baptist World

---

13. WCC, *Baptism, Eucharist and Ministry*, §7b.
14. WCC, *Baptism, Eucharist and Ministry*, §13.
15. WCC, *Baptism, Eucharist and Ministry*, §26.
16. WCC, *Baptism, Eucharist and Ministry*, §30.
17. WCC, *Nature and Purpose*, §93, and the special note on episcope that follows.

Alliance. Ministry within the local church congregation is placed in the context of an extended section on the ministry of oversight. A Baptist view of such episcope is summarized: "Oversight in the local community flows to and fro between the personal and the communal, since the responsibility of 'watching over' the church belongs both to all the members gathered in the church meeting and to the pastor."[18] It is then noted, however, that Baptists also recognize an interchurch or regional level of oversight, where again both communal and personal aspects apply.

Baptist understandings of the ministry of oversight were considered in some detail in the second round of dialogues between the Catholic Church and the Baptist World Alliance. Chapter 6 of the report, "The Ministry of Oversight (Episkope) and the Unity of the Church," explains that for Baptists oversight is mostly understood within the role of the local community of faith. Section 174 states:

> For Baptists, *episkope* (oversight) is exercised by the local church meeting in a communal way; the members appoint the pastor and deacons according to what they discern to be the calling of Christ, in order to "watch over" ("oversee") the body with competence and with fidelity to the word of God.

This local understanding of pastoral oversight is, however, "always in communion with the wider church," is established for the good of the church, and seeks to promote the unity of the whole church.[19]

Interestingly, the more recent *TCTCV* has somewhat less to say about the nature of ministry than the earlier papers.[20] It is noticeable that almost all of the discussion of ministry concerns the ordained ministry, but with no consideration of the *tasks* of such ministry such as we noted above. Instead, there is an extended consideration of the nature of authority in the church and its exercise, leading to a discussion of the ministry of oversight. The three elements of this ministry as personal, collegial, and communal are again cited, together with the important recognition that all such episcopal ministry is in various ways synodal—a recognition similar to the affirmation found in the Baptist-Anglican dialogue mentioned above.

It may seem that there is very little affinity between these ecumenical sources and the popular and well-established ideas of pastoral care considered earlier. Are these entirely different images of the church and

---

18. BWA and Anglican Consultative Council, *Conversations around the World*, §70.
19. BWA and Catholic Church, "Word of God," §§176, 179, 182, respectively.
20. Sects. 45 to 53 deal specifically with ministry within the church.

its ministry, or is there some way in which these two perspectives might enrich one another, into a more theologically based concept of pastoral care and its contribution both to the local church and its participation in the whole body of Christ? In the remainder of this paper, we will consider whether a Baptist vision of pastoral care of the church may provide at least one such integrative perspective.

Pastoral Care of the Church:
The Pastoral Life of a Baptist Congregation

Don Browning observes that historically pastoral care served two functions. First, "the incorporation of members and their discipline in the group goals and practices of the church and secondly the assistance of persons in handling certain crises and conflicts having to do with existential, developmental, interpersonal and social strains."[21] Commenting upon this view, Stephen Pattison observes that in recent times, "in Western liberal churches the second function seems to have almost totally supplanted the former."[22] The consequence of this movement has been that churches lose "any kind of distinctive identity over against the societies in which they are situated." These observations provide a helpful introduction to a more integrated understanding of pastoral care within the life of the church and specifically a Baptist view of pastoral ministry.

From its historical beginnings, the Baptist vision of the church has involved the ministry of oversight and care. This ministry can be seen to involve seven elements which are briefly described here.

i. Pastoral ministry involves oversight and shepherding of the church community.

The role of pastoral oversight of the community, "episcopacy," applies to local church ministry and not only to those who are area ministers, bishops, or superintendents. The task of pastoral care involves considerably more than individual counsel and personal care. To use the image of the church as the flock of God, it is at least as much concerned with the care of the flock as with specific sheep. The well-being of the local church *as church* is thus

---

21. Browning, *Moral Context*, 21.
22. Pattison, *Critique of Pastoral Care*, 63.

a central dimension of pastoral care and is more than the sum of caring for individual members of the congregation.

ii. Central to this oversight is the ministry of word and sacraments or ordinances.

Preaching and scriptural teaching are the means whereby the church tells its story and finds its identity, vision, and guidance. Similarly, the ordinances are also identity-forming. The community of faith communes with its Lord and is fed by his grace. The baptized disciples are incorporated into a body, where mutual fellowship enables each to live according to the gifts and calling of the Spirit. The nurture of the community life through word and sacraments is thus a means of pastoral care, both for individuals and for the community as a whole. These activities seek to build up the community, "equipping the saints" and "strengthening the Church's witness in the world"—elements recognized in the ecumenical understanding of all forms of oversight.[23]

iii. Pastoral care enables and empowers other ministries in the church.

One of the distinctive, though by no means exclusive, emphases of Baptist church life is an understanding of the priesthood of all believers, which is taken to mean that every person has both a gift and ministry to contribute to the life and mission of the church. Within this broad perspective, pastoral ministry includes the work of evoking these gifts and ministries, and thus enabling and empowering people to make their contributions. This does not mean that anyone or everyone has the same gifts and responsibilities as the pastor; rather it means that there is a diversity of gifts and ministries. Some will teach, some may provide counseling, others may administer, some will provide hospitality, others engage in community service well beyond the church itself. Simply belonging to the community life of the church can be a source of care for people. Where church activities allow people, including children and youth, to take a lead or to support and contribute, this can be very helpful to them. In this way, the community life is itself a form of mutual care.

---

23. WCC, *Nature and Purpose*, §§89–91.

iv. Pastoral care nurtures Christian living, within and beyond the church.

This vision of pastoral care within the life of a local church draws upon the Pauline vision of the garden of the Spirit in which there are many gifts and values, practices to be nurtured by the pastor and by the community life. In another image, Eph 4:16 suggests the whole body grows into maturity *as the various members exercise their gifts and contribution*.

One aspect of this care is the nurture of *ethical* lifestyle. A generation ago, Gaylord Noyce wrote of the role of the pastor as "moral counselor," to nurture a congregation's capacity for moral discernment. Through preaching and teaching, the minister can facilitate a willingness to engage complex and potentially divisive social issues, and thus enable not just individuals but the congregation collectively to act according to good conscience, for justice and peace, and so forth.[24] The "priesthood of all" includes the lives of Christians at work, in their homes and neighborhoods, as well as citizenship. Here, too, service and care for others is enabled and supported by the community life and vision of the local church.

v. Oversight in discernment

The ministry of pastoral oversight will nurture the community's vision and understanding of God's mission in the world. It will thus enable the church to discern what it means for them to be agents of God's reconciling, healing, and creative purposes. Pastoral care is thus not something other than mission and witness, but is one of the means of that evangelical hope. Historically, Baptists spoke of the church meeting as seeking "the mind of Christ." The pastor may lead this process of discernment but is not the sole source of such vision and insight.

vi. Pastoral care as mutual accountability

A crucial element in the Baptist vision of the church is the sense of mutual responsibility of the pastor and people. This accountability involves far more than matters of employment conditions. Critically, the pastor undertakes to engage in emotional and physical self-care, in professional

---

24. Noyce, *Minister as Moral Counselor*, especially chs. 5 and 6.

development and collegial relations. Many pastors find great benefit in forms of professional supervision. Regional ministers or associations may also provide forms of care and support. Similarly, the congregation has a responsibility to relate to its ministers in good faith and to exercise care for its pastors and their family members.

vii. Pastoral care participates in the love of God.

Along with all that has gone before, it is fundamental to affirm that pastoral care and oversight are grounded in the love of God for the church and its people. Baptists describe these ministries as gifts to the church. In this way, these ministries may be representative of God's care and may invite all people to know and participate in that creative and redemptive love.

God's redemptive pastoral care, the cosmic episcope, thus provides the context, the foundation, and the spiritual resource for all subsequent activities of pastoral care, authority, and watching over.

Thanks be to God!

Bibliography

BWA and Anglican Consultative Council. *Conversations around the World, 2000–2005: The Report of the International Conversations between the Anglican Communion and the Baptist World Alliance.* London: Anglican Communion Office, 2005.

BWA and Catholic Church. "The Word of God in the Life of the Church: A Report of International Conversations between the Catholic Church and the Baptist World Alliance, 2006–2010." *American Baptist Quarterly* 31 (2012) 28–122.

Browning, Don. *The Moral Context of Pastoral Care.* Philadelphia: Westminster, 1976.

Clebsch, William A., and Charles R. Jaekle. *Pastoral Care in Historical Perspective.* 2nd ed. New York: Rowan & Littlefield, 1983.

Clinebell, Howard. *Basic Types of Pastoral Care and Counseling: Resources for the Ministry of Healing and Growth.* Nashville: Abingdon, 1984.

———. *Basic Types of Pastoral Care and Counseling: Resources for the Ministry of Healing and Growth.* Expanded and revised by Bridget Clare McKeever. Nashville: Abingdon, 2011.

Hiltner, Seward. *Preface to Pastoral Theology.* Nashville: Abingdon, 1958.

Lartey, Emmanuel Y. *In Living Color: An Intercultural Approach to Pastoral Care and Counseling.* 2nd ed. London: Kingsley, 2003.

Lumpkin, William L. *Baptist Confessions of Faith.* 2nd rev. ed. Revised by Bill J. Leonard. Valley Forge, PA: Judson, 2011.

Noyce, Gaylord. *The Minister as Moral Counselor.* Nashville: Abingdon, 1989.

Pattison, Stephen. *A Critique of Pastoral Care.* 3rd ed. London: SCM, 2000.

WCC. *Baptism, Eucharist and Ministry*. Geneva: WCC, 1982.
———. *The Nature and Purpose of the Church: A Stage on the Way to a Common Statement*. Geneva: WCC, 1998.
Wright, Frank. *The Pastoral Nature of the Ministry*. London: SCM, 1980.

12

Theologizing Churches

Amy L. Chilton

SOME YEARS BACK WHILE serving as associate pastor in a local American Baptist church, I helped initiate conversation with our ministry council on the gendered language we use for God in worship. With the unmatched fervor of a seminary student, I was quite sure I had sound arguments for the best way forward toward more theologically sound worship. Other congregations in the Seattle area had already transitioned to gender-inclusive language in worship, and my own congregation had not heard me use gendered language for God in sermons, lessons, or prayers. Despite the assured astuteness of my arguments, I was surprised when one elderly member of the council, upon hearing our plan to "fix" the language we use in worship, slammed her fists down onto the table, leaned forward, and passionately declared, "God is my Father, and I won't call him anything else!" The image of this woman has stuck with me these years as I consider the complexity of gendered language use. Even more it has stuck with me as I consider the complexity of what it means to be church when the ways in which we practice our faith are both dear to us and make it incredibly difficult to find common ground with people who hold dear other Christian faith traditions, beliefs, and practices.

The ways in which we practice our faith, the words we use to pray, the songs we sing in worship, the ways in which we serve, our reading of the Bible—all of these practices and many more form our ways of theologizing.

Sometimes our practices form weak theologies, such as in the case of the many churches in the slaveholding southern United States in the seventeenth through nineteenth centuries, who both worshiped in racially segregated sanctuaries and believed God sanctioned slavery.[1] This chapter seeks to encourage stronger and more intentional practices of local theology in two ways. First, this chapter shows the importance of understanding how the things we do, especially those things that we do over time in our communities (our practices), shape the ways we think about God (our theology). In order to perceive the shape of our theology, to see where our reading of Scripture reflects our ways of living, we must see ourselves in the light of other theologizing communities. This requires that we in our faith communities find ways to evaluate critically how our theologies are shaped and formed by our practices, because in that light we see that our contextual realities quite obviously shape what we understand as truth. For Baptists, people "of the book," this necessitates critically evaluating how our readings of Scripture are shaped by our contexts, lest we confuse our own local readings with the full expanse of God's revelation. This increased awareness of theology in intercontextual light can then aid in the work we must do with other communities in finding Christian unity. Second, this chapter will explore the idea of learning a *second first language* as a means for bridging the gap between local and global communities by the sharing of faith practices across divides so that we can then evaluate how we and others read Scripture and understand divine truths. This sharing of faith practices in the intercontextual spaces can help both with Christian unity and with the growth of local faith communities in self-understanding of its practices and theologies.

Discerning Local Church Theologies

There is no doubt that speaking of theology as a practice of the church raises concerns among those who see right theology as being free from the complexities, and even volatility, of human experience. Because of the Baptist distinctive of local Scripture reading, theology easily gets reduced to attempts to find and maintain the perfect interpretation and, seemingly, absolute truth. This way of reading Scripture reduces the expanse of God's full revelation to one localized reading and way of theologizing. For this reason, the insights of other reading communities are necessary to shed

---

1. Newson, *Cut in Stone*.

light on the particularities of local Scripture readings and responsibility for ongoing contribution to the work of Christian unity: "Whenever [Scripture] speaks ... it challenges, corrects, and sometimes flatly defeats the tales we tell ourselves about ourselves."[2]

The complication for many Baptists is that this requires accounting for local experiences and the role of experience in theology having a fraught history, particularly for those of conservative evangelical descent for whom experience has historically been seen as a resource of liberal theologies that compete with, not complement, the truth of Scripture.[3] In response to this rejection of experience as a theological source, the last two decades have seen a turn to "practice" as a way of integrating both Scripture and experience. In theology this means better attending to the practices of local church communities that are reading Scripture and living their faith together over time. The way we live life together, the argument goes, shapes the perspectives we have on God. Yet, theologians are not united on the turn to practice. Kathryn Tanner argues that "one must not read into the ordinary functioning of Christian practices what theologians say about them," because practices are ambiguous and complex, and examining them takes concerted effort.[4] Indeed, given that it is *humans* who practice their faith, practices will always stand in need to correction.[5] Baptist theologian James Wm. McClendon Jr. declares practices to be "powerful" because they contain within themselves the ability to go off track and yet, done well or not, always shape practitioners toward some end or another. Understanding Christian theology as a set of complex practices in and between local communities and contexts can function as the impetus and tool for local Baptist communities to understand more fully the relationship between their own theologies and lived experiences. Understanding theology in this way can then help local churches better see and hear the global church by making experience more visible in the theological process, thus making visibly experience-shaped theologies less threatening.

---

2. McClendon, *Systematic Theology*, 2:41. Also, contributing the local reading to the plethora of global readings is "an ecumenical way, confessing the fullness of [the local church's] style of Christian existence and offering it to all in the hope that in the conversation that ensues it will be adopted by all" (2:46).

3. I am referring to my location in North America, aware that other Evangelicalism in other contexts may not be laden with such an aversion to experience.

4. Tanner, "Theological Reflection."

5. Winner, *Dangers of Christian Practice*.

After I outline some ways in which a practiced method can help local faith communities better perceive the connections between text and context, between Scripture and lived life, I will explore how attending to our practices can help theologizing communities "go on" in perceiving and discerning theological diversity—particularly going on to perceive and discern theology that unabashedly shows the lived experience of its context. For this I will explore the friendship between British Baptist lay-parson Muriel Lester and Gandhi as one example of how intercontextual practices understood as *learning a second first language* can help a theological tradition's own internal development and self-understanding.

Historically, Western Christian theologies have read like a "good old boys' club" populated primarily with Euro-American, supposedly context-free theologies, or perhaps like "touring clubs" that serve to give passing glimpses of exotic theologies without engaging them as serious dialogue partners (ooh, look, Asian theology!).[6] Western evangelical theology has too often discounted theologies that integrate visible experience into theological content. This then blinds us to the presence of our own lived experiences in our work and to the nature of theology as an active, ongoing task of the diverse global church.[7]

Certainly, an important question is whether theology understood as practice becomes captive entirely to the local practicing community.[8] Does a "practiced" theology become insular because practices necessarily happen in specific locations and communities? As a result of these specific contexts, is practiced theology unable to function as a space in which diverse communities gather in the "give-and-take of humane dialogue," which is McClendon's vision for theology?[9] In short, does theology as practice necessarily render theology itself a private language, understood only to the local community in which the practices occur? Baptist theologian Stanley Grenz proposes that theology must "explicate the implications, relevance, and application of the Christian faith to life in that particular social, cultural

---

6. For helpful commentary on this treatment of global theologies, see Martell-Otero, "From Foreign Bodies."

7. For helpful resources on the experience-blindness of conservative evangelicalism in the West, see Murphy, *Beyond Liberalism and Fundamentalism*, and Grenz and Franke, *Beyond Foundationalism*.

8. Along with my co-author and editor Steven R. Harmon, I explore this task of "seeing" and "hearing" the voices of the global church in Chilton and Harmon, *Sources of Light*.

9. McClendon, *Systematic Theology*, 1:35.

setting."[10] Indeed, this is an essential task, and one that theology as practice can help accomplish if it is done both in local faith communities and also intercontextually between communities. In this way light from other sources can illuminate local practices, because in these lights we see our own particularities, including our practice of Bible reading.[11]

For example, an examination of how praying to God as Father for seventy years had led my church council member to theologize about God as male might illuminate her own theology. But, perhaps placing that story in light of the perspective of Pastor Salvador might help as well. I worked alongside Pastor Salvador in rural Nicaragua. One day while I was shoveling mud side by side with him, he declared, "God is not a man; in the Bible, God also talks about God's self as a woman." By placing these two different theologies alongside each other, the very difference illuminates their particularities. How then, beyond illumination by comparison and self-examination, can a local community "go on" in order to bridge gaps of practice and theology between communities?

"Going On": Practicing toward Proficiency in a Second First Language

Practice has the potential to re-situate human experience and Scripture reading as the twofold context of our theological reflections on God's presence in our world. By extension it also necessitates accounting for the diversity of global theologies arising from different strands of the Christian tradition, because where practices differ, understandings and articulations of truth differ as well. To understand truth in this way is to understand that revelation "happens" in the give-and-take of faith communities. Furthermore, the articulation of theology reflects the realities and communities in which it is practiced.[12] Similar to philosopher Alasdair MacIntyre's understanding of tradition, which heavily influenced McClendon's theology, we can understand theology itself as a living tradition that is "historical

---

10. Grenz and Franke, *Beyond Foundationalism*, 16.

11. See my earlier work on the potential of using McClendon's speech-act theory for helping local churches better understand the relationship between the language they use for God and their lived experiences (Chilton, "How Do I Speak").

12. Grenz and Franke point to this need in evangelical theology, arguing that "a theology that seeks to take seriously postmodern sensitivities views itself as conversation" (Grenz and Franke, *Beyond Foundationalism*, 24).

extended" and "socially embodied."[13] As such, theology requires adherence to the community's sacred texts. Thus, we need not give up Scripture in order to accept theological diversity. Understanding theology as practice positions Christian theology as the ongoing work of Christian communities and allows the practices in which those communities engage to shape their theologies. McClendon is right, in that, precisely because practices are powerful and prone to failure, astute theological attentiveness is required by the practicing community.

Yet, local ongoing tradition can be insufficient for navigating the intercontextual lived and historical realities of the global church. This failure in theology as practice and the challenge of navigating *competing* tradition strands necessitates looking to the *shared* practices of overlapping tradition strands. By doing so, theology might not be enslaved to the limitations of any particular or singular context. By uniting faith communities in different contexts and attending to the theological work accomplished in shared practices we may better attend to the theological discernment of competing or differently nuanced faith traditions. As Grenz argues, differently practicing communities might, through shared practices, better see their "family resemblance."[14]

MacIntyre proposes a helpful way forward in disputes between "rival traditions" that might also aid us in thinking through the relationship between local practice and differently practicing communities: the learning of a "second first language."[15] Presupposing that MacIntyre is correct that rationality and language, and in this case the languages the global church uses to speak of God, are dependent on our traditions and are not easily translatable from one context to another, the question arises: can theology take place *between* different theologizing communities? Or, does practice take theology only deeper into its particular contexts and by doing so keep it from moving or happening between contexts? MacIntyre argues that when rational traditions cannot account for competing truth claims from within their own forms of enquiry, "the coming together of two previously separate communities, each with its own well-established institutions, practices,

---

13. MacIntyre, *After Virtue*, 222.

14. "A nonfoundationalist theological method leads to the conclusion that ultimately all theology is—as the 'postmodern condition' suggests—'local' or 'specific.' . . . Despite the specificity of all theology, these various local theologies share in common a 'family resemblance' . . . that comprises them as authentically *Christian* theology" (Grenz and Franke, *Beyond Foundationalism*, 25; emphasis in original).

15. MacIntyre, *Whose Justice? Which Rationality?*, 364.

and beliefs . . . may open up new alternative possibilities."[16] This coming together requires that the persons and communities involved are already developing their forms of rational enquiry by theologizing *locally*, in part through their socially embedded faith and life practices. It also recognizes that conflicting truth claims are a given and that the "coming together" positively allows development of theology across intercontextual encounter and relationship, thus theologizing *intercontextually*. Simply put, by doing theology with differently theologizing communities, we may find our own theology sharpened.

In our co-edited book *Sources of Light*, Steven Harmon and I have argued for "local Baptist communities in their practice of theology to take on the discipline of being formed by the faith witness of others through seeking out diverse sources of this 'fresh light that may yet break forth from the Word'—not merely as a preface to the practice of theology, but as a theological practice."[17] We conclude by showing how local congregations can be formed by such practices as hearing the voices of the global church from the pulpit and reading Scripture in light of those diverse contributions. Yet, simply hearing Asian or African interpretations of Scripture does not necessarily form the local reader as a more proficient theologian. Those voices can be heard as cacophony rather than the symphony we trust the Spirit is directing.

Many Baptist communities hear differently practiced theologies as deviant or unorthodox. The ongoing arguments of the last decades over women's roles in the church are but one clear example of this. MacIntyre argues that the solution to navigating this disordered way of hearing diversity is for persons in competing traditions to learn "the language of the alien tradition as a *new and second first language*."[18] But, to learn a second first language is not, in MacIntyre's estimation, merely to learn new words with which to formulate our own sentence structures, but rather to learn "how to go on and go further."[19] "Going on" is a learned proficiency acquired by knowing at a deeper level how language is embedded in the wider life of the competing community: "The boundaries of a language are the boundaries of some linguistic community which is also a social community."[20]

---

16. MacIntyre, *Whose Justice? Which Rationality?*, 353.
17. Chilton and Harmon, *Sources of Light*, 6.
18. MacIntyre, *Whose Justice? Which Rationality?*, 382; emphasis added.
19. MacIntyre, *Whose Justice? Which Rationality?*, 382.
20. MacIntyre, *Whose Justice? Which Rationality?*, 373.

Theological language and faith life cannot be separated, and theological language is learned by practice in one's community. MacIntyre argues that to learn the language of another community, one must "become a child all over again," learning both the competing language and also the parts of culture that correspond to that language's use.[21] Perhaps this requires a literal learning of another linguistic world from within; for example, learning Burmese dialects to understanding the theologizing of the Burmese refugee churches. But it also "requires a work of the imagination," which could be a learned through a variety of practices shared between contexts such as worshiping, sitting at table together, serving, or even friendship.[22]

Learning a first language is done within socially embedded practices. Learning *theological* language has its own peculiar requirements, because we learn to speak of God through the worship and service of God in and through our faith communities. So, it holds that learning a *second first language* also requires its own practices. Yet, if practices can go wrong, as discussed above, then practices can go wrong in learning a *second* first language just as they can go wrong in learning a *first* first language—theological or otherwise. Despite this, intercontextual encounter, discernment, and opening up to new possibilities are essential for theology. This is particularly so if we think of theology as a tradition that can and must "make internal progress through encounter with another tradition."[23] Theology as practice in a MacIntyrian/McClendonian sense needs other tradition strands for mutual growth and also sees intercontextual relations as important spaces for discernment and growth of all traditions involved. Thus, the complex concept and reality of perspective shaping practices must be shared between communities—by both learning to speak a second first language and imagining how to *go on*. Steven Harmon has argued that in the learning of a second first language, "one must try them on for size and live with their particularities of worship, spirituality, and doctrine."[24] I contend that this "trying on" is practicing the faith in the intersections of differing or competing faith traditions for the sake of the internal growth of all the intersecting strands of Christian tradition.

Let me offer here an example of shared practices across competing religious traditions, Muriel Lester's friendship with Gandhi, to illustrate how

---

21. MacIntyre, *Whose Justice? Which Rationality?*, 374.
22. MacIntyre, *Whose Justice? Which Rationality?*, 394.
23. Harmon, *Towards Baptist Catholicity*, 54.
24. Harmon, *Towards Baptist Catholicity*, 54.

shared practices between intersecting traditions led not only to increased understanding between Lester's British Baptist community and Gandhi's Ashram but also to substantive developments in Lester's own theology and faith practices. Lester, born in 1883 in Leystontone, Essex, England, to a middle-class family of Baptist preachers, encountered the poverty of London's East End slums at the age of nineteen. She, along with her sister and brother, spent much of the rest of her life in Bow where in 1915 she founded Kingsley Hall under the guidance of the East Enders, which functioned as a "teetotaling" pub, community center, sometimes preschool, church; most famously, it housed Gandhi himself in 1931 when he traveled to London for roundtable talks regarding India's independence from England. Although Lester did not methodologically address practices in relation to faith and theology, she did publish a few popular writings on prayer and worship in which she argues that these practices are the formative means by which a person and her community become transformed agents of peace, united across difference.[25]

One point of intersection between Lester and Gandhi that allowed Lester to learn a second first language was their shared practice of voluntary poverty. After her initial encounter with the East End, Lester increasingly took up a life of voluntary poverty, which she understood as an ancient Christian teaching. Similar to Gandhi's own argument, she believed that "if you possess superfluities while your brethren lack necessities, you are possessing the goods of others and are therefore stealing."[26] For Lester, voluntary poverty was the necessary outcome of her faith. She believed there were sufficient goods in the world to meet the needs of all if only those goods were distributed by need rather than power and privilege: "The only rational basis for the distribution of goods is need. And the only way to get goods distributed on this basis, is for all of us to stop seeking privileges for ourselves and to use all our resources for the common end of satisfying need."[27]

By 1921 Lester, with a community of like-minded but economically diverse folk, gathered in part by an invitation given in the *Daily News*, formed the Brethren of the Common Table. The Brethren met monthly for

25. Lester, *Ways of Praying*; Lester, *Why Worship?*
26. Lester, *Kill or Cure?*, 68.
27. Quotations of Lester taken from a "broadsheet" newspaper-format publication and the notes for one of her lectures given on her 1933 speaking tour of the United States (Wallis, *Mother of World Peace*, 118).

financial accountability, sharing intimate information of their daily expenditures. She described their meetings as "owning up to" exact details about how the member had spent her money and/or what were her financial needs. Excess money was placed on the table and those in need took it, for it no longer belonged to the one who did not need it. Lester describes this practice of sharing goods as transformative, realigning her needs, even enabling her to "go down Regent Street" without kid gloves![28]

It was these practices of voluntary poverty, embarked upon to "know if Christianity really could be practiced,"[29] that gave Lester a perspective that enabled her to notice the likeness between Kingsley Hall's and Gandhi's teachings and practices of poverty. She writes of her initial encounter with Gandhi's work:

> The strength of Kingsley Hall lies in the practice of the presence of God, as taught by Jesus Christ, and is an effort towards the Kingdom of God on earth. Our ideals and our aspirations at Kingsley hall have much in common with those of Mr. Gandhi's Ashram.[30]

Intrigued by the similar practices of poverty and peacemaking, Lester joined Gandhi for thirteen weeks in the winter of 1926–27. During that time, she joined in fasting, prayer, service, learning, and eventually political advocacy with and on behalf of Gandhi. From her place of practice, she entered into shared practices with Gandhi's people and ultimately reflected upon her Christian faith that "Christianity . . . outshines a thousand fold all of this . . . [something] I did not expect to feel . . . so strongly."[31]

While remaining active in her own tradition (theologizing locally), in her subsequent work and theological writings, Gandhi's own thoughts on peace and poverty contributed to her ideas (theologizing intercontextually). Lester, from a place of practice within her own tradition that has notable similarities to those in a "competing" tradition, shares practices of prayer, fasting, poverty, and service at the Ashram and Kinglsey Hall. In this way, in the intercontextual space between the two communities, she is able both to discern what is in the other tradition and to allow for her own faith, theology, and ecclesial community to grow and change in the interchange.

28. Lester, *It Occurred to Me*, 91.
29. Lester, *My Host, the Hindu*, 12.
30. Lester, *Entertaining Gandhi*, 2.
31. Quoted in Wallis, *Mother of World Peace*, 73, from a letter home written by Lester in Oct. 1926.

Conclusion

Certainly, practices are powerful, can lead astray, and require theological attentiveness. For this reason, correctly discerned practices in the local community are necessary for learning to see anew and to see aright, and also for learning to see in the light of contesting/competing traditions. Attending well to the practices of one's own community not only builds increased awareness of the particularities of that community's theology but might also build the perspective to see well another community. Experience-averse theology stands in need of a correction with which better attention to practice can help. Faith communities must attend to their own formative practices in order to develop inside perspectives on other traditions, such as Lester's practices of poverty. But practices must also be shared *between* communities so as to draw differing tradition strands a little tighter in the ecclesial tapestry and to help the local community *go on*.

Some shared practices between communities might include reading the Bible together with persons from other communities. So might the preachers using commentaries originating from other contexts.[32] On a practical, local level, faith communities might share in any variety of worship, faith, or service practices that can help a community learn a second first language and by doing so can participate in spaces of intercontextual encounter and growth. Theology itself requires practicing communities that are engaged in these kinds of intercontextual practices if it is to attend adequately to the gospel proclamation that occurs between both the proclaimer and the hearers. If we desire to avoid the error of dismissing the church's global symphony and better attend theologically to the work that practices do in shaping how we think and speak of God, then we must get together with those who practice and speak differently, both in order to learn a second first language to aid in discernment but also so that our own strands of the Christian tradition might grow in faith and faithfulness in their practices and theologizing.

Bibliography

Chilton, Amy L. "How Do I Speak of God from This Place? Navigating Religious Language Shifts in Baptist Contexts." *American Baptist Quarterly* 16 (2016) 52–62.

---

32. Chilton and Harmon, *Sources of Light*, 306–8, compile a bibliography of biblical commentaries originating from diverse social locations beyond the white, male, North American and European social locations typical of commonly consulted commentaries.

Chilton, Amy L., and Steven R. Harmon, eds. *Sources of Light: Resources for Baptist Churches Practicing Theology.* Perspectives on Baptist Identities 3. Macon, GA: Mercer University Press, 2020.

Grenz, Stanley J., and John R. Franke. *Beyond Foundationalism: Shaping Theology in a Postmodern Context.* Louisville, KY: Westminster John Knox, 2001.

Harmon, Steven R. *Towards Baptist Catholicity: Essays on Tradition and the Baptist Vision.* Studies in Baptist History and Thought 27. Milton Keynes, UK: Paternoster, 2006.

Lester, Muriel. *Entertaining Gandhi.* London: Nicholson and Watson, 1932.

———. *It Occurred to Me.* New York: Harper, 1937.

———. *Kill or Cure?* Nashville: Cokesbury, 1937.

———. *My Host, the Hindu.* London: Williams and Norgate, 1931.

———. *Ways of Praying.* Nashville: Abingdon, 1932.

———. *Why Worship?* Nashville: Cokesbury, 1937.

MacIntyre, Alasdair. *After Virtue: A Study in Moral Theory.* 2nd ed. Notre Dame, IN: University of Notre Dame Press, 1984.

———. *Whose Justice? Which Rationality?* Notre Dame, IN: University of Notre Dame Press, 1988.

Martell-Otero, Loida. "From Foreign Bodies in Teacher Space to Embodied Spirit in *Personas Educadas*: Or, How to Prevent 'Tourists of Diversity' in Education." In *Teaching for a Culturally Diverse and Racially Just World*, edited by Eleazar S. Fernandez, 52–68. Eugene, OR: Cascade, 2014.

McClendon, James Wm., Jr. *Systematic Theology.* 3 vols. Nashville: Abingdon, 1994–2000.

Murphy, Nancy. *Beyond Liberalism and Fundamentalism: How Modern and Postmodern Philosophy Set the Theological Agenda.* Valley Forge, PA: Trinity International, 1996.

Newson, Ryan Andrew. *Cut in Stone: Confederate Monuments and Theological Disruption.* Waco, TX: Baylor University Press, 2020.

Tanner, Kathryn. "Theological Reflection and Christian Practices." In *Practicing Theology: Beliefs and Practices in Christian Life*, edited by Miroslav Volf and Dorothy C. Bass, 228–42. Grand Rapids: Eerdmans, 2002.

Wallis, Jill. *Mother of World Peace: The Life of Muriel Lester.* Middlesex, UK: Hisarlik, 1993.

Winner, Lauren F. *The Dangers of Christian Practice: On Wayward Gifts, Characteristic Damage, and Sin.* New Haven, CT: Yale University Press, 2018.

13

Scattering Churches

Daniël Drost

Introduction

TCTCV IS AN INSPIRING document that reflects the committed ecumenical conversations over the last decades. It also reflects that we live in a time of change, in which the church has to find a new way of being church. Inspired by (ana)baptist history and ecclesiology, as articulated by Stuart Murray Williams and others, Urban Expression Nederland is a Dutch mission agency that intends to plant churches in the underchurched areas of the Netherlands. Their practices show some of the same sensitivities towards a changing society and a changing church as does *TCTCV*. This chapter engages and critically reflects upon Urban Expression's diasporic mission approach, to analyze how this core practice relates to and can contribute to the perspective of *TCTCV* and in doing so can function as a source of ecclesiological renewal in a western post-Christendom context.

Urban Expression

Urban Expression is "an urban mission agency that recruits, equips, deploys, and networks self-financing teams pioneering creative and relevant expressions of the Christian Church in under-churched urban neighborhoods."[1] It was launched in April 1997 through a partnership between Spurgeon's College and Oasis Trust, under the supervision of Stuart Murray Williams. Urban Expression started with Jim and Juliet Kilpin, who became part of the first Urban Expression church planting team in Shadwell. Juliet Kilpin was also appointed as part-time coordinator of Urban Expression and worked with Murray to establish this new mission agency. In the early years Urban Expression focused on East London; later on teams started planting churches in Manchester, Glasgow, Birmingham, Stoke, and Bristol. In 2007 Urban Expression Nederland was formed and in 2009 Urban Expression North America, with plans to plant churches in various locations in the United States and Canada. This chapter will focus on Urban Expression Nederland in particular.

In 2007 Matthijs Vlaardingenbroek, a church planter in The Hague, and Oeds Blok, a Baptist minister in Amersfoort, visited several Urban Expression teams in East London. They were inspired by the people and practices of these communities and the values they worked from. In 2008 Urban Expression Nederland was launched with teams in The Hague (team In de praktijk) and Rotterdam (team Thugz Church). In 2009 an Urban Expression team started in Amersfoort, Kruiskamp. In 2012 Oeds Blok started to work as a coordinator and coach for a new Urban Expression team. At the moment (2019) there are church planting teams in Amersfoort, Arnhem, Enschede, Rotterdam, Zaanstad, and Amsterdam. Villa Klarendal Arnhem and In de praktijk The Hague became "church teams," which means they are no longer plants but fully planted churches, with a senior function for the church planting teams.[2] There is a warm connection—both theological and relational—between Urban Expression Nederland and Stuart Murray Williams. Teams from the Netherlands regularly visit teams in Great Britain to be inspired, share stories, and build relationships. Likewise, Stuart Murray Williams regularly visits the Netherlands to speak, teach, and coach.[3]

A short remark on the terminology of diaspora or dispersion will be helpful. One of Urban Expression's commitments is "following God on the margins and the gaps, expecting to discover God at work among powerless

---

1. Urban Expression, "About Us."

2. See Urban Expression, "About Us"; Blok, "Creatieve gemeentestichting," 16–18; Blok and Vlaardingenbroek, *Survivalgids Pionieren*, 6–9; Vlaardingenbroek, *Grensverleggend*, 25–40.

3. Blok, *Avontuur van geloof*, 8.

people and in places of weakness."[4] This often means moving away from "Christian suburban areas" into inner-city neighborhoods with minimal Christian presence. I read this as a form of voluntary diaspora ecclesiology.[5]

Urban Expression and Baptists

Urban Expression was founded in Baptist circles and although not denominationally bound, it keeps attracting many Baptists.[6] This is visible in the UK but also in the Netherlands, where a substantial part of the team members are Baptist, and local Baptist churches and the Dutch Baptist Seminary work together with Urban Expression teams. Why is this the case?

Baptist theology and ecclesiology offer some convictions and intentions that are helpful for the teams praying, working, and living together in the inner cities and (other) deprived neighborhoods.[7] First of all, Baptists form a missionary movement. In the Netherlands the old saying goes "*Iedere baptist een evangelist*" (every Baptist is a missionary).[8] Second, the covenantal character of Baptist ecclesiology resonates with the forming of committed teams, willing to move into the neighborhood for the sake of the kingdom of God.[9] Third, the multivoiced approach of Baptist ecclesiology was helpful for the choice of working in teams, instead of working with ordained ministers.[10] Fourth, the Baptist ecclesial practice of communally discerning the mind of Christ proved very helpful for teams in

---

4. See Kilpin, *Urban to the Core*, 1–6.

5. See also Drost, "Diaspora as Mission," 254–61.

6. For an overview, see Kilpin and Murray, *Church Planting*.

7. Although Stuart Murray Williams started to develop an interest in anabaptist theology for ecclesiology and spirituality in his work as a church planter in East London, he has a British Baptist background. This anabaptist theology, to which he was introduced by Alan and Eleanor Kreider who were also staying in London at the time, was a helpful addition to his Baptist background. Because of the character of this book I focus in this chapter on Baptist characteristics of Urban Expression and why Urban Expression is attractive or recognizable by Baptists. For Murray's use of anabaptist theology, see Drost, "Diaspora as Mission," 239–49.

8. De Vries, *Gelovig gedoopt*, 119. This was the slogan of the "father of European Baptists" Johann Gerhard Oncken ("*Jeder Baptist ein Missionar*") who founded the first Baptist church on the European continent in Hamburg in 1834 and was involved with Baptist beginnings in the Netherlands in 1845 (Randall, *Communities of Conviction*, 49).

9. Fiddes, *Tracks and Traces*, 21–47.

10. Fiddes, *Tracks and Traces*, 7; see also Williams and Williams, *Multi-Voiced Church*.

ever-changing contexts.[11] Finally, Paul S. Fiddes describes the suffering of God as one of the main theological themes for Baptists at the beginning of the twenty-first century.[12] This might explain the willingness of Baptist believers to engage the suffering of people at the margins of society and the capability to reflect on this suffering from the perspective of the kingdom of God.[13]

Although Urban Expression is not an explicitly Baptist mission agency, Baptist ecclesiological roots have provided a helpful background against which Urban Expression convictions and communities were formed.

Urban Expression's Diaspora Practices[14]

Urban Expression communities embrace diaspora by moving to, or staying in the so-called Vogelaarwijken, which are underchurched neighborhoods. The stories of the communities show that in many cases the absence of churches, or Christian communities, is a reason to plant a church at the specific place.[15] This missionary presence is embodied by "seeking the welfare of the city." Several church planters have said that this was the way the teams started: getting involved in the neighborhood by contributing to whatever needs and projects were going on.[16] This involvement is not simply a means to an end but an essential part of what the gospel and the community are all about.[17] Connected with this welfare is a focus on the holistic character of the gospel. The word *shalom* is often used to describe this. The gospel is not some spiritual truth about spiritual lives but is about the whole person and his context.[18] This is visible in the different levels in which good news is offered to persons who engage or are engaged by the Urban Expression communities: from helping to clean or fix a house,

---

11. See Janssen-te Loo, *Samen ontdekken*, and in particular Drost, "Samen een weg."
12. Fiddes, *Tracks and Traces*, 57–61.
13. Kilpin, *Urban to the Core*, 1–6, 39–49.
14. I engage the practices of Urban Expression Nederland by way of document analysis. See Davie and Wyatt, "Document Analysis." I am aware that by doing so we will primarily engage "espoused theology"; see Cameron et al., *Talking about God*, 53–56.
15. Vlaardingenbroek, *Grensverleggend*, 25–40; Janse, "Villa Klarendal."
16. See, for example, Erwich, *Veelkleurig verlangen*, 99; Blok, *Avontuur van geloof*, 27–29, 50–56; Janse, "Villa Klarendal," 30.
17. Erwich, *Veelkleurig verlangen*, 103.
18. Blok, "Creatieve," 23; Blok, *Avontuur van geloof*, 51.

offering the gift of a bag of groceries, filling in juridical forms to becoming part of a community and eating together, hearing Bible stories, or receiving prayer. Presence in the neighborhood is embodied in these various levels. Inspired by the theological concept of *missio Dei*,[19] most teams have a strong sense of being part of God's mission, the reason to be a part of an Urban Expression team working in the neighborhood in the first place. In other words, Urban Expression teams are mission-focused.[20]

One of the characteristics of Urban Expression's approach is that mission is connected with living. Urban Expression teams do not work with revival campaigns, moving in and out of these deprived areas, spreading the message of the gospel in loud words. Mission is connected with living in these particular neighborhoods and becoming grounded there, embracing the place as home. Urban Expression requires therefore long-term commitment, at least five to seven years.[21] Teams try to find ways to be engaged in local communities,[22] which includes training indigenous leadership within and for the church that is developing.[23] Connected with this is the Urban Expression approach to work in teams. It is not a single missionary that relocates and works in a neighborhood but a team. They are self-supporting teams.[24] Team members have a job to finance their living and working in the neighborhood.[25] Sometimes initially funding is raised.[26] The teams try to find ways to involve everybody as much as possible in the services, and seek to stay away from a "religious specialist" leadership. They do so by finding ways of being multivoiced communities that are good news to the neighborhood and really fit with the specific context.[27]

Urban Expression's approach focuses on practices generated out of their own commitments. While they are attentive to the practices already

---

19. For a classic description of *missio Dei*, see Bosch, *Transforming Mission*, 389–91.

20. Urban Expression, "About Us."

21. http://urbanexpression.nl/raak-betrokken-als-pionier-en-leider.

22. See, for example, the commitment to be rooted in local communities and different ways to approach this: Erwich, *Veelkleurig verlangen*, 99; Blok, *Avontuur van geloof*, 27–29, 50–56; Janse, "Villa Klarendal," 30.

23. Den Hartogh, "Wie zijn wij?"

24. Urban Expression, "About Us." Urban Expression works with self–supporting teams. They recruit teams and work with them but do not financially support these teams. Every team is responsible for its own support.

25. See, for example, Blok and Vlaardingenbroek, *Survivalgids*, 30–32, 99.

26. See, for example, Blok and Vlaardingenbroek, *Survivalgids*, 99, 107–8.

27. See, for example, Blok, *Avontuur van geloof*, 63, 71.

embedded in the neighborhood and the lives of the people, they also invite people from the neighborhood into the practices of the communities. Urban Expression approaches church as a set of practices. The church is first of all a social reality. There are regular conversations about when an Urban Expression church plant has become a church: what is needed for that, what are the necessary conditions, and so forth. Although these are ecclesiological conversations about the very nature of the church, the underlying, unquestioned assumption is that the church (plant) is shaped by practices.[28]

This is how Urban Expression communities embody a diaspora ecclesiology. Summarizing, the core practice of these Urban Expression communities can be described as voluntary living at the margins and in doing so combining mission with neighborhood living. This brings us to the central question of this chapter: how does this core practice relate to and contribute to the perspective of *TCTCV*, and in doing so, how can it function as a source of ecclesiological renewal in a Western post-Christendom context?

Which Questions Do the Practices of Urban Expression Offer to TCTCV?

First, from the perspective of the diaspora practices of Urban Expression, the formulated ecclesiology of *TCTCV* suffers from being too theoretical or idealist in nature. When we look at the situation in the Netherlands, there is a tendency of Christians and churches to cling together in the so-called "Bible belt." Churches often lack the intention to embrace diaspora, instead looking for ways to avoid it and choose safety over mission.[29] If this is the case, what does the language of the church as being essentially missionary actually mean? It is biblical or systematic theological language, or even idealistic language. But how does this relate to reality? How do we move towards a practice in which this is actually the case? How do we move from believed ecclesiology to practiced ecclesiology?

Second, the "already" and "not yet" of the church is often an issue of debate in church planting contexts. In Urban Expression church plants

---

28. Van der Leer's *De kerk op haar smalst* on the question of ecclesiological minimum (what does it take for church to be church?) is regularly used in discussions about church planting and church. At the moment, Urban Expression distinguishes between church planting teams and church teams, who function as senior teams for the church planting teams. See urbanexpression.nl/teams.

29. See, for example, City-to-City Amsterdam, "Klonter als christenen."

one of the regularly posed questions is "Who is the church?" Is this only the (committed) team? Does it include the people who visit the meetings? And if so, when?[30] These are basic ecclesiological questions that come to the surface in a missionary setting. *TCTCV* does acknowledge this post-Christendom setting, but its ecclesial formulations do not shake up the basic framework. *TCTCV* states, for example:

> The local church is a community of baptized believers in which the word of God is preached, the apostolic faith confessed, the sacraments are celebrated, the redemptive work of Christ is witnessed to, and a ministry of *episkopé* exercised by bishops or other ministers in serving the community.[31]

This is a very correct formulation, dogmatically and historically speaking. But what about everyday post-Christendom life? Urban Expression practices provide questions mainstream churches will face in a couple of years.

Third, *TCTCV* states, "After the example of Jesus, the Church is called and empowered in a special way to share the lot of those who suffer and care for the needy and marginalized."[32] The terminology of "share and care for" is not always a helpful approach. Mission has historically often been understood as "a movement taking place from the center to the periphery, and from the privileged to the marginalized."[33] Urban Expression teams discover in their work that mission to the margins often actually appears to be mission from the margins. This resonates with a shift of the mission concept that is occurring, as *Together towards Life* (from now on, *TTL*) describes, from "mission to the margins" to "mission from the margins."[34] This shift is the result of various insights. One insight is that living on the margins provides a particular perspective on the gospel that is more difficult to grasp from the centers of power.[35] Another is that people at the margins (who were mostly viewed as recipients of missionary action) in fact often act as agents of the gospel.[36] Therefore, *TTL* states that their experiences and

---

30. See, for example, Blok, *Avontuur van geloof,* 70, 71.
31. WCC, *TCTCV,* 17.
32. WCC, *TCTCV,* 37.
33. WCC, *TTL,* 2, §6.
34. WCC, *TTL,* 2, §6; 6–19, §§36–54.
35. WCC, *TTL,* §38.
36. WCC, *TTL,* §§38–42. Urban Expression and some new monastic communities work from the same perspective. Not a mission for the margins but from the margins; not working for the people but with the people.

visions are crucial for reimagining mission and evangelism today.[37] These insights are not formulated in *TCTCV*, an ecclesiological document that seems to treat ecclesiology and missiology as two separated worlds. In the Western European context, however, these areas have become increasingly similar. This development makes clear that objects and agents of mission are no longer clearly distinguishable in classic frames such as Western and non-Western, center and periphery, the powerful and those at the margins. All are called to be agents of mission, and all are in need of being the object of mission as well.

Fourth, from the context of the everyday practices of Urban Expression, the clean ecclesiological formulation of section 66 needs to engage and struggle more fully some key questions.[38] It is one thing to formulate ecclesiological convictions. Urban Expression's convictions are surprisingly similar as to those formulated in *TCTCV*, section 66. The question of what it actually takes to be a church like that is yet another vital consideration. Urban Expression's approach to mission, which includes long-term living in deprived neighborhoods, has been very demanding on the missionaries.[39] One of the main questions within Urban Expression teams is: how can we survive? How do we deal with the pain and problems we are surrounded with every day? How do we raise our children in a neighborhood like this? How do we deal with financial stress (as Urban Expression teams are mainly self-supporting)? For this reason Urban Expression Nederland published a book about these issues, called *A Survival Guide for Pioneers* (*Survivalgids Pionieren*). Daniel de Wolf, one of the pioneers of Urban Expression Nederland, writes:

> Sometimes I feel sorry about the way I encouraged people to move to "a special needs neighborhood." I still encourage people to move there, but with more caution. I think living in "a special needs neighborhood" is not for everyone, nor do I think it is a

---

37. WCC, *TTL*, 2, §6; 7, §§38–42.

38. "The Church is comprised of all socio-economic classes; both rich and poor are in need of the salvation that only God can provide. After the example of Jesus, the Church is called and empowered in a special way to share the lot of those who suffer and to care for the needy and the marginalized. The Church proclaims the words of hope and comfort of the Gospel, engages in works of compassion and mercy (cf. Luke 4:18–19) and is commissioned to heal and reconcile broken human relationships and to serve God in the ministry of reconciling those divided by hatred or estrangement (cf. 2 Cor. 5:18–21)" (WCC, *TCTCV*, 37, §66).

39. Bremer, "Waardevast wonen," 48; Blok and Vlaardingenbroek, *Survivalgids pionieren*, 6–7.

> Christian obligation (a summit of Christian discipleship), but I came to see it more as a specific calling.⁴⁰

This is the reason that Urban Expression recruits people who have a specific calling for this kind of neighborhood: pioneering, creative people. They become almost like an order, sustained by their values and commitments. The key questions that Urban Expression practitioners raise are: Who is actually trying to embody the ecclesiology formulated in section 66? Does the church know what it takes to be a church so described, and does she calculate the costs? As formulated in the *Survival Guide for Pioneers*, the diaspora practices of Urban Expression show that to survive as a church you need to be centered around a strong team. The local church needs a strong network, for example, a strong connection with the pioneering network of Urban Expression. A church like this needs a theology or spirituality that expects everything from God and is honest enough to engage the brokenness within the neighborhood, within the church community, and within the believer's heart. In other words, old Baptistic practices such as covenanting, discerning the mind of Christ, and the conviction that the church is a community of believers are rediscovered as constructive within this post-Christendom missionary setting.

A Way Forward

The question of this chapter is how the diaspora practices of Urban Expression can function as a source of ecclesiological renewal in a Western post-Christendom context. For the second half of the twentieth century until now, church and Christian culture lost most of their influence in Western Europe and North America and has moved to the margins. This phenomenon is often referred to as post-Christendom, post-Christianity, or (post-)secularization.⁴¹ It has had a major influence on the everyday life of the church but also on her theological reflection. Urban Expression teams have embraced these marginalizing diaspora conditions before mainstream churches will be forced to do so. In that sense they are a few steps ahead.

---

40. Blok and Vlaardingenbroek, *Survivalgids pionieren*, 23 (my translation).

41. See Paas, "Post-Christian, Post-Christendom," for the terminological differences between post-Christian, post-Christendom, and post-modern. Habermas, amongst others, uses the term *post-secular* to describe the current time in which the modernist dilemma of reason and faith does not seem workable anymore. See, for example, Habermas, "Secularism's Crisis of Faith."

Urban Expression's questions today are those of the mainstream churches tomorrow. Which questions and insights from Urban Expression practices can function as a source of ecclesiological renewal? Let us consider two recommendations under which the insights described above can be gathered.

First, ecclesiology is in need of the practices of the church and of church plants like Urban Expression as a source of ecclesiological reasoning. It is necessary to bring the insights of the communities in conversation with the ecclesiological discourse. This has in fact already been going on for some time, as the work of Nicholas Healy, Pete Ward, and Charles Marsh shows.[42] This raises questions such as: what kind of spirituality is needed in times of diaspora? The context of church practices also raises social economical questions: what is the right way of doing mission or being present in this particular setting? How do you prevent a paternalistic way of offering care? How do you prevent gentrification or other problematic consequences of idealistic missiological ideas? Margins of society are often created by a failing government policy. What is the role of the church in this? Should it turn to an ecclesiological presence in deprived areas, or is a more political approach needed? In post-Christendom times the church lost most of her political influence, which might be a good thing. But the practices of Urban Expression show the need of stating the question of political influence again. These questions rising from the grassroots of church practices need to be engaged within the ecclesiological discourse, to prevent idealistic, nonrealistic descriptions of church.

Second, ecclesiology and missiology need each other. Ecclesiology and missiology used to be two different disciplines. In post-Christendom times, however, they find themselves asking the same questions. This is visible in ecclesiological communities such as Urban Expression, which find themselves confronted with classical missiological questions, such as what is good news for this neighborhood? Urban Expression practices show that ecclesiology and missiology do need each other. The insights of *TCTCV* and *TTL* could be more profound if they were combined. The practices of Urban Expression show the need for this interdisciplinary cooperation, because Urban Expression's questions of today are the mainstream church's questions of tomorrow.

---

42. Healy, *Church, World*, 154–85; Ward, *Perspectives on Ecclesiology*, 2–3; Marsh, *Lived Theology*.

Bibliography

Blok, Oeds, ed. *Avontuur van geloof: Praktijkverhalen van gemeentestichting met reflectie voor heel de kerk*. Baptistica Reeks 11. Amsterdam: Unie van Baptistengemeenten, 2016.

———. "Creatieve gemeentestichting in aandachtswijken van de stad: Theologie, praktijk en spiritualiteit van Urban Expression." *Soteria* 27 (2010) 16–28.

Blok, Oeds, and Matthijs Vlaardingenbroek. *Survivalgids pionieren: Praktijkverhalen van creatieve gemeentestichting*. N.p.: Urban Expression, 2016.

Bosch, David J. *Transforming Mission: Paradigm Shifts in Theology of Mission*. New York: Orbis, 1991.

Bremer, Pauline. "Waardevast wonen: Onderzoek naar wonen in een aandachtswijk vanuit de waarden van Urban Expression." Bachelor thesis, Hogeschool Windesheim, 2012.

Cameron, Helen, et al. *Talking about God in Practice: Theological Action Research and Practical Theology*. London: SCM, 2010.

City-to-City Amsterdam. "Klonter als christenen niet samen in de Biblebelt, maar verspreid je." *Nederlands Dagblad*, Nov. 19, 2019. https://www.nd.nl/opinie/opinie/940388/klonter-als-christenen-niet-samen-in-de-biblebelt-maar-verspreid-je.

Davie, Grace, and David Wyatt. "Document Analysis." In *The Routledge Handbook of Research Methods in the Study of Religion*, edited by Michael Stausberg et al., 151–60. London: Routledge, 2011.

Den Hartogh, Jaap. "Wie zijn wij? Een kwalitatief onderzoek naar de rol van gemeentestichtende teams op de identiteitsformatie van gemeenschappen aangesloten bij Urban Expression Nederland." Master thesis, Evangelische Theologische Faculteit Leuven, 2013.

De Vries, Olof H. *Gelovig gedoopt: 400 jaar baptisme, 150 jaar in Nederland*. Kok, Netherlands: Kampen, 2009.

Drost, Daniël. "Diaspora as Mission: John Howard Yoder, Jeremiah 29 and the Shape and Mission of the Church." PhD diss., Free University Amsterdam, 2019.

———. "Samen een weg vinden als Urban Expression in de wijk, met Yoder op de boekenplank." In *Samen ontdekken: De uitdaging van de vergader(en)de gemeente: samen de wil van Christus onderscheiden*, edited by Ingeborg Janssen-te Loo, 56–73. Baptistica Reeks 10. Amsterdam: Baptisten Seminarium, 2016.

Erwich, René. *Veelkleurig verlangen: Wegen van missionair gemeente-zijn*. Zoetermeer, Neth.: Boekencentrum, 2008.

Fiddes, Paul S. *Tracks and Traces: Baptist Identity in Church and Theology*. Studies in Baptist History and Thought 13. Milton Keynes, UK: Paternoster, 2003.

Habermas, Jürgen. "Secularism's Crisis of Faith: Notes on Post-Secular Society." *New Perspective Quarterly* 25 (2008) 17–29.

Healy, Nicholas. *Church, World and the Christian Life: Practical-Prophetic Ecclesiology*. Cambridge: Cambridge University Press, 2010.

Janse, Rick. "Villa Klarendal: Van brug naar de kerk tot gemeentestichting." *Soteria* 27 (2010) 29–34.

Janssen-te Loo, Ingeborg, ed. *Samen ontdekken: De uitdaging van de vergader(en) degemeente: samen de wil van Christus onderscheiden*. Baptistica Reeks 10. Amsterdam: Baptisten Seminarium, 2016.

Kilpin, Juliet. *Urban to the Core: Motives for Incarnational Mission*. Leicester, UK: Matador, 2013.

Kilpin, Juliet, and Stuart Murray. *Church Planting in the Inner City: The Urban Expression Story.* Cambridge: Grove, 2007.

Marsh, Charles, ed. *Lived Theology: New Perspectives on Method, Style, and Pedagogy.* Oxford, UK: Oxford University Press, 2017.

Paas, Stefan. "Post-Christian, Post-Christendom, and Post-Modern Europe: Towards the Interaction of Missiology and the Social Sciences." *Mission Studies* 28 (2011) 3–25.

Randall, Ian M. *Communities of Conviction: Baptist Beginnings in Europe.* Schwarzenfeld, Germany: Neufeld, 2009.

Urban Expression. "About Us." Urban Expression, n.d. https://www.urbanexpression.org.uk/about-us/.

Van der Leer, Teun. *De kerk op haar smalst: Op zoek naar een ecclesiologish minimum voor de kerk aan het begin van de eenentwintigste eeuw.* MA thesis, University of Amsterdam, 2006.

Vlaardingenbroek, Matthijs. *Grensverleggend: Hoe de kerk opnieuw missionair kan zijn.* Heerenveen, Netherlands: Medema, 2011.

Ward, Pete, ed. *Perspectives on Ecclesiology and Ethnography.* Grand Rapids: Eerdmans, 2012.

WCC. *The Church: Towards a Common Vision.* Faith and Order 214. Geneva: WCC, 2013.

———. *Together towards Life: Mission and Evangelism in Changing Landscapes.* Geneva: WCC, 2013.

Williams, Stuart Murray, and Sian Murray Williams. *Multi-Voiced Church.* Milton Keynes, UK: Paternoster, 2012.

14

Remembering Churches

Elizabeth Newman

REMEMBERING THE FUTURE IS about remembering who we are. As beings in time, we live not only in the past and present but also in the future, our lives formed by our sense of where time is going. In this essay, I argue that remembering the future well is key to a rich understanding of freedom. Baptists have rightly championed the freedom of the believer before God. Taken in a certain direction, however, this emphasis coincides with a modern understanding of freedom as self-determination. This trajectory easily leads to a loss of memory, an occlusion of time that atomizes the person as an "individual." In light of this challenge, I argue that Baptists and all Christians remember the future well when we remember freedom as a liturgical reality.

Baptists, Memory, and Freedom

Debates surrounding Baptists and freedom are well-traveled ground. On one end of the continuum is a strong emphasis on the "sacredness of individual choice."[1] A well-known representative of this understanding, E. Y. Mullins, embedded freedom in "soul competency," a term he described as the distinctive contribution of Baptists to the religious world. Mullins

---

1. Shurden, *Baptist Identity*, 23.

defined soul competency not simply as human self-sufficiency, however, but rather as a competency under God, one that excludes human interference or any form of "religion by proxy."[2] Religion, rather, "is a personal matter between the soul and God."[3] Mullins prioritizes freedom as noninterference: nothing or no one should come between the soul and God.

Efforts to correct or at least modify an individualistic soul competency have turned to community as also important for Baptist self-understanding. Thus, the community has a legitimate role, and is an "altogether valid hermeneutical 'core value' for understanding the Baptist identity as long as one does not ignore the role of the individual."[4] To resolve the temptation to a hyper-individualism, some emphasis on community seems necessary. Still, which takes priority? Mullins himself believed that "Protestantism is first individual and then social."[5] No community should take precedence over individual conscience. Others, however, worry about a devaluation of the community and a divisive individualism. Thus, as Douglas Weaver says, "Baptist ecclesiology in the twenty-first century will do well to incorporate a balance between the individual and the community of faith."[6] Yet this balance, Bill Leonard notes, is difficult to maintain in Baptist polity. There is an "untenable tension between individualism and community," a tension that makes conflict and schism "not merely possible but probable, indeed, in many cases essential," perhaps even central for the survival of the church.[7] Is this apparently inevitable tension, when amplified, a version of a commonly noted difference between Protestants and Catholics? Mullins would say yes; contrary to Protestantism, "Roman Catholicism is first social, then individual,"[8] a position, he believed, that underwrote the soul's incompetency.

For my purposes, it is significant that this debate typically places individual freedom in competition with that of the community. Thus, the freedom of the individual and the freedom of the community appear to exist in a zero-sum game. In order for x to follow her conscience, she must

---

2. Mullins, *Axioms of Religion*, 53. Religion by proxy included, for Mullins, infant baptism and episcopacy.

3. Mullins, *Axioms of Religion*, 54.

4. Shurden, "Baptist Identity," 325.

5. Dunn, "Church, State," 69.

6. Weaver, "Baptist Ecclesiology," 30.

7. Leonard, "Baptist Polity."

8. Dunn, "Church, State," 69.

be free *from* y and vice versa. Resolving this tension between *x* and *y* seems to require the acceptance of a pluralism of values embedded in the subject's free choice. Within this framework, the resolution to pluralism makes sense as a way to allow for individual freedom as noninterference and helps to understand how Mullins himself is seen as a unifying figure.[9]

The difficulty with this whole framework, however, is that it ultimately relies on a distorted ontology. As I will discuss more fully, this distortion can be seen in at least three ways. *First* is simply the belief that competition fundamentally marks our being. Of course, we are in competition with one another in all sorts of ways: for scarce goods, in education, in the global market, etc. Is competition, however, a mark of true being? *Second*, the above framework relies implicitly on a separation or even dualism between facts and values. We see this most fully in the belief that a person's choice constitutes freedom. This seems commonsensical in our modern context; is not the alternative some sort of coercive imposition? Such an understanding, however, as I engage more fully, relies upon a closed ontology: one in which being is neutral and values are subjective entities. *Finally*, this framework flattens out time. A flat understanding of time is strictly linear—measured by the clock—the individual (or community) using it or making of it what he or she will. In what follows, I respond to these challenges in turn in order to give an account of freedom ultimately grounded in liturgical life.

Being as Communion

David L. Schindler states that modernity, while no doubt contributing to the good in many ways, has nonetheless grown accustomed to a "distorted anthropocentrism." The problem is not that we have simply focused on humans, "but that we have done so while forgetting being and God." Such forgetfulness "helps to bring about the forgetfulness of our own *creatureliness* and that of all other *cosmic entities*."[10] In contrast to the assumption that being is essentially neutral—a tree, for example, is basically roots, leaves, and branches—Schindler claims that being and communion are convertible. Being is inherently oriented toward communion. Thus, a proper anamnesis (remembrance) presupposes that "all human beings have some primitive experience of restlessness for love and for God, however much this

---

9. Timothy Maddox, for example, refers to Mullins's "unceasing effort... to bring the broad citizenry of Baptists into a community" (Maddox, "E. Y. Mullins," 88).

10. Schindler, *Ordering Love*, 5; emphasis added.

experience gets diverted in our culture into a pursuit of happiness conceived largely as the consumption of commodities."[11] Such anamnesis involves a "recollection of our origin from another."[12] Being is "always being-with."[13]

This understanding of recollection and being could sound like a Platonic, or even gnostic, ideal, as if we were creatures trapped in creation who have forgotten our true selves. Schindler is describing a theological anthropology, however, that flows from a proper understanding of *creatio ex nihilo*. To say God creates *ex nihilo*, "out of nothing," means that creation itself rests on God's own freedom in love. Nothing exterior to God compels God to create. Creation is not neutral but already a communion of love apart from any choice on our part. Augustine reflects such anamnesis in his well-known prayer, "For you have made us for yourself, and our heart is restless until it rests in you."[14] So understood, the natural is "ontologically inseparable from the lure of the supernatural."[15] Desire for God constitutes, however dimly, the memory of all creatures.

There are certainly strong currents in Baptist life that register this anthropology. In Keach's catechism (1677), for example, the response to the question, "What is the chief end of man?" is "Man's chief end is to glorify God, and to enjoy Him forever."[16] Being has purpose: communion with God. In a Baptist Love Feast liturgy, participants pray: "We desire to love thee above all things... and to love one another above all people, that so we may bear in our bodies the marks of the dear Lord Jesus!...We invite Jesus to the feast! Come to it, Lord Jesus, come and make one in the midst of us!"[17] The desire to love God and so also to love one another, made possible through Christ, enables the community to become *who they truly are* and so bear in their bodies the marks of Christ. One could include other prayers

11. Schindler, *Ordering Love*, 24.
12. Schindler, *Ordering Love*, 5.
13. Schindler, *Ordering Love*, 446.
14. Augustine, *Confessions of Saint Augustine*, 1.
15. Milbank, "Hume versus Kant," 289.
16. Keach, "Benjamin Keach's Catechism." Mullins, in more modern fashion, relates the *imago Dei* to the "possession of a will," an emphasis that shapes his understanding of freedom as "self-determination" (Mullins, *Christian Religion*, 258). In a similar vein, more recently, James Dunn has related the *imago Dei* to "[our] ability to exercise free will"; "we are programmed to be choosers"; "God does not make puppets" (Dunn, as cited and paraphrased in Canipe, *Baptist Democracy*, 172).
17. Edwards, *Customs of Primitive Churches*, cited in Thompson, "Re-Envisioning Baptist Identity," 293.

or hymns describing being as communion, such as this contemporary version of the well-known passage from Irenaeus: "The glory of God is a human being fully alive, and the life of human being is the vision of God."[18] The key point for my purposes is the conviction that being and communion are convertible: intrinsic to each other.

One might well ask, however, how can communion be integral to all being if a person does not freely choose it? There are at least two responses to this question. First is perhaps the more obvious one. If a child (of whatever age) denies her mother, she does not negate the reality that she has a mother. Second, even a personal denial of the telos of one's being cannot ultimately negate it. As Augustine prays, "All those who wander far away and set themselves up against you are imitating you, but in a perverse way; yet by this very mimicry they proclaim that you are the creator of the whole of nature, and that in consequence there is no place whatever where we can hide from your presence."[19] Whenever one follows a distorted love, he is in reality seeking his true end in God. Augustine thinks "it is impossible for humanity to exist in any kind of an autonomous and 'self-constituted' fashion apart from God."[20]

So understood, true being is marked not by competition but by abundance. The more one enters into communion with God, others, and indeed all creation, the freer one becomes. The whole scriptural narrative points to the abundance of being/communion. Far from being a zero-sum game, this anthropology is one of ever more abundance. Dorotheus of Gaza (sixth c.) describes this freedom as follows: "Imagine that the world is a circle, that God is the center, and that the radii are the different ways human beings live. When those who wish to come closer to God walk towards the center of the circle, they come closer to one another at the same time as to God. The closer they come to God, the closer they come to one another. And the closer they come to one another, the closer they come to God."[21] Such freedom, because grounded in true being, is essentially noncompetitive.

Of course, this kind of noncompetitive freedom might sound like an ideal. Baptists (like all Christians) can be a contentious lot: our stories and

---

18 See Irenaeus, *Haer.* 4.20.7.

19. Augustine, *Confessions*, 71.

20. Kimbriel, *Friendship as Sacred Knowing*, 82. As Kimbriel develops it, Augustine relies "heavily on the idea that *not all that is interior is one's own*" (Kimbriel, *Friendship as Sacred Knowing*, 81; emphasis in original).

21. Dorotheus of Gaza, as cited in Taizé, "Dorotheus of Gaza."

lives wounded by conflict, division, and separation. Freedom understood as noninterference can seem crucial in order for us to avoid tearing one another apart. Even Bonhoeffer in his profound description of life together acknowledges the need to separate, to be free *from* others.[22] Communion with God and with others does not, it seems, always coincide. Bonhoeffer, though, emphasizes that communion is "not an ideal but a *divine* reality,"[23] calling for a particular way of life. Confession, forgiveness, speaking the truth in love are thus key practices through which God heals the body of Christ, all of which lead to greater freedom and communion.

Freedom as Consent

David Burrell rightly notes that freedom is less a question of self-determination and more about "attuning oneself to one's ultimate end." Such direction is not itself a choice but a consent to one's very being: "Any good choice will presuppose an orientation to the end, where the orientation itself is not a choice but a consent to the orientation of one's very being."[24] The difference between choice and consent might seem negligible. If I consent to your visiting me, for example, am I not choosing to have you visit me? Consent, however, indicates that the visit is first your offer. By analogy, consenting to our being is a way of indicating we are receiving our *telos* as gift from Another. We do not determine it for ourselves. Rightly understood, the goodness of the cosmos "is not rooted most basically in human freedom or intelligence, and thus in human spirit. . . . On the contrary, it is rooted in the creative freedom and intelligence of the creator, in which *all things of the cosmos truly participate*."[25]

Perhaps the saint or Christian figure who most embodies freedom as consent is Mary. As *TCTCV* states, "The response of Mary, the Mother of God (*Theotokos*), to the angel's message at the annunciation, 'Let it be done with me according to your word' (Luke 1:38), has been a symbol of and

---

22. "Where Christ bids me to maintain fellowship for the sake of love, I will maintain it. Where his truth enjoins me to dissolve a fellowship for love's sake, there I will dissolve it, despite all the protests of my human love" (Bonhoeffer, *Life Together*, 35). Bonhoeffer is distinguishing between fellowship based in authentic love in contrast to "togetherness" sustained by distorted loves.

23. Bonhoeffer, *Life Together*, 26; emphasis added.

24. Burrell, *Faith and Freedom*, 110.

25. Schindler, *Ordering Love*, 5; emphasis in original.

model for the Church and the individual Christian."[26] Mary, I would emphasize, is a figure of freedom, her yes to God and thus to the truth of her own being opening up a heretofore unimaginable abundance for the world.

It could sound as if an emphasis on freedom, being, and communion leaves little space for personal freedom of conscience. Yet, an understanding of being as communion disallows the use of force and coercion against another, acts which negate true communion.[27] The witness of conscience, however, is not simply one of personal values but of seeing and pointing to a truth and goodness not merely one's own. Consequently, the reception of a faithful witness takes time: time for the wider community to discern, consent, and so hopefully turn more fully to the freedom of a fuller communion. If a person turns away from the good, then he (we) are like the rich young ruler whom Jesus looks at with deep compassion. Of course, like Augustine, we all struggle towards the good. If being is communion, however, then it is also first of all true that God gives us communion to sustain us in our journey. Moreover, it is always grace that enables anyone both to see and receive this reality.

Memory, Time, and Freedom

As indicated, this understanding of freedom and communion takes time. However, what kind of time? Here we meet an obstacle because so much of modern time opposes being/time as communion. Political philosopher Michael Gillespie, for example, argues that modern people imagine themselves as being in time in a novel way; no particular time is more determinative than any other time. "To understand oneself as new," Gillespie writes, "is also to understand oneself as *self-originating* . . . not merely as determined by tradition or governed by fate or providence. To be modern is to be self-liberating and self-making, and thus not merely to be *in* a history or tradition but to *make* history."[28] Benedict Anderson relates this understanding of time—as self-originating—to the "imagined community"

---

26. WCC, *TCTCV*, §15.

27. As Curtis Freeman notes (citing Heinrich Bullinger), the "earlier [Baptist] conviction of soul liberty served a negative and delimiting function: 'One cannot and should not use force to compel anyone to accept faith, for faith is a free gift of God'" (Freeman, *Contesting Catholicity*, 194).

28. Gillespie, *Theological Origins of Modernity*, 2; emphasis in original.

called the nation.²⁹ The creation of the nation signals a break with the past; the newness of the nation, he argues, parallels the sense of time that makes possible the self-creating individual.

This kind of time is enacted in a wide range of liturgies. If liturgy as the "work of the people" has to do with concrete rituals, practices, and conceptions of the good, then some liturgy of freedom is always at play, if only implicitly. James K. A. Smith analyzes, for example, the "liturgy" (in the US) of standing for the national anthem. The silence and reverence surrounding the practice easily elevate it to a kind of holy ritual on par with standing for the Gospel. Smith observes that the lack of tension between "Christian and American nationalism is not a function of the generosity . . . of the American ideal but rather a sign of a Christianity that has accommodated itself to these American ideals of battle, military sacrifice . . . individual (negative) freedom, and prosperity through property."³⁰ As Stanley Hauerwas quips, "As is well-known, Friday night high school football is the most significant liturgical event in Texas."³¹ Within this formation, the individual and the communal are folded into the time of nationalism and into freedom as self-determination.

Such an example illustrates that memory lives in us before we live in it. Memory is as much exterior as it is interior. Words, gestures, and traditions enable us to arrive at understanding. In a scene from *Dead Man Walking*, a father kneels before his murdered son; all he knows to say is the Lord's Prayer, words given to him as a child but now signifying a forgiveness beyond human understanding.³² In the face of tragedy, his prayer—repeated through the ages—pulls him into time as hope: "Thy kingdom come."

Faithful anamnesis, then, provides an alternative to "pure modernity" in which, Stratford Caldecott observes, "there can be no up or down, no getting closer to hell or heaven, and there are no sacred places and times

---

29. Anderson, *Imagined Communities*, 6. "It is difficult today to recreate in the imagination a condition of life in which the nation was felt to be something utterly new. . . . The Declaration of Independence of 1776 makes absolutely no reference to Christopher Columbus, Roanoke, or the Pilgrim Fathers, nor are the grounds put forward to justify independence in any way 'historical,' in the sense of highlighting the antiquity of the American people" (Anderson, *Imagined Communities*, 193).

30. Smith, *Desiring the Kingdom*, 107. Smith is not arguing against standing for the national anthem, but rather analyzing the quasi-holy rituals surrounding it.

31. Cited by Smith, *Desiring the Kingdom*, 106.

32. Robbins, *Dead Man Walking*.

which participate in the divine."³³ But what makes time sacred? Abraham Heschel describes the Sabbath as a "palace in time," that aims at "the *sanctification of time*."³⁴ Sacred time begins with divine action: God creates the Sabbath, God raises Christ from the dead, the day of resurrection. Human anamnesis depends upon divine anamnesis. When the Hebrew slaves cry for help, "God *remembered* his covenant with Abraham, Isaac, and Jacob" (Exod 2:23; emphasis added). The penitent thief pleads, "Jesus, *remember* me when you come into your kingdom" (Luke 23:42; emphasis added). According to Joachim Jeremias, divine remembrance is always "an effecting and creating event." To say "God remembers his covenant . . . means that he is now fulfilling the eschatological covenant promise."³⁵

To remember time faithfully is to allow ourselves to be remembered by God. How do we do this? When Martin Luther was tempted by the devil, he would look at the words written in chalk on his desk: "*baptizatus sum*" (I am baptized). He was remembering not his own efforts, but God's action on his behalf, which freed him to live not in his own anxious time but in the time of new creation.

We see an emphasis on the priority of divine anamnesis in Baptist prayers surrounding both baptism and the Lord's Supper. An eighteenth-century baptism prayer states: "Thou that didst come from Galilee to Jordan come now also from heaven to ____ and meet us on the banks of this river. . . . We know that thou art present every where, but ah! Let it not be here as at first on the banks of the Jordan when thou didst stand among the croud, and they knew it not! O let us find the messiah here!"³⁶ Just as Jesus came from Galilee and was baptized in the Jordan, so also worshipers pray for the Messiah to meet us "here" in this time and place. The prayer is looking to God to create (remember) those gathered anew through the waters of baptism. In the Orthodox Creed of 1679, we read, "And as [Israel] had the manna to nourish them in the wilderness to Canaan; so have we the sacraments, to nourish us in the church, and in our wilderness condition."³⁷ Just as God provided manna for Israel in the wilderness, so does God now

---

33. Caldecott, *Beauty for Truth's Sake*, 139.

34. Heschel, *Sabbath*, 8; emphasis in original.

35. Jeremias, *Eucharistic Words of Jesus*, 251.

36. Edwards, *Customs of Primitive Churches*, cited in Thompson, "Re-Envisioning Baptist Identity," 291.

37. "Orthodox Creed" (1679), cited in Thompson, "Sacraments and Religious Liberty," 40.

nourish the church in her wilderness wandering. Such examples—and there are many more—illuminate how time is not simply linear. Rather, as Geoffrey Wainwright states, "the Christian liturgy bursts [the] closed world by dint of its language of praise and prayer, of thanksgiving and intercession, of anamnesis and epiclesis."[38] This is time as communion rooted in the ongoing reality of God's mighty and efficacious deeds, culminating in the Word made flesh. Such time is not our own. Rather, in and through the gift of time, we are being made part of God's triune *koinonia*, not simply for ourselves but for the sake of the world.[39]

Genuine freedom flows from living fully in this liturgical time of communion. James McClendon reminds us that we live in the past time of the early Christians as well as the future time of God's eschatological reign.[40] How is this even possible? After all, the past is gone, and the future is not yet. The faithful liturgy reminds us, however, that God has transformed time in a way that joins us to those long gone and opens us to a future yet to be. We can thus sing with the communion of all saints, "Holy, holy, holy/ All the saints adore Thee/ Casting down their golden crowns / Around the glassy sea."[41] Christ has redeemed all time, enabling us to be who we are created to be: creatures living in communion with God, one another, and indeed all of creation. We may close ourselves to this communion. In doing so, however, we become less free, unlikely to notice how even "the common thornbush is aflame with your glory."[42]

Bibliography

Anderson, Benedict. *Imagined Communities: Reflections on the Origin and Spread of Nationalism*. New York: Verso, 1983.

Augustine. *The Confessions*. Translated by Maria Boulding. Hyde Park, NY: New City, 1997.

———. *The Confessions of Saint Augustine*. Translated by John K. Ryan. New York: Doubleday, 1960.

Bonhoeffer, Dietrich. *Life Together*. Translated by John W. Doberstein. New York: Harper & Row, 1954.

---

38. Wainwright, *Embracing Purpose*, 23.

39. "The unity of the body of Christ consists in the gift of *koinonia* or communion that God graciously bestows upon human beings" (WCC, *TCTCV*, §67).

40. McClendon, *Systematic Theology*, 1:30.

41. Heber, "Holy, Holy, Holy."

42. Walter Rauschenbusch, "Thanks for Creation," cited in Hauerwas, *Better Hope*, 240.

Burrell, David. *Faith and Freedom: An Interfaith Perspective*. Malden, MA: Blackwell, 2004.

Caldecott, Stratford. *Beauty for Truth's Sake: On the Re-Enchantment of Education*. Grand Rapids: Brazos, 2009.

Canipe, Lee. *A Baptist Democracy: Separating God and Ceasar in the Land of the Free*. Macon, GA: Mercer University Press, 2011.

Dunn, James. "Church, State and Soul Competency." *Review & Expositor* 96 (1999) 61–73.

Edwards, Morgan. *The Customs of Primitive Churches*. Philadelphia: N.p., 1774.

Freeman, Curtis. *Contesting Catholicity: Theology for Other Baptists*. Waco, TX: Baylor University Press, 2014.

Gillespie, Michael. *The Theological Origins of Modernity*. Chicago: University of Chicago Press, 2009.

Hauerwas, Stanley. *A Better Hope: Resources for a Church Confronting Capitalism, Democracy, and Postmodernity*. Grand Rapids: Brazos, 2000.

Heber, Reginald. "Holy, Holy, Holy." In *Baptist Hymnal*, #2. Nashville: Convention, 1991.

Heschel, Abraham Joshua. *The Sabbath: Its Meaning for Modern Man*. New York: Farrar, Straus and Young, 1951.

Jeremias, Joachim. *The Eucharistic Words of Jesus*. New York: Scribner's, 1966.

Keach, Benjamin. "Benjamin Keach's Catechism." Reformed Reader, 1677. http://www.reformedreader.org/ccc/keachcat.htm.

Kimbriel, Samuel. *Friendship as Sacred Knowing: Overcoming Isolation*. New York: Oxford University Press, 2014.

Leonard, Bill J. "Baptist Polity: (Im)perfect Methods for a (Post)modern World." Cooperative Baptist Fellowship General Assembly Workshop, Union Theological Seminary-Presbyterian School of Christian Education, Richmond, VA, 2004.

Maddox, Timothy. "E. Y. Mullins: Mr. Baptist for the 20th and 21st Century." *Review & Expositor* 96 (1999) 87–108.

McClendon, James Wm., Jr. *Systematic Theology*. 3 vols. Nashville: Abingdon, 1994–2000.

Milbank, John. "Hume versus Kant: Faith, Reason and Feeling." *Modern Theology* 27 (2011) 276–97.

Mullins, E. Y. *The Axioms of Religion*. Philadelphia: Judson, 1908.

———. *The Christian Religion in Its Doctrinal Expression*. Philadelphia: Judson, 1917.

Robbins, Tim, dir. *Dead Man Walking*. Universal City, CA: Grammercy, 1995.

Schindler, David L. *Ordering Love: Liberal Societies and the Memory of God*. Grand Rapids: Eerdmans, 2011.

Shurden, Walter B. "The Baptist Identity and the Baptist *Manifesto*." *Perspectives in Religious Studies* 25 (1998) 321–40.

———. *The Baptist Identity: Four Fragile Freedoms*. Macon, GA: Smyth & Helwys, 1993.

Smith, James K. A. *Desiring the Kingdom: Worship, Worldview, and Cultural Formation*. Grand Rapids: Baker Academic, 2009.

Taizé. "Dorotheus of Gaza (Sixth Century): Humility and Communion." Taizé, last updated Oct. 4, 2007. https://www.taize.fr/en_article5234.html.

Thompson, Philip. "Re-Envisioning Baptist Identity: Historical, Theological, and Liturgical Analysis." *Perspectives in Religious Studies* 27 (2000) 287–302.

———. "Sacraments and Religious Liberty: From Critical Practice to Rejected Infringement." In *Baptist Sacramentalism*, edited by Anthony R. Cross and Philip E. Thompson, 36–54. Milton Keynes, UK: Paternoster, 2003.

Wainwright, Geoffrey. *Embracing Purpose: Essays on God, the World and the Church.* Peterborough, UK: Epworth, 2007.

WCC. *The Church: Towards a Common Vision.* Faith and Order 214. Geneva: WCC, 2013.

Weaver, C. Douglas. "The Baptist Ecclesiology of E. Y. Mullins: Individualism and the New Testament Church." *Baptist History and Heritage* (2008) 18–34.

www.ingramcontent.com/pod-product-compliance
Lightning Source LLC
Chambersburg PA
CBHW021914180426
43198CB00035B/586